The Diggers of COLDITZ

Also by Jack Champ

The Wind is Free: A History of the Royal Geelong Yacht Club

Also by Colin Burgess

Australia's Greatest Escapes: Gripping Tales of Wartime Bravery
(revised edition of *Freedom or Death*)
Aircraft
Pioneers of Flight
Prisoners of War (with Hugh Clarke and Russell Braddon)
Laughter in the Air: Tales from the Qantas Era (with Max Harris)
More Laughter in the Air: Tales from the Qantas Era
Barbed Wire and Bamboo: Australian POW Stories (with Hugh Clarke)
Freedom or Death: Australia's Greatest Escape Stories from Two World Wars
Destination: Buchenwald
Australia's Dambusters: The Men and Missions of 617 Squadron
Bush Parker: An Australian Battle of Britain Pilot in Colditz
Space, the New Frontier
Oceans to Orbit: The Story of Australia's First Man in Space, Paul Scully-Power
Australia's Astronauts: Three Men and a Spaceflight Dream
Teacher in Space: Christa McAuliffe and the Challenger Legacy
Fallen Astronauts: Heroes Who Died Reaching for the Moon
(with Kate Doolan)
NASA's Scientist-Astronauts (with David Shayler)
Animals in Space: From Research Rockets to the Space Shuttle
(with Chris Dubbs)
Into That Silent Sea: Trailblazers of the Space Era, 1961–1965
(with Francis French)
In the Shadow of the Moon: A Challenging Journey to Tranquility, 1965–1969
(with Francis French)
The First Soviet Cosmonaut Team: Their Lives and Legacies (with Rex Hall)
Australia's Astronauts: Countdown to a Spaceflight Dream
Selecting the Mercury Seven: The Search for America's First Astronauts
Moon Bound: Choosing and Training the Lunar Astronauts
Freedom 7: The Historic Flight of Alan B Shepard Jr
Liberty Bell 7: The Suborbital Mercury Flight of Virgil I Grissom
Friendship 7: The Epic Orbital Flight of John H Glenn Jr
Aurora 7: The Mercury Space Flight of M Scott Carpenter
Interkosmos: The Eastern Bloc's Early Space Program
Sigma 7: The Six Mercury Orbits of Walter M Schirra, Jr
Faith 7: L Gordon Cooper, Jr and the Final Mercury Mission
The Last of NASA's Original Pilot Astronauts: Expanding the Space Frontier in the Late Sixties (with David J. Shayler)
Shattered Dreams: The Lost or Canceled Space Missions

The Diggers of COLDITZ

The classic Australian POW story
about escape from the inescapable

JACK CHAMP *and* COLIN BURGESS

SIMON & SCHUSTER

London · New York · Sydney · Toronto · New Delhi

THE DIGGERS OF COLDITZ
First published in Australia in 1985, 1997 by Kangaroo Press Pty Ltd
This revised edition published in 2019, 2020 by Simon & Schuster (Australia) Pty Limited
Suite 19A, Level 1, Building C, 450 Miller Street, Cammeray, NSW 2062

10 9 8 7 6 5 4 3 2

Sydney New York London Toronto New Delhi
Visit our website at www.simonandschuster.com.au

NATIONAL LIBRARY OF AUSTRALIA

A catalogue record for this book is available from the National Library of Australia

Cover design: Luke Causby/Blue Cork
Cover images: 'Australian Officers and Orderlies in Colditz' (P07203.001) and 'Slouch Hat' (RELAWM13656.003) courtesy of Australian War Memorial; 'Colditz Castle' Julie G Woodhouse/Alamy Stock Photo.
Typeset by Midland Typesetters, Australia
Printed and bound in Australia by Griffin Press

MIX
Paper from responsible sources
FSC www.fsc.org FSC® C009448

The paper this book is printed on is certified against the Forest Stewardship Council® Standards. Griffin Press holds FSC® chain of custody certification SGS-COC-005088. FSC® promotes environmentally responsible, socially beneficial and economically viable management of the world's forests.

This book is dedicated to two Pats – Pat Champ and Pat Burgess. It is also dedicated to the indomitable spirit of mankind under adversity.

Australians in Colditz

Name	Rank	Capture Date	Arrived in Colditz	Departed Colditz
Officers				
Rex Baxter	Captain	26/05/41	23/06/43	*
George Bolding	Lieutenant	01/06/41	21/06/43	*
Jack Champ	Lieutenant	09/05/41	23/06/43	*
Doug Crawford	Captain	13/06/40	26/06/43	07/01/45
Clive Dieppe	Lieutenant	30/05/41	21/06/43	08/04/45
Bill Fowler	Flight Lieutenant	16/05/40	01/12/41	09/09/42
Jack Goodwin	Lieutenant	01/06/41	13/01/45	*
Ralph Holroyd	Lieutenant	15/04/41	29/04/42	*
Mark Howard	Lieutenant	26/05/41	23/06/43	*
Malcolm McColm	Squadron Leader	27/12/40	08/10/41	*
Jack Millett	Lieutenant	30/05/41	30/06/43	*
Vincent 'Bush' Parker	Flight Lieutenant	15/08/40	05/05/42	*
Johnny Rawson	Lieutenant	01/06/41	02/10/43	*
Medical Personnel				
Dr Roger Playoust	Captain	01/06/41	19/04/42	28/07/42
Orderlies				
Lionel Archer	Sapper	01/06/41	16/04/43	13/12/44
Frank Brown	Private	30/05/41	27/06/43	12/12/44
Harry Henley	Private	01/06/41	03/08/43	**
Vic Jeffries	Private	27/04/41	28/05/43	**
Claude Patterson	Private	28/04/41	16/04/43	02/10/44
P.M. Ray	Private	30/10/42	28/11/44	**
Eddie Walker	Private	01/06/41	03/08/43	13/12/44

* Liberated from Colditz 16/04/45.
** Date of departure not recorded.

Contents

Foreword to the 1997 Edition xi
Introduction 1

1 Out of the Frying Pan 7
2 Warburg: Planning the Wire Job 39
3 First Escape 72
4 Eichstätt: The Second Escape 96
5 Colditz 141
6 Some Intrepid Internationals 156
7 The Old Boys 167
8 Home Run 200
9 Austrian Escapade 211
10 Burning the Candle 230
11 The Colditz Glider 248
12 Beginning of the End 268

Epilogue 295
Index 304

Oflag VIB: Warburg

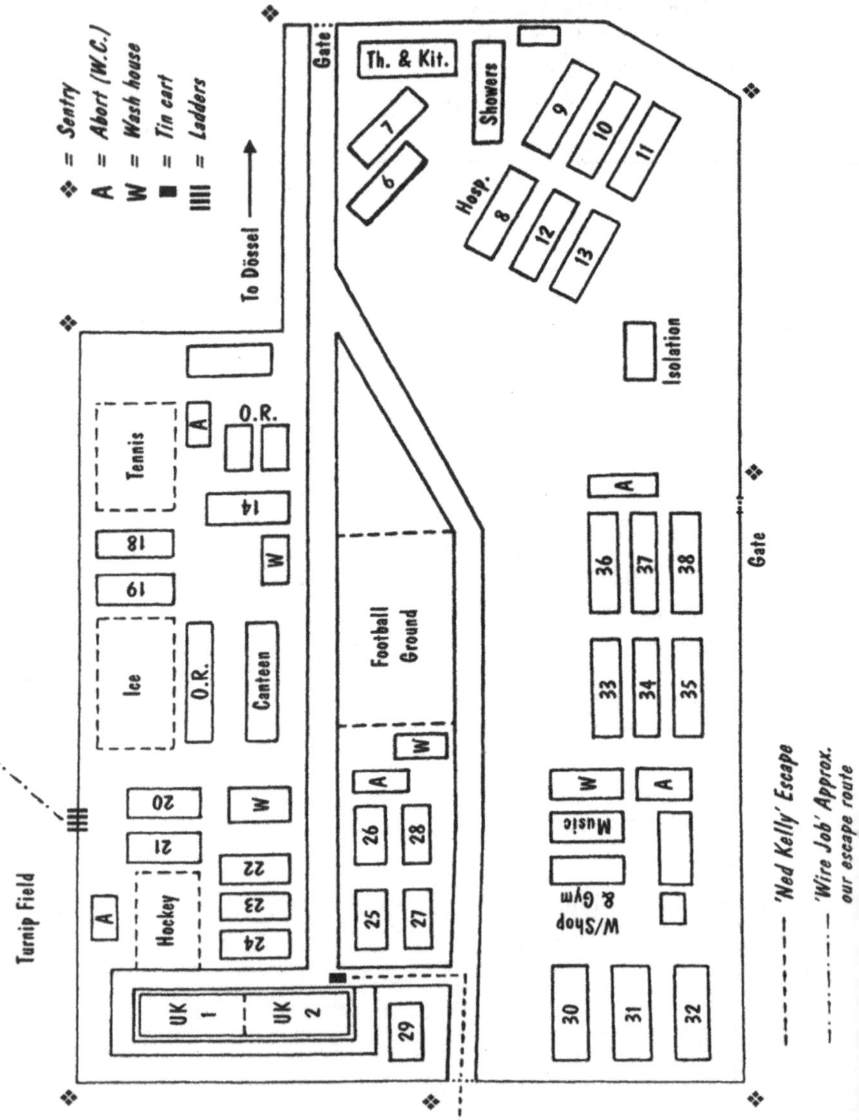

Oflag VIIB: Eichstätt

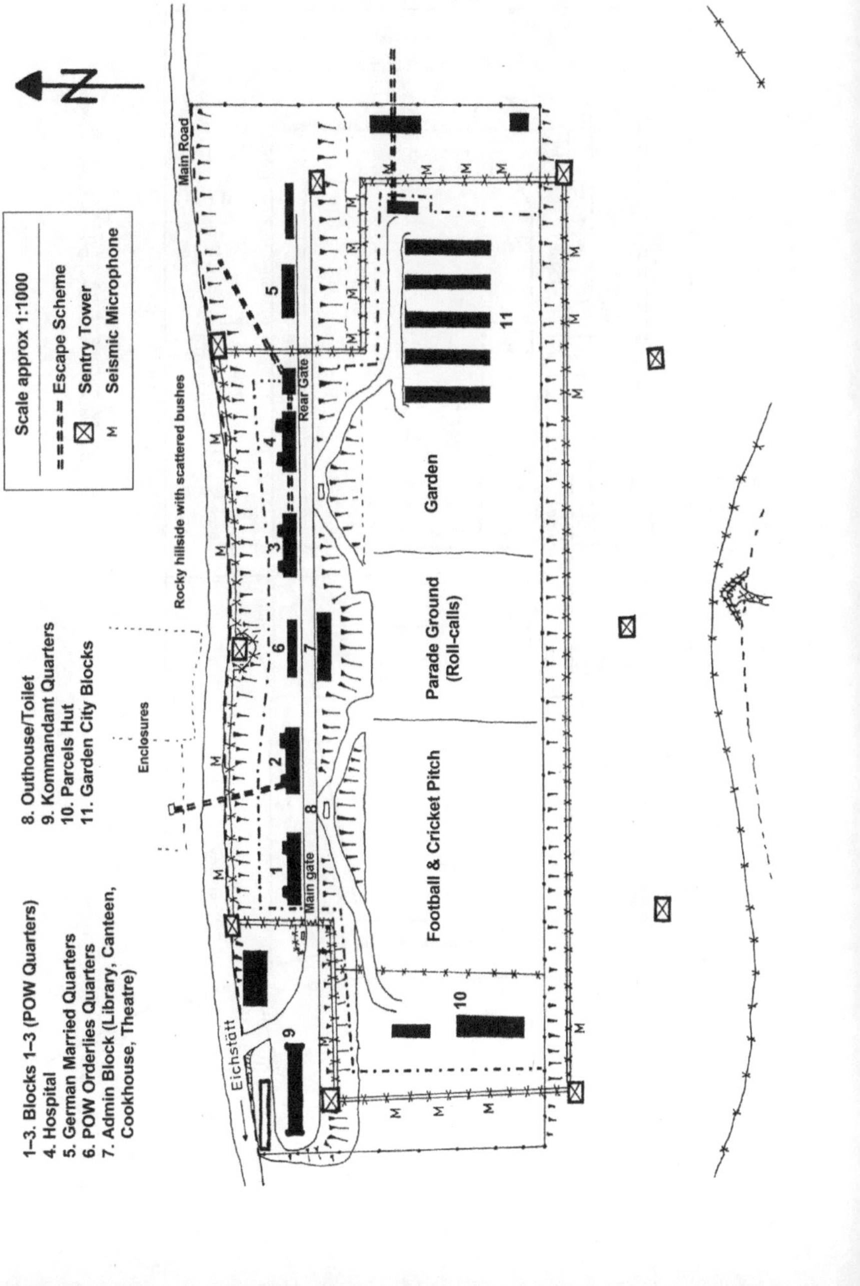

Oflag IVC: Colditz

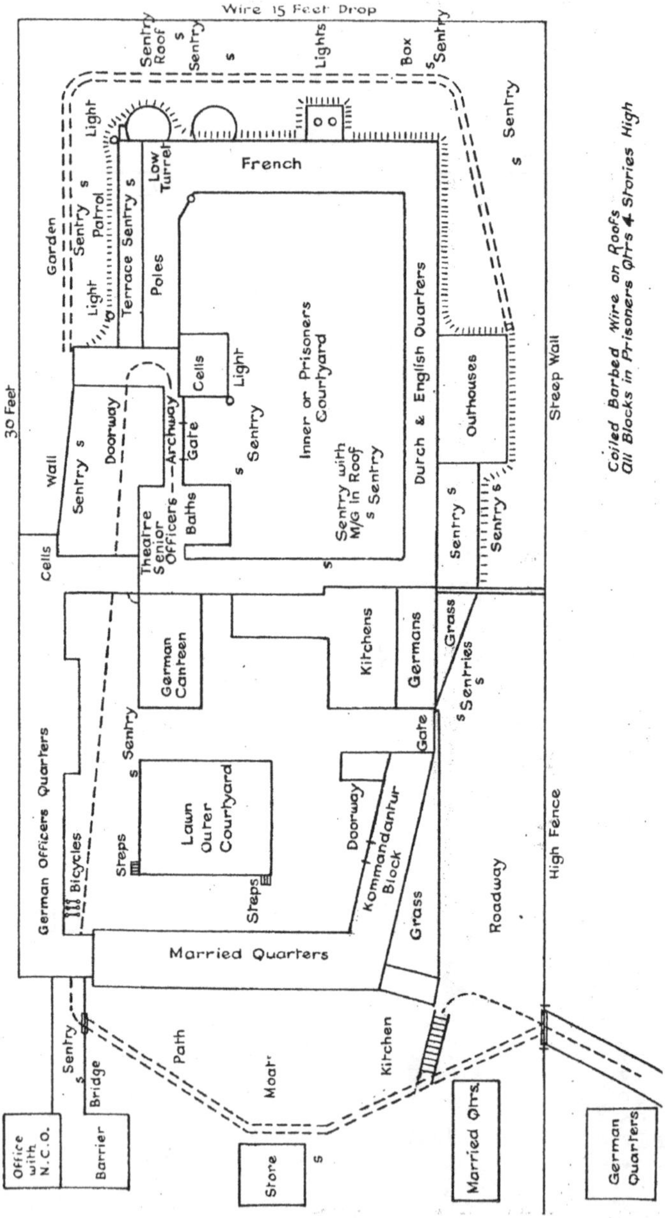

Foreword to the 1997 Edition

I was delighted when Lieutenant-Commander Mike Moran, 'Duty Stooge' of the Colditz Association, told me that Jack Champ and Colin Burgess were planning to write a book about the Diggers in Colditz. Since then, Colin Burgess and I have met on several occasions and any doubts I may have had before getting to know him were very soon dispelled. To him, this book was clearly a labour of love.

There were about twenty Australians in Colditz Castle, and without exception their personalities were intriguing; sometimes larger than life, generally very individualistic, never dull. They were a group of bold and resourceful men. Their presence testified to the global nature of the conflict of the Second World War as also to the intrinsic nobility and selfless courage of their participation in it. Their story is long overdue.

Almost a year before Jack Champ arrived in Colditz, I went 'AWOL'. I met him for the first time at our 1980 reunion at the Imperial War Museum. I am, of course, well informed about the escaping feats of the Diggers who landed up in Oflag IVC and their part in the life of that camp. It is nowadays a recognised 'honour' to have been in Colditz.

It says something for the resilient spirit of man that those Allied prisoners, the inveterate escapers who were sent to Colditz, mostly survived the ordeal. For such men, much more than for others, the hours were days and the weeks were years. They were men of action by nature, and they lived a long time the torture of forced inactivity. They were prisoners expiating no other crime than the unselfish service of their country.

The desire to escape was paramount among the men of Colditz. They were of all nationalities fighting on the Allied side: Englishmen, Scotsmen and Irishmen from Britain and every corner of the Commonwealth – Canada, Australia, New Zealand and Africa.

This book tells the story of the Colditz Australians. Eminently readable, it will I am sure earn a distinctive place in Colditz literature, which now includes some seventy books written in at least five languages.

P. R. Reid, MBE, MC
Author of *The Colditz Story*

Introduction

To Jack Champ and the men of Colditz I was a comparative youngster when this book was first conceived; I had not even been born at the time of their liberation and return to their homes and loved ones.

For most of them the transition from the deprivation, loneliness and degradation of the prison camps to the security, warmth and freedom of their own home environment caused many varying and profound emotions. The majority wanted to forget those lost years, to re-establish civilised human contact, and move freely again in a life without guards, locked doors, barred windows and barbed wire. Let Colditz become a memory.

And thus it was until Major Pat Reid, who had successfully escaped from the ancient castle, wrote his deservedly classic book, *The Colditz Story*. In the ensuing years the many stories about Colditz were perpetuated through his second brilliant book, *The Latter Days*, the excellent black-and-white film based on his books, and the rather ostentatious but highly successful television series.

In a lesser propagation of the legend (as it has now become) there have been books written by former British, Dutch, French, American and Polish POWs from the infamous castle. There is even a Colditz board game.

It was Pat Reid who first inspired me to tackle this book when he told me that the story of the Australians he had known in Colditz was one of the great untold tales of the war.

Jack Champ and I first met in late 1981 after I had contacted the surviving Australians to ascertain their interest in a book on their exploits. Jack told me that he had quite a lot of information in the form of an unpublished manuscript to which he would happily give me access. Having read the manuscript I put it to him that we co-author a fresh book, this time incorporating the stories I would obtain from the rest of the Aussies. We shook hands on this agreement, and subsequently became not only complementary writers, but lifelong friends.

I feel I must emphasise that in the German POW camps described throughout the book, and in particular Colditz Castle, the Australians were a minority contingent. Although the reader may gain the impression that they were all to the fore in the escaping game, they had their counterparts – obviously stronger numerically – in other nationalities. To attempt to tell the stories of these fine men is to travel over ground already well covered in previous books. Their omission is regretted, but the admiration for their deeds is undiminished.

There are several to whom Jack and I owed (and owe) our sincere thanks for their kind assistance. The mere listing of names can in no way suggest our tremendous feelings of gratitude towards these individuals. We are greatly indebted to all of them. Without their interest and cooperation it would have been literally impossible to collect, transcribe, organise or publish the information and stories contained in this book.

First, and indeed foremost, to Mike 'Mugsie' Moran. As principal motivator of the Colditz Association he tirelessly assisted when information or verification was needed, and his gracious support lent much of the soul to this book. Mike and his wife, Rena, remained very dear friends until they passed away within months of each other in 1993. Likewise, Pat Reid gave unflinching help despite being embroiled in writing his final work, *Colditz: The Full Story.* This intrepid escaper, a man I am proud to have called a friend over the latter years of his life, died on 22 May 1990, aged 79.

We enjoyed the wonderful support given us by other Colditz veterans such as David Walker, a courageous leader and author of such literary masterpieces as *Geordie*, *Harry Black and the Tiger* and *Lean, Wind, Lean*. When he knew our book was under way he wrote the following tribute to the Australians he had known during the war:

> Without exception the Australians were tough, and some (not all) were rough too; not always the most appealing of people to us hidebound Pommies when things were easy. But when bread was to be measured and treasured by the millimetre, it was quite another matter. They were champions in adversity, 'the best men in prison' as I wrote later in a novel called *The Pillar*. In 1965 I went to Australia to see my old cobbers again, and to make new friends. Since then I have been back twice, to be treated with kindness all along the way. A good hard breed from a good hard land about sums it up for me.

So many other former Colditz POWs assisted us throughout the research and writing of this book, and their help – either requested or spontaneous – is gratefully acknowledged. They were Jock Hamilton-Baillie, Don Donaldson, Hugh Bruce, Dominic Bruce, Ken Lockwood and Mike Wittet. Family members and friends who supplied information and photographs were Peter Champ, Phyllis Holroyd, Nell McColm, Malcolm McColm Jr, Bonnie Bolding, Kit Rawson, Harley Baxter, Mona Whalley, and George and Mary Watson. Post-war members of the Colditz Society also demonstrated their willingness to help: Michael Booker, David Ray, Mario Bosch and Dave Windle in England, and Jonathon Vance in Canada. In pre-personal computer days, Val Mills volunteered to type out our original manuscript and did so superbly and expeditiously. In copying and reproducing many irreplaceable photographs from the war years, my ongoing thanks goes to a great mate, Rob Croft.

Last, but certainly not least, to the men known as the 'Diggers of Colditz', who gave freely of their time and memories. Scattered throughout Australia, they and their families made this book a lot easier to put together through their enthusiasm and support.

Sadly, since this book was first published back in 1985, all of the Colditz luminaries named within its pages – including Jack Champ – have passed away. It was nevertheless a pleasure and a privilege to have shared many memorable days with these remarkable men, and I know they all took great (if somewhat modest) pride in the fact that their stories had finally been told.

In March 1996, my wife, Pat, and I enjoyed making a trip to Colditz Castle, and it was truly the experience of a lifetime. We were cordially greeted by the Curator of the Colditz Museum, Jens Mahlmann, and he took us on a personal tour of the museum and the ancient Schloss. As I stood in the small cobbled courtyard I had first read about as a youngster, those adventurous tales of the Colditz POWs came back to me, and I could feel all around me the spirit that was Oflag IVC. Nowadays the castle is floodlit by night, just as it was during the war years, and is a truly dramatic and even spectral sight. As Jack Champ once reminded me, we probably saw more of the exterior of the castle in two days than he did during his two years as a prisoner at Colditz.

A visit to Colditz is a relatively easy accomplishment these days, and I urge anyone who has ever thrilled to the Colditz stories to pay the picturesque town and old Schloss a visit. There is no disappointment in store except that the town's brewery has recently closed down and a tall glass of Colditzer Bier is no longer available – bad news for any Australian!

The chance to revise and enlarge this book some 35 years after it was first published came as a very welcome surprise. I am therefore grateful to publisher Brandon VanOver and editor Shannon Kelly from Simon & Schuster Australia for recognising the potential in releasing an updated version of what, over the decades, has become a classic tale in Australian military history and of heroic circumstances under adversity.

Following the release of the original edition of this book, many reviewers took the opportunity to point out the difference between life as a prisoner of the Germans, and those in Japanese hands. It is recognised that the Germans, to varying degrees, obeyed the strictures of the Geneva Convention, while the Japanese viciously applied their own code of Bushido, which entailed the most monstrous activities ever perpetrated on members of the human race. While some readers may find it curious to read for instance about an

Anzac Day feast in the heart of Germany, while such horrors as the Sandakan death march and the attempted annihilation of Gull Force on Ambon were being carried out elsewhere, it was nevertheless the way things were in the European theatre of war for Jack Champ and tens of thousands of other prisoners of war. Without the salvation of Red Cross parcels, which undoubtedly saved the lives of incalculable numbers of men, the story of the Australian POW experience in Europe may also have been far grimmer and more tragic. All former POWs in Europe have spoken of the insuperable debt they owe to the Red Cross. It is a pity and a disgrace that the Japanese did not permit any such humanity and compassion.

Jack Champ would have been delighted beyond words to know that our book was being republished in this wonderful new edition. Therefore, on behalf of Jack and myself, I trust that you enjoy reading this book every bit as much as we enjoyed putting it together.

Colin Burgess

1

Out of the Frying Pan

THINGS WERE DEFINITELY NOT ALL FUN AND GAMES in Oflag IVC, Colditz. Some chaps were suffering from varying degrees of insanity, while several more teetered on the edge. This of course is hardly surprising given the circumstances, but it was sad to see good friends in the castle prison gradually going to pieces. The repatriation system was iniquitously slow, and the cause of much outrage and continual heated sessions between our Senior British Officer and the Kommandant.

I remember seeing one fellow go demonstrably off his rocker at an Appell (roll-call), crying and pleading with the guards to shoot him. How powerless I felt and how less than a human being to witness such a tragic and easily avoidable spectacle. It was at such moments that a deep loathing for anything German would rise in one's gorge, and a hollow desperation eat at one's guts for days.

However the majority of days in Colditz passed with each of us trying to make the most of the dull routine, searching for some activity to enliven the daylight hours. What we did to alleviate our boredom ranged from serious studies and helping to organise the various camp utilities, to a schoolboy-like malevolence, when grown men engaged in elaborate pranks simply to confound and upset their so-righteous captors. I should know – I was involved diligently in both the serious side of camp life, and the games. The latter diversions were usually quite innocent. Great satisfaction was to be had from seeing the Germans frustrated and confused. On rare occasions shots were fired, but most times this was the prime objective of the prisoners' exercise, and they made sure they were well out of the way of the bullets …

Stuffed dummies were lowered out of the windows at night, wasps released into the small courtyard carrying tiny inflammatory messages tied to their legs; workmen had their ladders sawn in half while their backs were turned, visiting German dignitaries had their hats pinched. All good, high-spirited fun, and the subjects of many of the hilarious anecdotes that are part of the story of Colditz, lovingly related in many post-war books.

But it was for escaping that the name of Colditz is forever enshrined in the annals of war history. The medieval castle was a heavily guarded, maximum security fortress, created by the German echelon as a punishment camp for difficult prisoners and inveterate escapers. By the end of the war it boasted the largest number of 'home run' escapes of both World Wars!

By the time I reached Colditz in mid-1943 most of the secret exits had been discovered and plugged following literally dozens of brilliant and well-chronicled escape attempts. It is a tribute to the remarkable men of Colditz that they never gave up, never stopped seeking that possibility of escape, and never lost sight of their duty to country and self.

* * *

On the last day of April 1944, I happened to stroll into the large recreation room on the top floor of our quarters in Colditz. On the way up the stairs I had passed one of our 'stooges', who gave me a friendly smile. Their purpose was to station themselves in a strategic position and keep an eye on the guards' movements, giving a warning if any German approached an area where for one reason or another the prisoners did not want unexpected visitors. These stooges were part and parcel of the make-up of the camp, and I did not think twice about his presence on the stairs.

As I walked into the room four British officers were already there. One of them, John Beaumont, was behaving in a most peculiar manner. John, a lieutenant in the Durham Light Infantry (and later an Anglican priest) had been a tunnelling companion at our last prison camp in Eichstätt. He was standing at the far end of the room dressed only in shorts and gym shoes, with a blanket folded under his arm. He began walking towards me, but suddenly, when halfway across the room, he leapt to his left, fell to the floor and dragged the blanket completely over him.

'Quite good, John,' said Dick Howe, who was standing near me. Dick, a captain in the Royal Tank Corps, was the appointed head of the Escape Committee. 'But still not fast enough. I suggest that just before you leap you change step, turn left and jump with both feet. Try giving that a go.'

Also in the room was Western Australian infantryman Lieutenant Jack Millett. He helped Beaumont fold the blanket, and watched with interest as the procedure was tried once more. This time it went a lot quicker, leaving Beaumont inert on the floor completely covered by his blanket. I turned to Captain David Walker of the Black Watch who was standing beside me. David, a highly respected officer and a good friend of mine, was deep in thought.

'What's going on?' I asked, and David glanced across at me. 'John's had a bit of an idea for an escape,' was the noncommittal reply. 'I'll probably need your help later on; I'll let you know.'

John Beaumont kept rehearsing his act over the next few days, assisted by Jack Millett. Dick Howe was finally satisfied and gave his approval for the attempt, with David Walker appointed to 'manage' the escape. A few days later David had a meeting of around twenty selected prisoners and outlined the plan.

At that time, the Germans allowed a party of about forty to be taken to a nearby park about twice a week, where we could exercise and play limited football and basketball. It was quite a small area, adjacent to the camp, and enclosed by a single high barbed wire fence.

The walk would start about 1pm, after those wishing to go had gathered just inside the main gate to the camp. Once the gate was opened, we would form up under strong guard outside. Here we were counted and then moved off in columns of threes with sentries spaced about every ten feet on either side of the column.

On arrival at the park we were counted again and then let in through the gate. The sentries spread themselves around the enclosure and a machine gun was mounted just outside the wire at the northern end. We spent our time exercising, or in good weather simply lying on the grass. Two hours later we were formed up outside, counted and marched back to the camp where we were counted again before re-entering the courtyard. It was only a short walk, and on the way back there was a spot just outside the camp where the road turned left almost at right angles.

'You all know the sharp left-hand turn by the outside of the castle on the way back from the park,' said David. 'Well, John Beaumont is going to leap sideways from the column next time the park walk is on, just after he rounds the corner. He will conceal himself until the rest have passed and then go like hell, hopefully to make some distance and get into hiding before dark.

'John needs to be positioned on the left-hand side of the column, just behind the second sentry, and surrounded by some of you taller chaps. It will also be necessary to straggle a bit as we near the corner, forcing the sentries to drop back. Then, with luck, they won't spot him making his break. The people in this room have been selected to help. I know you all will.'

'But David,' said someone. 'It won't work; there's nowhere to hide just there, and the guards in the rear will spot him easily.'

'They will not,' he responded, 'because John intends to turn himself into a pile of rubbish.' Several of the men chuckled involuntarily, and then Walker continued.

'To explain: John has a blanket, on which will be tied old tins, rags, paper, vegetable peelings and an assortment of other junk. This will be concealed beneath his greatcoat. Just before the turn he will remove the blanket and, covered by us, carry it in front of him. As he leaps sideways the specially folded blanket will flip open, he will fall to the ground and pull it over him. Thus the heap of rubbish. He's now darned good and I am sure it will work.

'Now another important thing. We must give him as much time as possible to get clear. It will only be a few minutes after we leave John that we arrive back at camp for the final count. We'll certainly cop a bit of abuse, but hopefully we can delay a final count for fifteen minutes or so.'

Everyone seemed impressed with the scheme and Walker selected the taller officers to cover John's movements. My Victorian chum Rex Baxter, six feet tall, was one; Tony Rolt another. For my part I would be about five ranks behind John, flanked by two German-speaking Englishmen whose job it would be to distract the guards at the crucial time.

Three days later, on 2 May, a walk to the park was announced for that afternoon, and all of us in the team were informed. After being counted we marched down to the park under guard, the twenty of us in the know, and about twenty others. All went well, and two hours later we were formed up for the march back.

Just before we reached the corner those of us to the rear of John began to straggle behind, and the column lengthened. The guards were annoyed. *'Schnell, schnell!'* they shouted, but were ignored.

The chaps alongside me began to pester the guards on either side in order to distract them. 'What's the bloody hurry?' they argued. 'We're nearly there!' The guards just snarled at them and kept yelling at us to move faster. As we turned the corner I glanced to the left. There, lying against the wall, was a heap of rubbish! We marched on to the camp, about another 400 yards, and halted outside the gate. Then the fun began. They just could not count us. We refused to keep in line and moved about, some in four ranks, some in two. Confusion reigned supreme as the Germans yelled at us. Finally the Security Officer, Hauptmann Eggers, arrived. He singled out David Walker whom he knew spoke German.

'You must get the group in order to be counted,' he commanded.

'Sorry, can't do anything about it,' was the casual response. 'I'm junior in rank to a number of these officers. They don't, and won't, take orders from me.'

Eggers was furious. He spluttered and screamed but got nowhere. Eventually we were forced to enter the camp under a strong armed guard.

In this manner they were finally able to get a correct count and realise our number was one short, but twenty precious minutes had passed. Mobile patrols were immediately despatched by the Germans.

Unfortunately John Beaumont was caught walking rapidly along a track about three miles from the camp, just 200 yards short of some good afforestation cover. Thus a well thought out, carefully planned and perfectly executed escape came to an untimely end.

This, in effect, was one of the last escape bids to take place in Colditz, for not long after our Senior British Officer Colonel Tod received news of German reprisals on escaped POWs. To the chagrin of the German officers at Colditz, he reminded us at Appell that an Allied victory was now assured, and it was pointless risking a bullet in the back of the head with liberation so close at hand.

For my own part, I had now been an unwilling guest of the Third Reich for more than three years, and in that time I had been involved in some of the most incredible and spectacular escapes of the war.

I was born in Geelong in southern Victoria, Australia, on 6 August 1913. After the usual number of years of scholastic endeavour, the latter nine at Geelong College, I was confronted at the age of sixteen with one of the worst depressions of all time, and the inherent problem of finding a job.

By sheer perseverance I was lucky enough to get work in a fertiliser company as a junior clerk, 'stamp licking' at the princely wage of one pound per week. I remained with this company until 1936, when I joined the staff of the Ford Motor Company of Australia as a junior accountant. After qualifying as an accountant in 1937 I moved into a more senior position, and remained there until war broke out in September 1939.

With the formation of the Sixth Australian Division in October 1939 I left Ford and joined the Australian Imperial Forces as a raw private on the twenty-third of that month.

Following ten weeks' training, during which I had risen to the exalted rank of Lance Corporal, I was selected for a two months' intensive officer training course at Liverpool in New South Wales. During this period I attained the rank of Corporal, and the sixty-four members of the course were returned to their units early in March the following year.

We were very proud of ourselves, and the eight members of my unit who had all graduated successfully were ordered to present ourselves to the commanding officer, Lieutenant-Colonel (subsequently Brigadier) Arthur Godfrey DSO MC. We were prepared for a resounding 'Well done!', but instead the colonel took the wind out of our sails by reminding us that while we had been enjoying the relative comforts of Liverpool, our unit, the 2/6th Infantry Battalion, had been training hard in preparation for embarkation to an undisclosed destination, and we were expected to knuckle down immediately.

Two days prior to our departure I was surprised to be called before the Colonel once more, and with little ceremony informed that I was promoted forthwith to Lance Sergeant. The day before we sailed I was granted commissioned rank and embarked with the unit, the most junior of junior officers in the whole of the 17th

Brigade. I did not even have officers' uniform, and sailed in battle dress with one small pip proudly worn on each shoulder.

After seven months of hard training in Palestine and Egypt we saw action in the Western Desert at Bardia, Tobruk, Benghazi and El Agheila before returning to Alexandria where, after a brief period of rest and relaxation, we sailed for Greece to support the Greeks in their struggle with the Italians. We arrived early in April 1941, at which time I was a member of Brigadier (later Lieutenant-General) Sir Stanley Savige's staff, as Liaison Officer to the 2/6th Battalion.

Greece was a fiasco. With the arrival of the 17th Brigade Headquarters staff at Larissa, Savige's staff captain, Ab Gray, was called to a conference of British staff personnel, and he was given the operation orders for the evacuation of British troops from Greece. Our three battalions – the 2/5th, 6th and 7th – were at that time still in Egypt awaiting embarkation orders for Greece, where they arrived a week later! Perhaps 'fiasco' is too mild a word for such a monumental balls-up.

After several wasted days languishing around a deserted airfield, from which all aircraft had either been flown back to Egypt or destroyed, we received our evacuation orders and travelled to what was known as 'T' beach on the south coast of Greece, where we arrived just too late for the departure of the last ships.

We were trapped, surrounded by an ever-closer enemy, and it was time to make ourselves scarce. A last order came through as we were making ready to leave Argos: we were to disperse and make our own way to Crete, from where we would be evacuated. Crete? Bloody hell!

Ten of our unit decided we would set off on foot from the area, and by next morning we found ourselves in a small fishing village about 35 miles north-east of Argos. Here five of us commandeered a fishing boat which we sailed to a small island about two miles from Spetsia, and after trekking to the other side of the island found two fishermen who nervously agreed to row us over.

Once on Spetsia we were fortunate enough to meet some benefactors almost straight away, including a nurse who spoke perfect English. We were given a very welcome meal at the local hospital, and spent that night at a small inn about half a mile away. The next morning the five of us walked down to the jetty, where we met up with an English sergeant and several other British troops. As the day wore on we were joined by seventy-five infantrymen, all in the same position as ourselves. We learned that a fishing boat with ten officers and forty men had left the previous night for Crete, and our hopes began to rise, knowing that our troops were being evacuated by ship from Crete.

Lieutenant Archie Walker and I found a Greek fisherman with a 50-foot diesel-powered boat and crew, and he grudgingly promised to take us to the island of Milos, about eighty miles to the south-east, and roughly halfway to Crete. His fee was eighty thousand drachma – equivalent to nearly 500 dollars today. He said there was a British naval station on Milos, and as we could only scratch up about forty thousand drachma he agreed to be paid the balance on arrival at Milos. We all crowded onto the boat, and the Greeks set sail.

A storm blew up that night, and we had to shelter for two days on the uninhabited island of Glaronissia, which was little more than a rocky outcrop. The boat's captain was reluctant to press on to Milos, but we promised him another ten thousand drachma, and as the weather seemed to be abating he finally agreed.

We set out that night, and five hours later we anchored offshore from a quiet-looking village inside Milos Harbour. A faint light flashed from the beach, and we were asked in Morse for identification. A signalman aboard our boat answered with the captain's torch, and soon several rowing boats came alongside and ferried us all ashore. Once there, Colonel Courage of the British army informed us there were already fifty British personnel with him, and the island's commandant had assured him he was in touch with Crete. A British naval vessel was expected to pick us up within 24 hours. The next day we woke to find our Greek fisherman and his boat had vanished during the night, and we were stuck on Milos with only a vague assurance of help from the navy.

Help did not arrive that day, and the day after we were instructed to march to the other side of the island, about ten miles away, where we would be picked up by a boat. On the way across we killed and barbecued some sheep before pressing on. Once again the promised boat did not turn up, and the next morning we were instructed to return to the village, as new arrangements had been made for our evacuation.

We tramped back, tired and dispirited, and the following morning received word that we would be evacuated on a Greek schooner we could see moored in the harbour. Our patience was running just a little thin by now, but the sight of the vessel was encouraging. Together with about fifty civilians, mostly women and children, we were ferried out to the schooner, only to be told on arrival that there was a problem with the engine. A message from the village assured us that a replacement part was being rustled up and would be brought out soon. Meanwhile we were to sit tight.

We spent an uncomfortable night crowded together on the cramped schooner. We had water, but nothing to eat, as the island's commandant had told our officers there was very little food on Milos.

At 11am we were still aboard the immobile boat when someone observed plumes of smoke from two vessels racing through the harbour entrance. We waved our hats and jumped for joy, but our cheers soon ceased when we realised they were German gun boats. Panic ensued as everyone scurried for cover; some leapt overboard, while others concealed themselves where they could. I crawled under a dirty piece of canvas beneath the forward deck.

A few minutes later the gun boats hauled alongside, and German soldiers began leaping aboard. Resistance was impossible because of the civilians, and in any case it would have been futile. I peeped out from under the canvas just in time to observe a timid Greek woman pointing out my hiding place to an armed soldier.

'Raus! Raus!' screamed the soldier as he strode over and prodded me savagely with his rifle. *'Hände hoch! Hände hoch! Raus!'*

I crawled out from beneath the ancient piece of canvas, stumbled onto the deck and into the brilliant sunshine where I paused for a moment. Impatiently the German jabbed me in the back with his rifle barrel, forcing me amidships. German soldiers were everywhere, and orders were being shouted all over. As I was marched roughly along I casually dropped my right hand to my Smith and Wesson revolver, still resting unnoticed in its holster on my hip, and with one movement drew the weapon and tossed it overboard. At least they wouldn't get that! As it splashed into the clear blue water the German whacked me behind the ear with his rifle butt for my insolence.

In a dazed condition I was pushed towards a milling group of English and Australian troops. With my ears ringing, and in a confused state, I heard a guttural voice addressing me. 'For you, the war is over.'

Sullenly I looked up into the gloating face of a German soldier.

Slowly it began to dawn on me; I had become a prisoner of war. A deep sense of despair washed over me. To be wounded, maybe; to be killed, impossible – not Jack Champ! But to be captured – I had never given it much thought. The date was 9 May 1941.

Thirteen of us had been crowded into a small room in an old Greek house.

As officers, we were separated from the other men and marched off to this house, from where we would eventually be transported to Athens.

On 12 May we were informed that we were being shipped back to the mainland. After our evening meal we were loaded onto a Greek caique (a small schooner type of vessel). The guards kept us in the hold until we were under way, but then allowed us onto the deck. They were taking no chances; machine guns were mounted fore and aft, and a warning given that any attempt at mischief would result in the lot of us being shot.

Weather-wise it was a glorious day, and the sea was a lovely blue, but as we sailed along I became quite morose and depressed. My mood was not aided by the sight of two bloated bodies floating nearby in the twilight seas. At nightfall we were once again secured in the hold, and when we woke the caique was pulling into Piraeus Harbour. The city of Athens lay off to our starboard, and the pleasant atmosphere was offset by the incongruous field-grey uniforms of our guards. They did not fit in with these tranquil surroundings and war seemed a faraway reality.

A rather antiquated bus pulled up and we were ordered to board it for the short drive to German Headquarters. We were kept here for a few hours, during which time spurious Red Cross forms were handed out for completion. We had all been forewarned in training about these, and while we readily pencilled in our names, ranks and service numbers we left blank the areas concerning our battalions, senior officers and unit strength. It was an old trick, and no one there seemed too surprised when we refused to divulge this information. Later that day we reboarded the bus and travelled the sixty miles to Corinth, where we were told we would be 'billeted' in our first prisoner-of-war camp. It was here we received our first nasty shock; until this time we had been under the impression that very few British troops had been left in Greece. We were absolutely astonished to find that almost ten thousand men were now 'in the bag'.

Our names were taken by an arrogant German officer, and it became immediately apparent that our treatment was about to change for the worse as we were literally shoved into the camp.

The camp in Corinth sat on a sandy area of nearly fifteen acres and had formerly been a Greek army barracks, with room for only half the number that were now squeezed in. Decent accommodation was a thing of the past and most prisoners elected to sleep outside on the ground. The barely tenable quarters were old stone buildings and unventilated, verminous wooden sheds. The sanitary arrangements were crude – three long trenches had been dug at one end of the compound, and with many prisoners now suffering from dysentery these were constantly in use. At any time of the day there would be anything up to 600 men using these communal 'toilets' and soiled bits of paper were blown all over the compound, eventually accumulating at the foot of the fences.

Soon after we'd arrived I discovered that some of my battalion officers were there. Ab Gray, Jack Paterson, and Jack Young were sleeping in a two-storey stone building, and once I'd located them they very kindly took me in and let me sleep on the floor with them.

My memories of the nearly four weeks I spent at Corinth are rather hazy now. I recall days of almost unendurable boredom and frustration; of falling into a day-to-day routine of searching for food, killing lice, and trying hard to keep the incessant hunger at bay until one could fall asleep in order to shut out the anxieties for a few hours.

Towards the end of May a rumour reached us that we would shortly be moved to more permanent camps in Germany, and early in June our departure was announced. We were to leave on the fifth.

Two days before we left, I met up again with a new arrival – a young 2/7th lieutenant I had known during gas school in Cairo and later in the Western Desert. His name was Mark Howard, and his ship the *Hellas* had been sunk during their evacuation from Greece. Mark had been wounded, and ended up in hospital before being sent to Corinth. He had impressed me a great deal during the gas training and in the desert, and struck me as a solid, courageous soldier. It was good to strike up our friendship again – one that endured even after the war. Our lives as prisoners of war in Greece and Germany ran very much on a parallel from that day, and we would share many fine adventures.

On 5 July all the officers in the camp began the first stage of their journey into Germany. We were told that our first destination would be Salonika in north-eastern Greece, and from there we would be dispersed into various officer camps in Germany.

Dulag 183, Salonika, was an infamous transit camp for all the prisoners taken in Greece and Crete. The Turks had originally built the camp as barracks during their Occupation, and it had later been used by the Greeks as an artillery barracks.

By the time we arrived on 7 June after a long, appallingly overcrowded train journey in cattle trucks, conditions were absolutely disgusting – worse even than Corinth – and the resident German guards completely ruthless. The prisoners, although revolted by the filth and hideous stench of the place, knew very little about adjustment to life as a POW, and most of us meekly allowed ourselves to be bullied and maltreated by our captors. We had scant idea about self-preservation under these conditions, let alone of entertaining any thoughts of making an escape. Every waking moment was dedicated to a pitiful struggle to obtain even the smallest scrap of food, and a lethargy born of hunger began to sap our will.

Some prisoners actually managed to escape, but most attempts were crude and ill-conceived, with desperation the prime motivation. Those caught were either shot or savagely beaten. The price of failure at Salonika was very high.

Our guards thought little of whipping or beating prisoners on the slightest pretext, sometimes tying them down for days in the heat and filth of the compound as 'reprisals'. The savage beating or killing of prisoners was actually condoned by the guards' superiors, because of rumoured atrocities against German soldiers in the Cretan campaign.

Corruption was bred of hunger. Many escape attempts were allowed to continue their course by the Germans, who had been given previous knowledge of the plans by informers. In one forlorn bid five Cypriots crawled out to the barbed wire fence under cover of darkness, but the guards had earlier been told about the escape.

As the men reached the wire the Germans rushed out and shot them down in cold blood. The bloody corpses were left tangled in the wire and on the ground as a warning to others. After a couple of days in the searing heat the stench was overpowering, and the area was respectfully avoided if possible.

Food supplies at the camp were irregular and barely adequate for survival. It consisted mostly of any old garbage the Germans cared to issue. By now I had also become good friends with Captain Rex Baxter of the 2/5th Battalion. He had been wounded in the hip in Greece, and was hospitalised in Athens with Mark Howard, who had a thigh wound. Because of his wound Rex was allowed to work in the camp kitchen, and he summed up our food issue in just one word: putrid. Lumps of maggot-riddled horse or goat, rotten vegetables and filthy, undrinkable water was our daily fare. We became inured to seeing fur and even hooves in the meat supply. Little wonder that morale slumped to an almost desperate level, while disease and dysentery caused despair to course like a cancer through the camp. Mosquitoes swarmed around the stagnant water intended for both drinking and daily ablutions, and bed bugs ran rampant through the huts.

We were demoralised, hungry, and weak as kittens, and the bed bugs – they would get into every crevice of our bodies and the lining of our clothes, and we were forever scratching and searching them out. We either crushed them between our thumbnails or burnt them off with matches. When we burned them they exploded with a satisfying little pop, but the resultant stink was dreadful.

Finally, to the relief of everyone, orders were posted for six hundred men to prepare themselves for the train journey into Germany. We gathered our few belongings into a bundle, and on

9 July were paraded in the barracks ground for a slow and thorough roll-call.

Then we were carefully searched, but I managed to hang onto my little compass by the simple ruse of holding it in my hand. After two hours we were on our way.

At the station the guards quickly distributed our food for the trip. This comprised a small chunk of cooked meat, three rock-hard Greek biscuits, and a small loaf of coarse black bread, the main ingredient of which was sawdust. This was our entire food issue for the week-long journey.

Naturally enough many of the hunger-crazed prisoners could not contain themselves, and tore into their food straight away. It was a torment not to follow their example. Later, those who had eaten the rations regretted their impulsiveness; their hunger may have been temporarily satisfied, but those with dysentery suffered badly when their bowels rebelled, and life on the train became unbearable.

Days passed in a sickening haze of dysentery, the stench of urine, and unrelenting hunger in the stifling, overcrowded cattle trucks. It was almost a relief when we realised we were well into southern Germany. The train finally pulled up at a large station and the guards threw our sliding doors open. As we gulped in the sweet fresh air we discovered we had arrived at East Munich. The day after we pulled in to another big city, this time Ulm. The officer in charge told us we would reach our destination that night, and right on six o'clock we slowly rolled into the station of a small Bavarian village called Biberach.

Filthy, unshaven and dispirited, we were bundled into an untidy line and marched uphill, through some otherwise beautiful and lush countryside, until we arrived outside a large camp with the inevitable barbed wire fences and sentry boxes. We were halted outside the main gate. Owlishly, we looked into the compound of our new camp, where some curious British officers had gathered to scrutinise us, searching perhaps for an old chum or two. Listlessly we allowed ourselves to be checked off and passed through without a search. Little wonder – we must have smelt pretty ripe by this time.

As we entered the camp, shouts and cheers in clear British voices gave us a rousing welcome. The camp at Biberach already contained about 400 officers who had been captured at Dunkirk and Calais. These chaps were mostly shut up in their barracks for our arrival, but had clustered by the windows, shouting their heads off. Suddenly we felt a lot better – there was a friendly element in a hostile place. It did us good after that terrible trip. Next we were lined up in the camp square, led off in groups for a welcome and refreshing hot shower, and then given some assorted clean clothing to wear. As if by a miracle a cup of strong English tea was handed out to each of us. We later found out that the resident British officers had pooled their tea rations to provide us with our first good drink for weeks.

Never has tea tasted better!

Our new quarters consisted of long concrete huts. Assorted rooms opened off a long, central passageway, and we found a good-sized one, into which eight of us fitted quite comfortably. Our room contained four two-tiered wooden bunks, and each was equipped with two blankets and a straw paillasse. The walls were plaster, and the floor made up of a smooth composition material. Above all else, we were pleased to note that the rooms were clean.

Oflag VB, Biberach, was the best camp I was held in during my involuntary stay in Germany. The guards were not overly friendly, but they were reasonable, and responded to most grievances about conditions. Every Friday we enjoyed a hot shower, and the rations, although by no means adequate, were wholesome. But to an escaper's eye the greatest encouragement of all was provided by the sight of the Swiss mountains, just visible to the south past Lake Constance, which was a bare 45 miles away. The nearest possible crossing point was Schaffhausen, which we estimated to be around 70 miles away.

The Germans had us all photographed and fingerprinted, and noted down any distinctive scars or marks on our bodies. We were then issued with a metal identity disc – mine proclaimed me to be Kriegsgefangener (prisoner of war) Number 102. They gave us three letter-cards and four postcards to send home, and we were permitted to write to our loved ones immediately. This was the allowance for one month, and never changed over the years.

I slept quite a lot in those early days as my body recovered from the journey into Germany, but as time wore on I slept less (as did the others) and we took to having long walks around the camp compound for exercise. About this time we also received our first 'pay' from the Germans. As a lieutenant I received 81 lagermarks per month. These camp marks were printed on ordinary paper and were totally useless anywhere else but the camp canteen. As there was practically nothing there to buy, one could either save the notes or gamble with them. Records of pay were kept by our own British paymaster and it was possible, by not drawing money, to build up a sizeable credit. The military authorities back in Australia deducted the sum of 4/6d (45 cents) per day from our army pay to represent the money given to us in Germany.

Towards the end of July, amid great excitement, we received a consignment of Canadian Red Cross parcels, and each of us was to be given one whole parcel. Our euphoria was then dampened by the German Kommandant Hauptmann Gomel, who directed that all tins inside the parcels were to be opened and inspected for contraband. We set up an immediate howl of protest; to suggest that illicit items would be in Red Cross parcels was ludicrous (in all my years as a prisoner of war, and in all the POW accounts I have ever read, there was never a single instance of contraband being smuggled inside a Red Cross parcel. To have infringed this precious lifeline would have meant immediate cancellation of the parcels and the subsequent death of hundreds if not thousands of prisoners).

Our Senior British Officer, Major-General Victor Fortune, was livid at the Kommandant's stance. As commander of the 51st Division he had elected to stay with his men and face capture rather than be evacuated to Britain, and was a tremendous fellow to have on our side in the camp. Enraged, he issued immediate instructions that a 'go-slow' policy was to be adopted.

The Kommandant's directive stated that if we did not wish to draw certain items we could leave them in a store with our name on them, to be opened only when we drew them out. All others were to be opened in front of us. General Fortune's strategy was for each officer to claim his parcel at the store, and point out the tin cans required. Just as the corporal was about to open the cans the officer would change his mind and decide to draw out different cans. When he had finally made up his mind he would take out a piece of paper and carefully note down what cans he had deposited. All this took time, and by midday only twenty-five parcels had been drawn. As there were more than eight hundred of us it was obvious they would never get through. This was pointed out to the Kommandant and he finally relented, allowing the remaining parcels to be issued intact.

To this time we had been existing on German rations. Suddenly we had eight lovely Red Cross parcels, and we were as excited as kids at Christmas. Parcels were carefully opened and the contents arranged on our little table in the centre of the room. Gleefully we surveyed our bounty: we had tinned meat roll, herrings, apple puddings, bully beef, sardines, salmon, meat and vegetable stew, biscuits, sugar, tea, coffee, cocoa and, most impressive of all, chocolate. The tins were carefully classified and Ab Gray appointed our quartermaster. He arranged a menu for the week, and that evening we enjoyed the finest meal we'd eaten in months. We were excited, everyone was talking at once, and each of us had their opinion as to how the food should be treated. That night we sat up until midnight talking, laughing, singing and telling jokes. With the parcels came a supply of English cigarettes, and we each received a tin of fifty Gold Flakes to last us for a week. And weren't they bloody marvellous.

During our stay in Oflag VB we received a regular issue of one Red Cross parcel and fifty cigarettes per week, and the nutritious food kept us in relatively good health, enabling us to participate in sport and exercise.

We now began to talk seriously about escape, and the probability of making it back to England. In the Greek camps the position had been rather hopeless, and like most prisoners we had decided to wait until we were settled in a permanent camp in Germany before we made any serious attempt.

The camp boundaries at Biberach consisted of barbed wire double fences about sixteen feet high and six feet apart. In between these fences were coils of wire and wooden stakes. The entire perimeter was lit by arc lights by night, and the sentry boxes were fitted with powerful search lights. In addition to the sentries in the towers, two guards were positioned on both sides of the camp each night. These guards were visited at frequent intervals by a patrol of two German NCOs with a ferocious-looking dog.

At 10pm all lights in the camp were turned off and the doors locked. Anyone caught outside after this time was liable to be shot.

Mark Howard and I had taken a good look at the camp's defences and decided that escaping would be a difficult proposition. So much for our misgivings; when we finally left Oflag VB in October – just four months later – no fewer than fifty-two officers had escaped from the camp, five having reached safety in Switzerland.

We heard a whisper on parade one day that an officer was missing, and had been absent for two days. His place had been filled by an accomplice in the camp hospital who, as soon as he had been counted in his hospital bed, would dash outside and be counted again at the general Appell. The escape itself had been made in a sack used for carrying waste paper from the parcel room. The escaper had hidden himself in the sack and friends had placed paper on top of him. He was then loaded onto a hand cart by a British working party and taken to a shed outside the camp. After dark it was a simple matter to cut his way out of the bag and take off. Unfortunately he was recaptured near the Swiss frontier and returned to the camp. His name was Captain Hector Christie. He had almost made it – he had been within sight of the Schaffhausen crossing area when, by rotten chance, he had accidentally tripped over a sleeping sentry, who quickly recovered from his rude awakening and ordered the violator to put his hands up. Because the Germans had not worked out Christie's exit route it was tried again. This time Lieutenant Chandos Blair succeeded in crossing the frontier after ten days on foot, and eventually made it back to England. First away!

There was an escape committee in the camp, headed by an officer who could be approached if one had a scheme for getting out. The principal task of this committee was to coordinate escapes in order to prevent any overlapping by two simultaneous efforts, which could ruin many months of planning and preparation. As well, they had in their possession a supply of maps of the local and Swiss frontier areas. At this stage we were still very green prisoners, and not up at all in the politics of the escaping business, so most of us had no occasion to register a plan with the committee and talk it over with them. As many of the officers in the camp were keen on escaping, competition was quite fierce and original plans few, but some did work well.

One example was the 'bath-house racket'. Every Friday the whole camp had a hot shower in a block just outside the gate. These showers started at 9.30am and prisoners went in batches of about twenty-five every fifteen minutes. The scheme itself was simple; those escaping (generally two) went to the showers in the usual way. Once in the changing room they put on workmen's overalls, which had been made from pyjamas dyed to a blue colour with indelible pencil. When they were ready they would emerge from the shower house and proceed in a leisurely fashion around the outside of the wire. The get-up was very good indeed, as there were frequently workmen about the place dressed in this manner, and the Germans' suspicions were not aroused. Over a period of two months, eight prisoners escaped using this method, and the Germans did not know how it was being accomplished until two men were caught just a few yards from the shower house by an exceptionally alert guard.

So good was the security surrounding these escapes that it was not until the last two were caught that the majority in the camp knew how they were getting away.

A few days later two British officers dressed in German fatigue outfits (more dyed pyjamas) walked boldly up to the gate, presented their faked passes, and strolled off in the direction of Switzerland. They were Terrence Prittie (who was to make eight escapes during the war before finally reaching home) and Peter Brush. Some time after, two more bogus Germans passed through the gate using the same method – this time Tony Rolt and Ronnie Barter. They had given the first pair a good four hours start in order to get well clear of the camp, and they too encountered no difficulty in passing through the camp gates. Sad to say they were all picked up by the Germans within a few days and returned to Oflag VB, earning a spell in the solitary confinement cells for their audacity.

The day after our arrival I was standing outside my barracks when I noticed a British officer in artillery uniform pass me several times, staring quite pointedly at me with a puzzled expression on his face. Eventually he stopped and introduced himself as Captain Tom Westley.

'Please don't think me rude,' he said, 'but you remind me a great deal of a chap I used to know in the Great War – my AIF platoon commander. I was in the AIF before taking up residence in England.'

'Jack Champ,' I rejoined, shaking his hand. 'Pleased to meet you.'

He looked astonished. 'Would you be related to Finlay Champ?'

'Why yes,' I replied. 'He's my uncle.'

'Well how about that,' he cried. 'We were in Egypt together during the war. You looked so much like him that I just had to come and ask you. It's nice to meet you, although I wish it were under better circumstances.'

I ushered Tom into our quarters and introduced him to the other Australians. In the weeks to come he was very good to all of us, and was more than instrumental in getting me involved in my first escape scheme. We'd been in Biberach a little over a month when Tom called me aside one day and said he was working on a tunnel, which was being dug from a small room on the barbed wire side of Block 6, quite near the perimeter fence. I heard nothing more until August, when Tom told us they were short of manpower, and asked if we wanted to join in. There was a strong rumour going round that we would soon be on the move again, and with a considerable distance still to be dug it was crucial they proceed with maximum effort. Tom told us from the outset that we would not be escaping through the tunnel as the numbers were already too great, but we decided to pitch in and help anyway.

Soon after, we commenced our duties. We would go to the room in question two at a time, and work two shifts every day. The room was occupied by five officers – Michael Duncan, Simon Molloy, Peter Onions, Dennis Atkinson and Michael McNab, all part of the tunnel team. A barred window overlooked the wire, and just inside the door was a slow combustion stove on a concrete block about two feet square.

The tunnel had been started by lifting the stove off the concrete block, then lifting the slab itself and cutting a hole in the composition flooring below, with a diameter a little less than that of the slab. A wooden trap was constructed which fitted exactly into the hole, and this was then painted to resemble the surrounding flooring in case the Germans decided to lift both the stove and the slab during one of their searches. With the block back in place over the trap, and the stove replaced, the whole affair looked very innocent.

Digging tools were pieces of iron bedstead about three feet long and two inches wide. The shaft went down for two feet and then gradually sloped downwards towards the wire at a 30-degree angle for about fifteen feet before going horizontal. The tunnel was revetted with bedboards or any other timber that could be pinched from within the camp.

By this time the tunnel was nearly ninety feet long, with about half that distance still to be excavated. The man digging at the face of the tunnel would gouge away at the dirt and clay and fill small wooden boxes with the spoil. A second man, in a specially widened chamber about fifteen feet from the end of the shaft, would haul the boxes back as they were filled. In the room above them two 'stooges' were on constant lookout duty. One watched at the wire-side window for any approaching guards, while the second was posted at the door listening for signals from another stooge monitoring German movements around the compound. A third man would haul up the boxes from the man in the chamber and empty them into Red Cross cartons. When these were full a lid was fitted and they were stacked beneath a bed.

The tunnel was lit by means of a wire connected to the electric light socket in the room. The diggers below received fresh air by means of an ingenious camp-made bellows and some cardboard tubing, which took the air right up to the face of the tunnel. As the tunnel got longer, so more tubing was added.

It was possible to close the whole show down in just fifteen seconds following a warning. The light wire would be pulled from its connection and thrown down into the hole, and the resultant darkness would alert those in the tunnel, who would stay motionless until the lights went back on. The bellows and tubing were also thrown down the hole, the trap fitted, the slab lowered over the trap, and the stove replaced on top of the slab. Someone would hurriedly sweep any stray dirt under a bed, and we would then assume positions of innocent relaxation – reading, talking, or writing letters.

The jobs we Australians were allocated were for the most part carried out in the escape room itself. We pumped the air, filled the boxes, watched out the window and did stooging duties on the door. We had some very narrow squeaks in this time. On one occasion something went wrong with the outside monitoring system, and a knock came on the door. Our stooge opened it a fraction of an inch, and to his complete astonishment looked straight into the eyes of a German NCO. His immediate reaction was to slam the door in the NCOs face and yell, 'There's a German outside!' We crash dived in record time, but fortunately the guard went away, probably puzzled by the rude treatment meted out to him. It was a close call.

The soil from the tunnel was eventually dragged out from under the beds and passed up through a trapdoor into the roof, where there was quite a large area between the ceiling and the roof. On the days this happened two extra helpers would go up into the roof and spend the day spreading the dirt evenly over the ceiling timber, after which they would pass the empty boxes back down ready to be refilled.

And so the job moved to completion. Michael Duncan, who was engineering the tunnel, worked out his distances and calculated that the required length had been dug. In order to double-check his calculations it was decided to thrust a poker up through the surface at the work face, and observers by the wire-side window would note where it came up. Bobby Barr went down the shaft with a poker and we watched from the window. To our amazement we suddenly saw the end of the poker sticking up out of the ground, twenty feet short of where it was supposed to be. To make matters worse, a sentry was doing his rounds and his dog began sniffing at the area where the poker had been withdrawn moments earlier. The dog began barking, just inches above a petrified Bobby Barr, who was holding his breath. Finally, to our relief, the dog and the sentry moved on.

It took ten more days to dig the extra twenty feet, but eventually everything was set for the mass break-out. A few days' delay occurred while the escape team waited for a suitably wet night, which came on 13 September. At 10pm they began to break through to the surface, and things went quite smoothly. I was not involved in this part of the operation, and did not learn of the break until we went into Block 6 the next morning. We were told, amid much satisfaction, that all twenty-six officers were safely away.

At Biberach the Germans counted us twice a day; the first Appell at 8.30am and the second at 4.30pm. That morning we trudged down for roll-call wondering what the goons (as we now called our captors) would do once they realised they were a few officers short. We writhed in silent satisfaction as they went about their routine, but knew the balloon would soon go up. We duly lined up in five ranks by blocks, each block being counted separately. As the missing men came from just about every block in the camp the ensuing confusion was quite amusing. The first block was three men short, the second five short, and the third two short. The German adjutant responsible for conducting the Appell finally strode over to General Fortune, and in a classic case of understatement declared, 'There seems to be something wrong!'

Fortune, who knew exactly what the problem was, had the trace of a smile on his face. 'What seems to be wrong?' he asked the flustered German. 'After counting three blocks I am already short by ten of your officers!' the worried man replied.

'Well, that's nothing really,' came Fortune's laconic reply. 'Count the rest, and you will find there's a damn sight more missing!'

The red-faced adjutant nearly collapsed on the spot, and rushed off to inform Kommandant Gomel.

Needless to say the German authorities were not amused. Immediately suspecting a tunnel they sent patrols around the camp perimeter, and soon discovered the exit hole. We were kept on parade for about four hours while they meticulously checked our names and found out who was missing. The whole of the German guard company was turned out, and patrols assisted by sniffer dogs began scouring the countryside. Guards were placed in the room from which the tunnel had been dug, and around the exit shaft. By afternoon a relative calm had returned to the camp.

Eventually we started hearing reports of the escape party being picked up. Some were only free for 24 hours, while others, just failing to make it across the Swiss border, were away for up to three weeks. But at last came the best news of all; four out of the 26 had actually made it across the border into Switzerland, and were waiting to be transported home to England. They were Michael Duncan, Barry O'Sullivan, Angus Rowan-Hamilton and Hugh Woollatt.

Having worked on the tunnel the eight of us knew all the officers involved, and as each came back after recapture he would relate his adventures to us. Bobby Barr, a big lump of a man who had once played rugby for England, had a humorous story to tell. After his capture he had been placed in a French POW camp, where he spent two days in the solitary confinement cells. On the second day, while being taken across the compound under guard for a wash, he suddenly heard a voice with a strong American accent calling to him. It was some moments before he realised the speaker was one of the sentries on a watch tower by the wire.

'Hey fella!' the guard had called down. 'Are you English?'

'Why yes, I am,' an astonished Barr had yelled back.

'Christ it's good to hear English again!' said the guard in rich American tones. 'I lived in the States for fifteen years, and arrived back in this goddamn country just in time to get caught up in the goddamn war! Wouldn't that just shit you to tears?!!'

On 7 October word came through General Fortune that the camp would be evacuated in the next couple of days. The Germans refused to disclose our destination, and speculation was rife.

Very early on the day of the move we were roused from our beds and told to gather our equipment together for a final Appell, at which we endured another thorough search. Then it was down to the kitchen until the Germans were ready to march us down to the station.

As my name started with a 'C' I was in the first lot to go, and a German interpreter carefully briefed us regarding our behaviour on the train. It was *verboten* to open any windows, *verboten* to go to the toilets unless accompanied by a guard, and we would be shot if we attempted to escape. Decent carriages this time, thank God, not cattle trucks.

And so, on 10 October, with a touch of winter in the air, the Germans began evacuating the remaining 700 POWs from Biberach. During the train journey we found out that our destination was a place called Warburg, near the Westphalian city of Kassel.

Steadily our train headed north, through Swabia and Franconia, and over the Neckar and Main rivers. Word was passed when we reached Kassel, the capital of Hesse, and one of the guards mentioned that Warburg was another 25 miles on. It was two days since we had left Biberach.

On arrival at Warburg station we were again lined up into our squads of fifty to be marched up and away from the village. Two miles on, we arrived at the main gate of Oflag VIB, which for many of us was to be our new 'home' for the next eleven months.

All seven hundred of us were split up into three groups, and allocated three large huts, where we were searched all over again. Once this was done we were permitted into the main compound, where we could finally talk amongst ourselves and work out some satisfactory billeting arrangements. Our Aussie team elected to stick together.

We learned from some maps which had survived the searches that Warburg was about 250 miles from the Swiss border, and around 100 miles from Holland.

After four months at Biberach, where the Swiss Alps could be seen on a clear day, the distance seemed insuperable.

2

Warburg: Planning the Wire Job

Our new camp at Warburg (pronounced Vaarburg) was situated on an open plain in an agricultural district, and the view, particularly looking out from behind barbed wire fences, was certainly cheerless.

Oflag VIB had been built about three miles from the tiny village and railway station of Warburg, first set up and used as a captured officers' camp in October, just days before we arrived. It had been hastily constructed on a high, windswept plateau, and was meant to contain around 2500 officers and 300 orderlies. Each wooden hut was designed to hold about 200 prisoners. When we moved in it was painfully obvious that the control of fleas and rodents was to be a major problem, along with the ever-prevalent lack of food. After a few months in Warburg we had just about eradicated the first problem, but the second was still cause for anxiety. Thoughts of escape and ways to achieve this freedom always pervaded our day-to-day activities.

The rooms in each of the huts ran off a central hallway. I ended up in one about twenty feet by fifteen with nine other officers. In the centre of the room was a deal table, and each of us was supplied with a wooden stool. Around the walls were the standard two-tiered bunks, and near the door was an iron stove on which we were expected to do all our cooking. When we placed the stools around the table it was impossible to get from one side of the room to the other without walking over the bunks. Our washing facilities consisted of a series of trough-like arrangements situated in another wooden building about 100 yards from our living quarters. There were no inside lavatories, and it was necessary to walk 200 yards to a very open-air toilet.

It was in Warburg that we first met up with a number of fellow Australians who had been captured on Crete. They had arrived just two days before us, having endured a most unpleasant four months. For six weeks they had been in the bug-ridden compound at Salonika, then, after a nightmare cattle truck journey up into Germany, they had spent two months in a repulsive camp at Lübeck. Since capture they had been completely without Red Cross food or clothing, and even after such a short time on German rations most of them were in a poor state. A number were suffering from beri-beri and all had lost a lot of weight. I met several men from my own brigade whom I knew quite well, and it was difficult to recognise them.

A few days after our arrival supplies of Red Cross parcels came in, but it was another eight days before they were issued to us. The usual argument about opening all the tins took place, and eventually the Germans allowed us to have sealed food cans until such time as they could make arrangements to provide a store in which to keep them. When the parcels were handed out our new camp Senior British Officer, Colonel Kennedy, sought and received the approval of all prisoners to give two parcels per week for one month to the men captured on Crete.

We were about to face the coldest winter that Germany had experienced for fifty years. Conditions were indescribably dirty and crowded, but the spirit of the men in that camp was (apart from Colditz) the finest that I experienced as a prisoner of war. One compensating feature of the place was a fairly adequate coal allowance. It was possible by careful management to keep our stove going from seven in the morning until ten at night.

Shortly after our arrival I received my first clothing parcel from England. This parcel contained warm underclothing, shirts and pyjamas, and was an absolute godsend during the coming winter. By this time I had been issued with a new battledress tunic sent out by the Red Cross, who had also sent me a blanket to supplement the two thin ones supplied by the Germans. In the depths of that winter of 1941–42 I would go to bed with two pairs of long underpants and two heavy singlets under my pyjamas, a thick woollen sweater on top and a knitted balaclava cap on my head. All the clothing that I had taken off would be carefully placed on top of the blankets in a manner designed to give as much warmth as possible. The huts in which we slept had large gaps between the boards, and the windows were badly fitted. At one stage the temperature reached minus 54 degrees Fahrenheit (–47°C), and believe me that was bloody cold.

It was just twelve months after our capture on the island of Milos that my first real opportunity to escape came along. Spring had finally come around, the snow had melted and the sun was appreciably warmer. The days were becoming longer, the winter mud and slush was drying out and firming beneath our feet, and our spirits began to rise anew.

Although we had helped in various ways in other peoples' schemes we were never really in the front line of activities, but built up instead a reputation for reliability and alertness in assisting with even the most menial of tasks involved in an escape bid. Then one day in mid-May 1942 after the 8.15 Appell, Rex and I were invited to attend a top-secret meeting in the long brick hut which lay adjacent to our own hut 24. The atmosphere in the dimly lit room was restrained as a slim English officer opened proceedings. 'Thank you for coming, gentlemen,' he began. 'My name is Stallard – Tom Stallard. Some of you I know already, but the rest of you are here because you were recommended to me. Very broadly, some people are working on a bit of a blitz out of this place, and we are selecting men from whom we can expect the fullest cooperation to be involved in the scheme.'

His gaze swept the faces before him.

'Now, before I go on, I must ask that each of you make a solemn oath not to repeat anything you hear today. The plans are not to be discussed with anyone apart from those in this room, and then only in the open, well out of earshot.'

I stole a look across at Rex. Did he know what this was about? Rex looked back and shrugged his shoulders; he was as much in the dark as me. Major Stallard waited as each of the twelve men gave his solemn word, and then he relaxed a little.

'Please smoke if you wish, gentlemen,' he said. Several of our group pulled cigarettes from their pockets and lit up. 'We are going to assault the wire. A considerable number of us are going over the double barbed wire fence at night – the exact number will be determined a little later on. We will use ladders to climb to the top of the wire, and platforms to straddle the two fences. The apparatus we will use is simple but effective; one has already been made, and it works.

'Each ladder is twelve feet long, and the longitudinals of the platform about fourteen feet.' Stallard bridged his arms to demonstrate. 'The inner end of the platform forms two handles for launching, and the farther end, which will protrude beyond the outer fence, has a trapeze-type bar. The middle of the platform has slats made from bed boards two and a half feet long by six inches wide. They are spaced about five inches apart. With me?' We all nodded.

'There is a very important feature of the platform. On both longitudinals at the position of the cross piece there is an inverted V-slot. The top rung of the ladder protrudes about nine inches beyond the laterals. These protrusions are designed to click into slots on the underside of the platform and so prevent it from sliding forward.' Again he demonstrated this using his forearms as the ladder and platform. The principle was easy to grasp.

'We will operate from huts located close to the wire, in which the apparatus will be placed the evening of the day we go. Your particular assault area is the wire between huts 20 and 21. Each assembly will be pushed out of the window with the platform resting on the ladder. Ten men will be designated to each apparatus. Numbers 1, 2, 9 and 10 will run to the fence with the apparatus and place it upright against the wire. Number 1 will then grab the handles of the platform and push it up and out until it straddles the two fences. He will then crawl quickly across, grab the trapeze bar, and drop to the ground. The remainder of the team will follow in rapid succession, and you will then run like blue blazes! Now, you are probably wondering about the search lights, and the German patrols.'

I had indeed: arc lights illuminated every square inch of the wire, and powerful searchlights swept the compound from regularly spaced sentry towers. The sentries were under orders to shoot anyone who crossed a warning trip-wire a few feet from the inner fence, and signs had been planted inside the trip-wire which read *'Halt! Lagergrenze! Bei Überschreiten des Drahtes wird geschossen!'* ('Stop! Camp boundary! Anyone crossing the wire will be shot!')

As well, following the recent breaking of a tunnel just beyond the wire, additional guards were now patrolling outside the perimeter of the camp. Stallard continued. 'We have discovered a way around these problems, and have a positive way of fusing the lights – and I mean the entire camp lighting system. The method is secret but flawless, and we can put them off and on at will. You may recall that all the lights went out for about ten minutes a few nights back. That was us – the Germans thought it was an air raid.' I remembered it happening, and had jumped to the same conclusion. I was becoming increasingly impressed with Stallard's scheme.

'Now, as for the patrols. We realise this is a rather difficult problem but we are confident that it can be taken care of by creating a few simultaneous diversions. Full details have yet to be worked out. Your assault point, as I have said, will be on the southern wire behind 3 Battalion's huts, and about equidistant between the two closest towers – that is, about 80 yards from each sentry box. The timing will be such that both sentries are as far away as possible. At this stage of the planning there may be other assault teams going over the wire elsewhere at the same time, but more details will be released later on.'

There was silence in the room as the men mulled over the scheme. Stallard began to wind up the session. 'I won't ask for questions at this time, although I'm sure you have plenty. I do ask that you go away and think about it overnight, and I'll answer your questions tomorrow. You may even point out something we've overlooked. I will also need to know if you are in or out, as we'll need to look at drumming up replacements should you decide not to participate. It's going to be a risky show, and no stigma will be placed on any man who feels he'd rather pull out now. That's all, gentlemen. Thank you.'

The meeting over, Rex and I strolled around the camp perimeter, having a good look at the fences behind 3 Battalion's huts. The wire was nine feet high, and composed of taut, closely spaced barbed wire between solid, concrete-embedded poles. At the top of the inner fence a section angled back into the compound to prevent anyone climbing over it. In the two-metre space between the two fences were masses of coiled barbed wire, which made for an almost impenetrable barrier for anyone trying to cut their way through. When I looked at Rex he was smiling.

Rex was the epitome of the Australian fighting soldier. Educated at Grammar School in Melbourne, he was an officer in a militia regiment when war broke out. He quickly transferred himself to the newly formed Australian Imperial Forces and soon rose to the rank of Captain. He saw service in the Middle East before being hit by a bomb splinter in Greece, and was recuperating in an Athens hospital when the Germans overran the city. Rex was ever cheerful, although I am sure that his tall rangy frame and boundless energy caused him to suffer the pangs of hunger more than most. Now, however, he was deep in thought. After a while he spoke.

'It's a bloody beauty, Champy!' he enthused. 'I'm sure it will work. Just what we've been waiting for. What do you think?'

'I couldn't agree more,' I responded. 'I've run it over in my mind, and I sure can't find any holes in the plan.'

We strolled on, both deep in our own thoughts, and the next afternoon we gave our answer: we were in.

* * *

The recreation hut at Warburg was situated near the centre of the camp, in a rather isolated position away from other buildings. It was mainly used as a music practice room and was therefore avoided by anyone with the slightest musical appreciation. Tom Stallard had asked us to meet him there a few days after our initial get-together.

By the time we arrived Martin Gilliat's stooging system had been set up to ensure we weren't bothered by any snooping German 'ferrets'. They acquired this name because they had the disconcerting habit of randomly ducking under our huts, either to search for signs of tunnelling or to eavesdrop on our conversations. Martin was in charge of security for us, and ran a well-organised team. Until Rex and I had been taken under Tom's wing we had made ourselves available to Martin for any stooging activities, and in this way had aided many earlier escape bids.

Tom Stallard was already there with Captain David Walker of the Black Watch, whom we both knew slightly. Our team of ten men, which included Stallard, was now assembled. The hut was sparsely furnished – just a battered old piano up against the far wall, a couple of racks along the wall containing sheet music, and two wooden beams about twelve feet apart which stretched across the room at a height of about seven feet. Two strong wires had been strung between the beams, about eight feet apart, with more music sheets strung over them. All very innocent, but I was in for a surprise.

Stallard and Walker crossed over to the music racks and removed the few bits and pieces of sheet music. They lifted the racks from the wall and carried them one on top of the other into the middle of the room. Then they swung one rack upright and leaned it up against one of the wires. All of a sudden it struck me – the 'rack' was actually one of the ladder assemblies, and the wires were meant to simulate the camp fences! It was ingenious in its simplicity and disguise. We watched intently as Stallard grasped the handles of the platform, stepped swiftly up the ladder assisted by Walker, and deftly pushed it across. The platform cleared the ceiling by a foot or two, dropped easily onto the far wire, and we heard the top rung click neatly into the slots. Stallard crawled across and then, grasping the trapeze, dropped expertly onto the floor. They were right – it worked simply and effectively.

Our primary objective that day was to nut out a launching team of four. Two would be at the top end of the ladder, and it would be their job to hoist that end onto the top of the angled inner wire and then steady the ladder as the other two went to work. The Number 1 would grasp the platform handles and step up two rungs in order to launch the platform. As he would be off balance and have no free hands, it was his Number 2's job, as well as that of the other two 'primaries' (9 and 10, who would be last over) to hold him steady as he pushed the heavy platform up and out. The other six in the team would scramble over behind Numbers 1 and 2, and then it would be the turn of the first two men. The practice apparatus was actually shorter than those which would be used in the break, as the perimeter fences were a couple of feet higher than the wires in the room. For security reasons, and because of restrictive room, the ladder and duckboard were kept as two separate units due to the squeeze between the beams and the roof.

One by one we all had a go at it. Because of his rangy build and obvious strength Rex was chosen as our Number 1, and because I was going with him if we got away I automatically became Number 2. The remainder drew lots for positions and Stallard, refusing any priority, drew Number 10. We continued our practice session for over an hour. It was rather fun, and we were almost enjoying ourselves, although a look at Stallard and Walker would remind us of the seriousness of the exercise. After this initial session we usually managed three practice runs at every rehearsal.

During the next week our team took its turn at stooging. Sometimes we were inside looking out through the window, eyes glued to the outside stooge, watching for the pre-arranged signal of an alert. On other occasions we would find ourselves outside, watching the approaches. This part of the operation was rather boring, but we didn't mind because this time Rex and I were part of the vanguard; when a break was made we would be part of it. For all its boring aspects stooging was still a vitally important part of the whole operation.

Our turn for team practice came around once again. Rex was now an expert launcher, and our teamwork had developed to the point where we performed automatically. One further hazard Stallard pointed out was the camp's electrical wires, which hung about six feet above the top of the inner wire. If the platform hit those the whole assembly could go awry, so we made the necessary allowances in our training runs.

Security was tight – so tight that we didn't even know who was on the other ladders. Then one day about a month later we had a sudden alert. 'Goons up!' yelled the stooge at the window. I was halfway across the duckboard section when the warning came. Rex had just dropped to the floor and five more of the team were right on my heels.

'Cripes Jack, *move*!' Rex cried. I moved alright, and dropped to the concrete floor. The fellow behind accidentally planted his heel on my unprotected foot and I let out a suppressed howl of pain.

As soon as we were all off the equipment Tom Stallard whipped the platform back over the wire, and we had our music rack once again. We quickly hung it on the wall and jammed the music sheets back into its recesses. Henry Coombe-Tennant straddled the piano stool, and by the time we had assembled around the piano he was well into 'Roll out the Barrel'. As we joined in I noticed that most of us were warm and perspiring. Not good – but hopefully the Germans would not notice. Just then the door swung open and in strutted Hauptmann Friedrich Rademacher, the head of the German camp security.

Rademacher was about 50 years old, grey-haired and with rather handsome Teutonic features. He was unashamedly theatrical, gesturing widely whenever he spoke. For dramatic effect he would often pull out his revolver and wave it about, even loosing off the odd shot or two into the air when it suited him. His other 'toy' was a beautiful sword, which he wore when wanting to create an impression. This would be unsheathed and brandished with vigour when his emotions got the better of him, which was often. The prisoners despised his eccentric behaviour – the Germans grudgingly tolerated it.

The man was ruthless, and would let nothing stand in his way. He was notorious for his 'bastard' searches – a cruel and unnecessary treatment of our few personal effects. On these occasions Rademacher and a couple of his henchmen would march into any hut, and with all politeness proceed to apologise for any inconvenience his search would cause. It was a necessary evil, he would explain. This gesture completed the search would begin, and as it progressed he would undergo a terrible personality change, and the less contraband he found the deeper his rage would become. Stamping back and forth, ordering his guards to find the radio and the tunnels he knew in his mind must exist, he would wave his revolver or sword to emphasise his superiority. It was easy to see why he was not in the front line in charge of fighting men. He would not tolerate interference from any British officer, and as this would only have infuriated him more it was best to bite one's lip and stay silent.

At the height of his rage Rademacher would order our belongings thrown out into the compound – even when the ground was covered in mud or snow. A tangled mess of blankets, clothing and personal effects would pile up outside the doors and windows, our tins of milk and jam would be tipped all over the floor of the hut and walked into a filthy, sticky glue. One of his favourite bits of bastardry was to squeeze our precious toothpaste all over our bunks. Once the hut had been turned inside out and Rademacher had vented his spleen, he would bellow out an order and then march out of the hut in all his vainglory, followed by his miserable guards. On a few occasions he did actually uncover some fledgling tunnels in various huts, and he would gleefully order these filled in with the contents of a local cesspit, which meant the residents of the offending hut would have to put up with the resultant stench.

Rademacher was absolutely loathed by Mark Howard, who despised the Germans for plunging the world once again into war. Mark had travelled quite a bit in Germany during his school days in England, before deciding to settle in Australia in 1937. On arrival in Australia he was engaged as a jackeroo on a large sheep station in New South Wales. The term jackeroo is indigenous to Australia and roughly translated means a poorly paid, well-educated young gentleman who works on a sheep station or larger farm, learning the trade. He works long hours and does what he is told, but being a gentleman lives in the homestead with the owner or manager and his wife. He's a cut above the other station hands socially, but gets less pay.

Mark came from a long line of soldiers. His father commanded a destroyer at Gallipoli, and his brother Henry won the Military Cross during the Palestine rebellion before the war, later commanding his regiment during the invasion of Europe in 1944–45. When war broke out in September 1939 Mark enlisted in the 6th Australian Infantry Division, and after some training was commissioned with the rank of Second Lieutenant in the 2/7th Infantry Battalion. He saw action at Bardia in January 1941 and was wounded in the hand. Mark was evacuated to a casualty clearing station behind the lines, but walked out and found his way back to his unit. He then went on to command his platoon for the remaining two days of the battle. Mark was wounded again in Greece, and with Rex Baxter was captured in an Athens hospital.

Because of his travels in pre-war Germany Mark had a good grasp of the language, but despite this he refused to speak any German throughout the war. He also considered it beneath his dignity to talk to any of the German officers or guards. There was one occasion when he broke this rule, and it was because of Rademacher, who had been up to his tricks again, this time in our hut, and all our precious belongings had been tossed out into the mud and slush. Rademacher was loving every moment of it; he strutted up and down like a peacock outside the hut while food, stools and books came flying out the window. We were livid, but as they held the guns we had to hold our silence. But Mark did something. He'd seen enough, and calmly walked through the cordon of guards, hands in pockets and puffing slowly on his pipe. Very deliberately he walked straight up to Rademacher, stood right in front of him puffing smoke in the man's face, and then told him in very explicit German just what he thought of him, Hitler, and the whole German race. Within seconds he had been surrounded by a strong cordon of guards, and Rademacher was speechless with fury. Mark was shoved away to the cells where he spent the next three weeks in cold and hungry isolation. Of course it was a foolish thing to do – foolish but courageous, and it was the only time I ever heard Mark speak German.

Little wonder that Rademacher was a much-hated bastard. There was an unsubstantiated rumour at the end of the war that he had stayed on as Security Officer in the camp, and when it was liberated the resident Yugoslavian prisoners had promptly strung him up. It's far from a Christian attitude, but more than a few of us wished we had been there.

However that was in the future, and we now return to the sudden appearance of Rademacher in the recreation hut in Warburg. On this occasion he was accompanied by a sallow, pimpled corporal. We stopped singing and stood meekly to attention as the two of them methodically searched the room. The corporal pulled some of the music sheets out of the wall racks, but had no idea what was right before his eyes. We may have seemed a little nervous, but there was nothing unusual in this when Rademacher was close at hand. Satisfied at last they strolled over to the door, where Rademacher swung around with an expansive gesture and pointed straight at the music rack.

'You practice for the concert perhaps?' he bellowed in his usual manner, and then smiled. 'Please continue; the music is good. I am sure you will give a good performance!'

We breathed a collective sigh of relief as they strode off, and our stooges, taking up their posts once again, gave us the all clear.

'Thank goodness!' sighed David Walker. 'That was a bit too close for comfort. However it was nice of the cretin to wish us well with our performance. We'll perform all right, but not the way he imagines! With a bit of luck he'll be sent to the Front after our little break-out, and some lucky blighter will fire a shell up his arse!' We all laughed, mostly with relief, and the tense atmosphere quickly evaporated.

'That's all for today, chaps,' said Stallard. 'But before you go I must impress upon you the tremendous importance of getting fit. I want you to run at least a thousand yards every day, walk at least three thousand, and play as much sport as you can without risking injury to yourself. You must realise that once you go over the wire you will have to run flat out for at least a thousand yards and you won't be in shorts and shirts – you'll be fully dressed and carrying a 10-pound pack, which is the maximum we will allow you to carry. You may be interested to know that we have decided only four ladders will be used on the night. At one time we planned on going with up to sixteen teams, but materials, training and diversions would have been too much of a problem. So we are concentrating all our efforts into your team and just three others, giving us a total of forty men to get over the wire and away.'

The escaping season was in full swing at Warburg as spring turned to summer. Travelling conditions were more suitable; it was not as cold and wet, and because the earth was warm it meant that food items such as potatoes and fruit were readily available.

Many tunnels were dug, but most were discovered by the highly active ferrets before they could be broken. Ironically, our efforts helped the Germans increase their knowledge of escaping tactics, which made successive bids even harder. The ferrets, dressed in their grey overalls, would suddenly invade a particular hut and go over it with the proverbial fine toothed comb. They would strip each room bare and go over each inch minutely, rapping on the walls, ceilings and floors, alert for hollow sounds, which would give away the tunnel or 'hide' they had been seeking.

But tunnelling was not the only way out of Warburg. Another method was to try a game of bluff with the rather nonchalant sentries at the gates by dressing up as German soldiers and going out under their very noses. This ruse had already been attempted several times but with only limited success. Once again, the Germans learned quickly.

Rex and I now had a vexing and difficult problem to contend with. It was Mark Howard. As Mark was not involved in the escape over the wire, and we had sworn not to discuss it with anyone other than direct participants, we could not tell him what we were up to nor where we went on our mysterious practice excursions. He knew we were onto something, and like Mark kept it to himself, but we could see it was burning him up. He was disappointed when we wouldn't join him for a game of hockey or some other sport, and we couldn't even spend much time with him. Rex and I knew that the situation would not last much longer, but we felt rather guilty about letting Mark down – especially since we were such close friends. One day as the three of us were strolling around the perimeter road the inevitable happened. We had been walking in silence for some time, when suddenly Mark spoke up.

'Listen, you chaps,' he said. 'I hate to bring up the subject, but it's getting me down. You two are up to something, and I'm sure you're in on some escape business. I may look dumb, but I can assure you I'm not. Hell, neither of you has eaten your chocolate ration for two months, and I know damn well how much you love the stuff. You're both exercising like crazy, and you vanish for hours at a time. What a nice pair of bastards you are – can't you let me in on what you're up to?'

It was Rex who answered. 'Look Mark, we are onto something, but we are also under strict orders not to talk about it to anyone. A time will come when I'm sure we can fill you in, but for now I must ask you not to mention it again.'

Mark looked crestfallen, but resigned. 'Okay,' he said after a while. 'I'm sorry and I'll drop it. But please let me know if there's any way I can help. For a start I'll give up my chocolate ration to you if you'll accept it.'

Up until now I'd remained silent. 'Thanks Mark,' I said. 'Rex is right – we can't say anything to anybody at the moment, and we sure can use your chocolate ration – it would be a big help.' I clapped my hand on his shoulder, and we walked on in silence.

At least he knew the score, and that we weren't excluding him by our own choice, so the three of us breathed a little easier. Mark was too good a friend to lose, and his quiet offer to help in the face of our stubborn silence was typical of the mighty spirit he had often displayed. Up to now the three of us had shared everything – clothes, food, tobacco, cigarettes and, most of all, our confidences. We even shared letters from home, while our mothers back in Victoria and England formed friendships and corresponded with each other.

It was just after 2pm when we heard the tractor chugging up the hill outside the camp gate. We watched in what we hoped was a desultory manner as it stopped at the entrance while the guard examined the civilian driver's identity card. A German soldier clambered onto the back of the tractor, the gate swung open, and the vehicle drove into the camp compound. We had a particular interest in this tractor. It had come to tow out a string of four-wheeled carts spread around the camp and into which were deposited the empty tins from our Red Cross parcels which had begun trickling through in reasonable quantities.

It had all started about eight weeks before in early May when Lieutenant Johnny Rawson had come to me, and in the security of an open air walk around the perimeter had told me that he and another Australian officer named Andy Benns were going to escape. Johnny was also from the 2/6th Battalion, and we had undergone the same officers' training course in Australia. He had joined the unit in Egypt as a reinforcement officer just before the battalion sailed for Greece. On the way from Greece to Alexandria Johnny's ship, the *Costa Rica*, was sunk by enemy bombing. She was part of the evacuation fleet taking troops back to Egypt. Fortunately there were few casualties, and the escorting British destroyers were soon alongside. With typical navy skill and seamanship they took the troops aboard, but due to a submarine scare the destroyer Rawson was on went straight to Crete where, along with many others, he was taken prisoner. He had been among the Lübeck group we looked after when we arrived at Warburg.

Before the war Rawson had been the District Secretary for British Products in Geelong and the Western Suburbs, and I had met him a few times in Geelong. He had the gift of the gab, and could have sold party ice to Eskimos. His father had been killed in action at Hamel during the Great War, and although Johnny never really had the chance to prove himself as a combat soldier, he certainly turned out to be an outstanding escaper. He would be Mentioned in Despatches for his persistent and courageous efforts, more of which occupy later pages in this story. Johnny sure had guts – tons of it – and was always tossing schemes around. This was yet another.

My mind was on other things, but then I realised Johnny had mentioned an escape plan. 'What method are you using?' I asked.

'We're going out in the tin carts,' he replied. 'You know, concealed under all those empty tins and towed out by the tractor. We've got it all worked out; when the carts get to Warburg station we'll get out of them with the help of the British orderlies in the working party and transfer to a railway truck still under the tins. We then enjoy the convenience of the German railway system to travel south and within reach of the Swiss border!'

I sighed. 'Look here, Johnny, I don't think there's a man amongst us who hasn't watched those bloody carts driving out of the main gate and thought about hiding in them. But it isn't possible; the guards aren't that stupid. Have you ever watched what they do when the tractor and carts are leaving? About four of them get these bloody great six-foot iron spikes and probe the entire stack of tins. They don't hold back, and always make sure their spikes hit the floor of the cart. No, it's too much like suicide, and furthermore I'd like to have a beer with you and Andy after the war. I'll even pay!'

Johnny was not at all put off by my pessimism. 'Remember Ned Kelly, Jack? Remember how he used to get about in a suit of home-made armour covering his body and head?'

'Yes,' I ventured. 'I saw it in a museum or someplace in Melbourne a few years ago. Why?'

'Well', he said, his eyes shining, 'we're going to make two suits of armour just like old bushranger Ned. We've discovered a couple of disused stoves in the kitchen and we intend to hammer out plates for our backs, legs and heads. We'll strap them on before we enter the tin cart, and then lie face down on the floor with the tins covering us. We'll know when the carts are going to be towed to the station because the Germans will notify the British corporal in charge of the working party the day before. All we need now is someone to stage-manage the show, and we thought – we hoped – that you would do it.'

We strolled on in silence – me in astonishment, and Rawson deep in thought. 'Suppose the iron spike strikes the armour?' I said at last. 'Won't the goons be suspicious when the spike doesn't travel all the way to the bottom of the cart? And what about air; how will you breathe?'

Johnny exuded confidence. 'First, Champy, should the spike strike the armour we are reasonably confident it will just glance off and the Germans will think they have just struck another tin on the way down. As for air, the tins are just thrown in, so there's plenty of space between them, and we shouldn't have any problems breathing. As well, the carts have wooden planked floors, and some air will come up that way. It's going to stink to high heaven – that's our only problem! How 'bout it, Champy? If you'll agree Andy and I will put it to the Escape Committee tomorrow.'

Rawson was always a cocky little bloke, and I never saw him down. He radiated confidence, and most importantly he had courage to spare. Conversely, Andy Benns was quiet and unobtrusive, and had spent almost the entire winter lying on his bunk reading all he could about pig farming. But then I had seen him in action in the Western Desert, knew him to be a good fighting soldier, and felt he and Rawson would complement each other perfectly in any escape scheme.

The plan, although fraught with danger, seemed feasible. But there were several dangers such as getting them into the cart undetected, surviving those frightening thrusts by the iron spikes, and then transferring them from the tin cart to the railway truck. However it was original enough to work, and I secretly loved the Australian flavour of the Ned Kelly armour. 'Okay Johnny, I'll do it. You get your approval from the committee and then we'll try to iron out a few details. For starters we'll need some extra help, but that doesn't present a problem.'

The following day a jaunty Rawson strolled over to see me. His grin told me all I needed to know. 'Well, it's been approved, but it took me a while to explain to those Poms who Ned Kelly was. When I'd explained it all they thought it was great fun, and we'll be given full support with maps, compasses, clothing and all sorts of help and advice if we need it.'

'That's great news, Johnny,' I responded, knowing full well that the Escape Committee would have gone over the proposal very thoroughly. They would need to be convinced any scheme had a good chance of success before giving their consent and committing precious resources. Just like Johnny to make light of it. 'Now,' I said, seriously, 'I want a meeting with you and Andy after Appell tomorrow morning.'

The next day we met as scheduled and took a slow walk around the perimeter wire. One of the tin carts stood beside the camp road near our hut, obscured from the view of the sentry on the gate by the hut itself, and also out of view of the sentry towers. This would be ideal and also convenient to our quarters, as well as those of Johnny and Andy, which were a short distance away. The cart was half full of tins already, and we calculated it would be full in about three weeks' time. This would give us ample opportunity to prepare the two escapers for the task ahead. I outlined the plan as I saw it.

'On the night before you go, the two of you will swap places with two men in our hut. All your gear will be brought up here the night before, and hidden as well as possible. As you know, the goons doing the inside night patrol go off at first light – about five o'clock – but only two of the day patrol come in at that time, and they always go to the other end of the camp first and work back.

'This is the time we go into action. Ab Gray and Len Isherwood will take up positions so they can cover approaches from both directions. They will only be about 30 yards from the cart and can alert us if any Jerries approach. Jack Paterson will watch the gate from a window in our hut. All of us, with the exception of you two, will wear shorts, pullovers and gym shoes. Should there be an alarm you two will either make a break for it back to our hut or, if the operation is sufficiently advanced, you will hide in the tin cart. The rest of us will disperse and jog around the camp as if we were taking some morning exercise. Rex Baxter, Mark Howard and I will do the job of getting you into the cart, which will mean tossing around a lot of cans. We'll pile the tins up one end and get Andy in first, and after covering him we'll do the reverse to get you in, Johnny. I calculate the whole operation should take about ten minutes, and of course after that you'll be on your own.'

The two men were silent for a moment, then Andy spoke up. 'I'd feel a lot better if we could rehearse it, Jack. We wouldn't get into the cart, just stand around it with you, but with the stooges in position. We could allow fifteen minutes to test the timing factor.'

'That's a good idea,' agreed Rawson, 'but let's have three rehearsals just to be on the safe side.'

I was pleased they were taking it so seriously, and the following day I got the stooging team together. We sat on the grass overlooking the sports field and pretended to play cards. They listened carefully as I outlined the plan, and of course they agreed to help.

'What happens if something goes wrong?' asked Ab Gray. 'Suppose the goons approach the area at some critical point?'

'Then it's my responsibility to either carry on or to abort the whole thing,' I replied. 'If, in my opinion, things become too hot to continue, then I will simply shout Stop!, and from then on it's every man for himself. The only ones likely to be caught are Johnny and Andy, and I have already discussed this with them. They are quite prepared just to give themselves up if the Germans catch them in the act.'

Two days later we had our first rehearsal. The fifteen minutes passed without incident. The second time the German patrol appeared after only twelve minutes, but we all started jogging madly in every direction, and no suspicions were aroused. On the third occasion the full fifteen minutes elapsed. We felt pretty confident, but the biggest advantage lay in the fact that we now knew what to do.

Slowly the cart filled up. It was quite agonising watching the progress as every day more empty cans were thrown in by POWs who had consumed their meagre rations. John and Andy were now ready, but it was four weeks after our initial meeting when we finally received word that the corporal and a working party of ten men were ordered to be ready for a detail to move to Warburg station the following afternoon, 15 June, where they would transfer the contents of the carts into some rail trucks. The tins would later be taken to factories in the Ruhr where they were reclaimed and the metal used to help the German war effort.

I slept badly that night and woke frequently to check the time on my luminous watch. Johnny snored gently in the bunk above me. He was sleeping like a baby. Andy, meantime, spent a restless night and was awake before any of us, brewing tea which he drank slowly, pondering the events of the next few hours.

At four o'clock I got up and dressed in the dark. Andy watched me silently as I woke Mark, who in turn went around and woke the others. John and Andy donned their camp-tailored civilian suits, and we treated them to a breakfast of biscuits and jam, washed down with English tea well laced with condensed milk. Johnny just sipped at his tea, and left most of it in his mug.

The whole party assembled in the passageway of the hut, except for Paterson, who was at his post by the window watching the gate. Right on five o'clock, with the new dawn slowly creeping through the camp area Paterson whispered, 'Guard out. New guard in!'

I watched through a crack in the front door until the new sentries had moved off towards the far end of the compound. 'Stooges out!' I hissed. Our two joggers stepped out and hurried to their assigned position. 'Rex and Mark,' I said, then almost immediately, 'Johnny and Andy.'

Clutching their gear under their arms the two escapers made off towards the tin cart. Rex and Mark were already in the cart furiously piling tins from one end to the other. The din was terrible. As Johnny helped Andy strap on his armour, I did the same for him.

'Andy in!' snapped Rex. Mark jumped down and together we heaved Andy over the side of the cart. Mark jumped back in with him, and soon Andy was buried under a mound of tins.

'Johnny up!' Rex called. Mark and I managed to get Johnny over the side, where the two 'tin-throwers' quickly covered him over and then arranged the cans to look as natural as before.

'That's it!' I said, and like rabbits into a warren we all disappeared into our hut. Five and a half minutes had elapsed from start to finish. So far, so good, but the greatest ordeal was yet to come.

That was one of the longest days I have ever known, but no doubt for our two mates buried beneath the tins it was one hell of a lot longer. From time to time, with stooges covering for us, we would sidle up to the cart and ask how they were. They could hear us clearly. Their first question was always, 'What's the bloody time?' and once when I told Johnny it was only nine o'clock he said, 'Now fair dinkum, don't kid us Jack – it must be at least midday!'

Understandably they both developed cramps, and then Andy wanted to urinate. All those early morning cups of tea were now causing a problem, but our stooges gave me the all clear, and I told Andy to be quick. A thin stream of urine soon trickled to the ground through a crack between two floor boards, followed quickly by a muffled bellow from the opposite end of the cart. 'Bloody hell, Andy! All over my flaming pants and boots. I'll smell like a bloody urinal!' Despite the situation I had to smile.

Lunch time came, but I had no stomach for tepid turnip soup. Apprehension grew within me as the hands on my watch crawled slowly towards zero hour.

My watch had just ticked over 2pm when we heard the tractor chug-chugging its way up the hill, heading straight for the main camp road. Ten minutes later it appeared around the corner with three carts in tow. It stopped alongside our cart, and the Germans coupled it up. Soon the trailer train was through the gate, and we watched as four guards jumped up on the first cart and with fierce, driving thrusts, banged the long iron spikes through the tins to the floor. The next two carts got the same treatment, and just as thoroughly. Then it was our turn.

The Germans had lost none of their vigour. A hearty lunge, then up came the spikes, the guards moved them a couple of feet and then down into the cans once again – down to where our friends crouched with all their faith pinned on a theory and their armour. The empty tins screeched horribly as the spikes were withdrawn from the metal, and I must have looked quite ghastly as I stood watching helplessly – waiting for that agonising human scream, for that pool of blood to form under the cart. Why had I let them do it? They had no chance, and the bile rose in my throat as each spike was driven home. Suddenly the guards jumped down from the cart, gave a signal to the driver, and the tractor with its train of carts rattled off down the road to the rail yards three miles below us.

I ran to the nearest latrine and vomited violently. 'Thank God!' I kept saying to myself. 'Thank God!'

Underneath all the cans, now clanking merrily on top of them, Johnny and Andy were at last able to flex their cramped limbs without fear of being heard, and to reflect on the past few minutes. It had been a near thing; they had both been struck by the spikes, but as planned the spikes had skidded off the rounded armour and ploughed into the floor of the cart. It no longer mattered that there had been several places where the spikes could have penetrated between the armour plating, nor that such a blow would probably have proved fatal. Now the grand adventure began, a simple transfer to a railway truck with the assistance of the British orderlies, and an express ride to somewhere near the Swiss border. Farewell Warburg!

In a little over half an hour the bumping and rattling ceased, and the road became smooth. They realised they must be in the vicinity of the station, and settled themselves down once again. The tractor stopped, and they could hear the hiss of steam and the cries of the station personnel all around them. A German barked some orders nearby, and said something about a delay. Then it went quiet; not a sound for a long, long time.

Curiosity finally got the better of Andy; he decided to stick his snout out and find out what was going on. Johnny heard his companion stirring at the other end of the cart, but elected to remain where he was. Andy would let him know …

Andy's head emerged from the cart like a beast from the depths, showering tin cans about him. He blinked once in the strong sunlight and found himself staring straight into the face of an astonished German guard! The guard quickly recovered his composure and swung his rifle up, pointed it at Andy and screamed, *'Hände hoch!'* Looking like the Tin Man from *The Wizard of Oz* and with grim resignation written all over his face Andy stood up, showering cans everywhere. A second guard ran over and motioned him to clamber down from the cart.

Rawson, hardly daring to breathe, lay stock still and waited for the search of the carts which must inevitably follow. But the Germans' full attention was on Andy, and shouting their heads off they shoved him down the platform, away from the carts. Johnny made his mind up in a flash; he thrust his head upwards and out of the tins. No Germans, but approaching him at a fast clip along the otherwise deserted platform was the group of orderlies. 'Jesus, sir!' cried the corporal. 'We thought they'd nabbed both of you. We had to help load some crates before tackling the tins, and I guess they posted the guards in case of scavengers.'

'No time for all that!' shouted Johnny. 'Help me get this bloody tackle off. They don't know I'm here yet, and if I can get into the rail truck there's still a chance they'll miss me.'

They quickly stripped off Rawson's armour cladding and hoisted him into the rail truck which was fortunately close to the cart. With feverish haste they began transferring the cans, slowly but surely covering the prostrate officer and his discarded armour. The transfer had almost been completed when a contingent of Germans angrily stormed down the platform to where the orderlies were now innocently engaged in tossing cans into the rail truck one at a time.

The Feldwebel in charge snapped an order and the orderlies were pushed back from the carts. A systematic search of the near-empty carts took place, and the soldiers finally reported that there were no more British officers concealed in them. They completely ignored the rail truck right beside them.

A bit more hue and cry ensued, and then the Germans marched off down the platform once again, leaving the orderlies to finish their task. This done, Johnny heard a whispered 'Good luck, sir!' and then there was silence. Once again he settled down for a long wait.

Rawson knew that the train would not pull out before nightfall. Trains travelling in daylight presented a fat target to Allied aircraft, so most rail traffic occurred after sunset. He had now been lying beneath those stinking cans for most of the day, and his body began to suffer cramps. The tins were not heavy, but the constant strain of lying prone for hours on end was beginning to tell. He sweated his way through numerous cramps, gritting his teeth and moving slightly, lest he make a noise.

Two hours later a lancing cramp shot through his right leg. He nearly screamed, but bit his bottom lip. However the pain was so severe that he had to move, and in an almost reflex action he swung his foot forward, causing a hideous noise. The shooting pain eased a little, and as he slowly massaged his aching leg he wondered if they'd heard him. He didn't have to wait for long.

'Raus! Raus! Schnell Raus!' This was from right above him, and he knew his little game was up. Slowly, reluctantly, he stood up and glared balefully at the little German corporal staring at him over the side of the truck, rifle wavering, but aimed straight at Rawson's stomach. Sighing deeply, he put his hands in the air and said, *'Ich bin Britischer Offizier. Nicht schiessen!'*

And thus ended one of the finest and certainly most unique individual escape attempts of the war. Ned Kelly would have been proud!

A few days after Johnny and Andy were picked up I woke quite early with a cramp, and could not get back to sleep. I decided to walk it off, rolled out of my bunk and put on my greatcoat.

It was a frosty morning, but after a brisk walk along the perimeter road I began to warm up and even enjoy the reverie of an early morning stroll. I had completed one circuit and was about to return to our hut when I saw a lone figure standing in the middle of the road ahead of me. He was tall, dressed as lightly as I was heavily, and the arms beneath the Australian short-sleeved tunic were tanned a deep brown. The only concession he made to the cold was that his hands were thrust deeply into the pockets of his shorts. As I drew nearer I noticed the little colour flashes on his sleeve. He was a member of the 2/7th Battalion. Right at this moment he was standing side on to me, gazing out into the countryside, head cocked to one side. I walked up to him.

'Morning,' I said. After a few moments, in which time I had begun to think he was going to ignore me, he turned around.

'Sorry mate, I was listening for any bird calls. No luck though – no bloody trees. I got so used to waking up back at home with the whole bush alive with noise. Funny how you can never appreciate such things until they're no longer there. All those magpies and cockatoos made a hell of a racket, but at least you felt as if you were in the middle of something. You're a Digger aren't you? My name's George Bolding – 2/7th.' He took his right hand out of his pocket and we shook hands. His hand was surprisingly warm, and the handshake firm.

'Jack Champ,' I responded. '2/6th.'

As if by mutual agreement we commenced walking in that familiar anti-clockwise route I had been pounding out. For some reason unknown to me we always walked anti-clockwise around the perimeter road at Warburg, puzzling the Germans. They always thought there was some ulterior motive!

George turned out to be a dairy farmer from Victoria, and as we strode along we talked of home. I had no way of knowing that our paths would run fairly parallel from then on, nor that we would both end up in Colditz. George had been born in Hazelwood North to one of the district's pioneering families. There were strong military influences as he grew up; an uncle of the same name had fought in the Boer war before dying of fever in Pretoria, and two uncles had died in battle during the Great War. George joined the 13th Light Horse in his early twenties and enjoyed the military and social aspects associated with the troop, especially the annual camps at different locations in Victoria. During one such camp at Broadmeadows his troop was involved in filming the Light Horse charge for the classic Australian film *Forty Thousand Horsemen*. He was commissioned as a Lieutenant in the Light Horse on 12 October 1939 but resigned the following March to enlist in the AIF. I asked him how he came to be captured.

'I was a bit older than the average recruit back in '39–40, Jack,' he said.

'So I was a lieutenant, brand bloody new and terribly proud, when the Sixth Division moved overseas. I lasted all of eight months. Like you, our unit pushed the Ities around for a while in Africa, then the Germans pushed us around in Greece. With most of my mates I was captured in Crete, and the Germans shipped us home – their home – and told us to bloody-well behave ourselves for a few months while they won the flaming war!'

We both enjoyed a good laugh at that, and by the time we had arrived back at our huts we had warmed to each other's company. We shook hands again.

'Cheerio Jack!' George said, with a broad smile across his tanned features.

'Nice meeting you. Be seeing you soon.' He waved, and was off, and I returned to the hut a mite happier for the early morning chat with a man who would later prove a good friend and staunch ally.

That same evening Rex came back to the hut in a miserable frame of mind, sporting a badly swollen nose. A few days earlier, for want of something better to do, he had decided to learn the gentlemanly art of boxing, and his coach was a very large redheaded Scot from the 51st Highland Division – a former champion boxer. Rex was certainly willing enough, and we grew accustomed to the spectacle of him jabbing away at imaginary opponents in the hut. Mark and I would just look at each other – we knew Rex would soon tire of this energy-sapping activity and go onto something a little less exerting.

However Rex had one great failing as a pugilist – he would not keep his guard up. His coach was disappointed, but determined.

'Get that bloody guard up, Baxter,' he would growl. 'Or one day I'll put your teeth so far down your throat you'll have to shove a toothbrush up your arse to clean them.'

At this particular evening session, Rex made one great howling error – he dropped his guard just as a thunderous left came sailing in. It landed with a shattering thud on the side of his nose, and Rex went down with blood streaming from a broken nose. His coach hardly paused as he hauled Rex to his feet. 'You've nearly got it, Baxter. I thought for a moment there you might get your guard back up in time!'

The desire for further bouts was gone, and Rex spent hours examining his misshaped appendage in a mirror. The nose eventually set itself comparatively well, but from that time on Rex was inclined to snuffle like a Corgi. A couple of years later he was able to use the excuse of having his nose fixed at a POW hospital, at a time when he was supposed to be in a German court facing a rather serious sabotage charge, so in a way it came in handy. That story is told a little later on.

Another amusing story dates from about that time. We were sitting in our hut reading, when a harmless young German interpreter asked if he might come in for a while. He was a pleasant enough, although highly gullible young chap, thoroughly brainwashed by the Nazi doctrine, and convinced that Germany would soon rule the world. In the interim he was quite keen to better his knowledge of our language and would drop in from time to time to engage us in conversation in English. On this particular day he started one up with Jack Paterson, who was lying on his bunk smoking.

'What will you do when we permit your return to Australia, Jack?' he asked innocently. 'Have you any plans for your future?'

Jack looked at him. 'It's back to the station for me, sport,' he replied. 'Right away from the bloody war, and home to my sheep and horses. What about yourself?'

A faraway look came into the youth's eyes. 'When the war is over and won, I will buy a new bicycle and tour all over the great German Reich!'

'Go on,' said Jack, in his usual laconic fashion. 'And what will you do in the afternoon?'

3

First Escape

The end result of all the recent escape activity was a general tightening-up of security, and preventative activities inside the camp increased alarmingly, seriously limiting our practice sessions for the Wire Job.

'You've got to build up your speed!' said David Walker as our team gathered around him. 'The target from go to finish is sixty seconds. Now come on – let's see what you can do!' We lined up with the apparatus on the rack. 'Go!' he yelled.

We sprang into action, banged the ladder into place, and Rex did a perfect launch. As last man Stallard hit the floor, Walker yelled 'Stop!' and consulted his watch. 80 seconds. Not bad, but we knew we could do a lot better with practice. And so we kept at it, and in our next session a week later we had reduced the time to 70 seconds, but David Walker was far from satisfied. 'It's still too bloody long,' he growled as he paced up and down. 'Every second you save is a second further away you'll be once the goons arrive on the scene!'

A week later our time was down to 63 seconds. There was a good deal of pride in our teamwork, and more than a little curiosity as to how we stacked up against the other three teams. Quite deliberately Walker let it slip that Doug Crawford's team was now below the minute mark, and this urged us on even more. This was actually the first I knew of Doug's involvement in the scheme. We had known him in Biberach, and as he later joined us in Colditz it is worth digressing for a few moments.

Doug was born in Queensland in 1914, and took his schooling at Brisbane Grammar School. His first job was in an insurance office, but he lost this due to the Depression in the 1930s. For a time he taught book-keeping at Queensland Tutorial College; and also tried his hand at tobacco farming for the princely wage of 15 shillings a week. He then worked on a banana farm for a short time before returning to Brisbane and taking a job selling typewriters. He later opened up a manufacturer's agency business.

In 1936 Doug was commissioned in the Citizens Military Forces unit. In October 1939 he and twenty-one fellow officers provided the nucleus of a 6th Division Field Artillery unit which, in March the following year, was reorganised as the 1st Anti-Tank Regiment. The unit was shipped to England on the *Queen Mary*, and underwent training on the Salisbury Plain. After a brief baptism of fire in Egypt the unit was sent to Greece. Here they were directed to the Veve Pass, overlooking the Florina plain, with orders to hold the German advance until the Greeks were evacuated from Albania, where they were fighting. Eventually, in the face of an overwhelming German thrust, the British forces were ordered to withdraw. On 12 April, while involved in the withdrawal of his own troops, Captain Crawford's truck was fired on, and his driver shot. His unit was quickly overcome and taken prisoner. Eventually they were transported north under heavy guard, marched across the Danube, and then crowded into cattle trucks for a nightmare train journey across Germany to their first camp, Oflag XC, Lübeck. After a short stay several of them were sent to the POW camp at Biberach (they were there before us) which was essentially for French POWs. As Doug was the highest ranking of the twelve British officers now in residence, he had the distinction of being appointed the first Senior British Officer at Biberach. Later some more British POWs arrived under Major Peter Brush, and he handed over the mantle.

Later, in Warburg, Doug was involved in digging a tunnel which was found by snooping ferrets. Foolishly the Germans only caved in the entrance, so the digging team promptly began a second tunnel which broke into the earlier one. Why waste a perfectly good and useable escape route? There was no electricity available to light this tunnel, just carbide lamps which would only burn at the face for about fifteen minutes. When they went out, so did the diggers.

The day the tunnel was due to break some heavy rain swept in, and water began to seep into the vertical shaft where Crawford was preparing to dig the exit hole. Suddenly there was a shout; the ferrets had somehow found out about the tunnel and were on their way. It was every man for himself. Doug slithered out as fast as he could, clambered up the entrance shaft into the now-vacant room, dove through the door and was safely out in the compound. His only real problem now was that he was absolutely covered in wet, sticky mud! Despite this he tried to look nonchalant and unhurried as he strolled away from the suspect hut. Incredibly the red-faced German Security Officer raced straight towards him and then ran past without so much as a second glance. Hardly believing his luck Doug made his way through a couple of huts and then threw himself under a tap. The tunnel was properly destroyed this time, but the Germans never caught up with Crawford, and the hubbub soon died down. For his arduous but unsuccessful work on the tunnel he was given a place on the Wire Job.

Now it was time to introduce another man, a Number 11, into each team. He was to be the 'anchor man', and it would be his task to climb the ladder on the heels of the last man, putting all his weight on the handles to prevent the platform from tilting until the man was over. He would then return to his quarters. We were given Lieutenant Bobby Barr, a tunneller we knew well from Biberach.

In our position of trust we learned a little more about our pending escape. It had originally been planned to catapult lumps of iron on long strings over the power cables and pull them down to extinguish the lights, but this may have caused injuries and was rejected by the Escape Committee. An army electrician was then called in and given the task of finding a better method. He finally located the main fuse box in the camp boot repair and tailor's shop. On the night Tom Stallard had told us about, the electrician had managed to fuse the lights, and the committee was satisfied. We also learned that two dummy ladders were going to be shoved against the fence near the sentry boxes while we were in action specifically to divert the guards' attention.

With the help of the Escape Committee Rex and I had been planning our route. We had put our heads together and decided to head west into Holland, a little over a hundred miles away. Once there we hoped to contact the Dutch underground movement and would put our trust in them. Our eventual target was Spain, and so on to Gibraltar.

Master maps of all areas were smuggled into camp in games parcels. They were printed on very fine tissue paper, exact in every detail, and our backroom boys had cleverly constructed a printing press enabling them to make multiple copies. Heavily strained jelly provided the base, and once the jelly had set hard they were able to etch the map details onto it in very fine relief. Then with ink made from indelible pencils they could run off as many copies as were needed. The results were surprisingly good.

We were also given handsome compasses with a magnetised needle set on a cork swivel. A small speck of luminous paint from a disused watch on the end of the needle would indicate north by night.

I swapped one of my precious blankets for a grey Greek army greatcoat, which I shortened to just above knee height. Dyed battledress trousers and a cap made from a piece of blanket completed my outfit. I had managed to retain my army haversack even though such items were forbidden, which I also dyed and converted into a pack. It was rough, and would not stand up under close scrutiny, but it would do the job.

Following instructions, we had all been hoarding nails which would be needed to make the assemblies. We pulled them out of doors and walls, found them on the ground, and pinched them from German carpenters. It was surprising how the quantity built up. The longitudinals for the ladders would come from the ceilings of the huts.

July dragged on and August came. A POW camp was a great place for rumours, and these stories usually concerned the progress of the war, but now a new crop of rumours spread through the camp like wildfire. They were most disturbing from our point of view, as they suggested that our camp was to be split up. Two weeks later confirmation came when all army officers with or above the rank of major were given a week's notice they were about to be moved.

When this took place there was one noticeable absentee – Major Tom Stallard had gone into hiding.

In order to keep our four teams up to quota, some air force fellows were recruited to fill the gaps created by the move, and they were given hurried instructions on what to do on the night. All ten were put on Ladder 4 and minor reshuffling took place on the others. The break would be late in August, so we began finalising plans.

Now that we were all set to go we became quite edgy, and kept an impatient watch on the weather. Our preferred conditions on the night of the break would be cloud, wind and possibly rain, but to our chagrin a full moon lit the compound and the skies were clear. Every day we pounded along the dust of the compound and perimeter road building up strength and gazing impatiently at the cloudless blue skies.

Our SBO, Colonel Kennedy, reassured us after discussions with the Kommandant that we would be given at least 48 hours' notice of any further evacuations from the camp, which at least made us breathe a little easier. On 28 August we were summoned to a meeting in David Walker's room. Tom Stallard was there, and he had some welcome news.

'From now on,' he began, 'you are on twelve hours' notice. We have decided the actual assault area will be between huts 20 and 21. Some rather noisy diversions have been organised for when the lights are put out, and I can assure you the place will be in complete uproar while our escape is in progress. Grapples with empty tin cans on them will be tossed into the coiled wire and jangled with a rope; there'll be people banging on drums, blowing trumpets, and generally creating as much ruckus as they can. Our departure will be timed so that the guards on patrol will be as far from the assault area as possible, and we're quite convinced that all the Germans will panic, having no idea what the hell is going on.

'As you know hut 20 is empty, and this is where our team will assemble. Those on Number 2 ladder will also assemble there, while the remaining two teams will be in hut 21. When we go over we will fan out, and David will show each of you the direction you should take. Now one important thing; we know there is a German standing patrol in the hayfield beyond the camp, but they change their position every night. Should you be unlucky enough to run into this patrol you are to surrender immediately and try to occupy them for at least three minutes to give the others a chance to get away. Understood?' After we'd muttered our affirmation Stallard continued. 'In conclusion, Captain Johnstone will be in charge of the entire operation from the compound, and his word will be law. He will give you the signal to start, and if he feels it is necessary he will call a halt. That's about it, gentlemen; no more practice sessions, and word will be passed to you when it is on.'

And so we waited. Waiting is a tiresome business and a time for worrying. I would find myself lying awake at night thinking about the scheme. Would I be up to it when the time came? Would I freeze with nerves or panic? Would the platform remain steady? It was fine on the practice wires, but how would it be on the actual wire? Perhaps it would tilt just as I was going over. I had this horrible vision of myself hopelessly ensnared in the coiled barbed wire between the fences. Would the guards shoot? Would I somehow let the others down? An uneasy sleep would eventually steal over me after much soul searching.

The following day Rex Baxter would always dispel any fears or doubts I had. Rex had to be the greatest optimist of all, and his complete confidence in the escape would pick me up no end. He was a great support to have.

As part of his post-escape preparations, Rex had constructed a mud oven around our coal-burning stove. In this we baked small nutritious cakes containing such high-energy ingredients as oatmeal, honey and fat, and packed them into cocoa tins. Together with the chocolate we had been hoarding, we felt we had enough food to sustain us until we reached Holland.

On Sunday, 30 August, Colonel Kennedy received his 48 hours' notice that we were to be evacuated. Although conditions were far from ideal it was decided that the Wire Job would be on that night. Then, at lunchtime, we heard some devastating news.

Concurrent with our training to assault the wire, a tunnel had been slowly snaking out from beneath hut 13, driven down from a coal cellar off the hut's kitchen. The working face of the excavation was lit by a small bulb hanging from some poorly insulated piecemeal wiring which ran along the roof of the narrow tunnel. A young English lieutenant, John Dupree of the Seaforth Highlanders, had been working at the face lying in water which had seeped into the tunnel. With him was his assistant Michael Borwick. Lieutenant Cruickshank, in charge of the scheme's day shift, was operating the air pump at the bottom of the vertical shaft supplying air to the two men.

Suddenly Cruickshank heard Borwick yelling down the tunnel to turn off the electric current, which he did immediately. Moments later Borwick emerged backwards from the tunnel.

'Dear God, help him!' he gasped. 'There's been an accident!'

Cruickshank dived into the dark hole and scrambled frantically along the pitch-black tunnel, eventually encountering Dupree's inert body.

Dupree had been hauling up a dispersal trolley with a new length of air pipe. The projecting end of this had caught in some live wire which had been coiled to enable the light to be moved progressively forward. This wire had fallen down and become entangled in the wheels of the trolley. Dupree had crawled back from the face to try and clear the tangle behind him – a difficult job in the tight confines of the tunnel – when a joint in the wire broke and a live end fell across his bare back, electrocuting him instantly. Cruickshank desperately tried to pull Dupree's body back along the tunnel, but the man's dead weight made this an impossible task.

There was no alternative; the tunnel had to be sacrificed in the faint hope of getting Dupree to the surface and reviving him. Cruickshank scrambled backwards out of the tunnel and clambered up the shaft into the coal cellar, where he found Borwick anxiously waiting with the others from the day team. A few moments later they were all pounding desperately on the locked cellar door, and a surprised orderly let them out. They quickly alerted a German sentry, and then someone rushed over to inform the Escape Committee. They had to get Dupree out in a hurry, and the quickest solution was to dig down into the shallow tunnel from the compound.

While Jock Hamilton-Baillie and some others frantically dug down over the area of the accident, Captain Frank Weldon ran into the coal cellar with a length of rope, squirmed up the shaft and managed to tie a rope around Dupree's ankles. Once back in the air pump chamber he and Johnny Johnstone hauled on the ropes, and after a superhuman effort they managed to drag the young soldier out of the tunnel. They hauled the body upright then others in the cellar, including some Germans, grabbed Dupree and carried him into the kitchen. Frank Weldon collapsed with his exertions. Then

British and German doctors worked side by side in an attempt to revive Dupree, but to no avail. He was dead.

Once the initial panic had died down and the sad news had swept the camp Colonel Kennedy found himself with a difficult and delicate decision to make. Should he allow our escape to take place in light of the tragedy? A hurried conference was held, and the members of the Escape Committee each stated their thoughts on the subject. Some insisted the escape be postponed, while others maintained that as the camp was being evacuated, and the escapers trained to the point of readiness, it should go ahead. Kennedy weighed it all up and made his decision.

'You go, Tom,' he told Stallard. 'You go because that's what young Dupree would have wanted you to do.'

That afternoon Rex and I joined Stallard and Dick Page (our Number 9) as well as the team from Number 2 ladder in hut 27. We entered the ceiling through a well-concealed trapdoor and found Jock Hamilton-Baillie waiting there for us. Known to us all as H. B., it was he who had designed the ladder apparatus. A deceptively young-looking and slim fellow, he had escaped from a camp at Tittmoning, east of Munich, and had been recaptured trying to cross the Swiss border eighty miles away.

The timber and nails were already there, as well as some purloined hammers and saws. Under H. B.'s direction, and covered by a strong cordon of stooges, we worked fast. In two hours we had two perfect sets of gear, which we then stained purple using indelible lead dye so they would not stand out as much. An identical twosome was being made in the ceiling of an adjacent hut by the other two teams.

After the evening check parade we told our close friends that we were breaking out that night. We told them out in the open, two at a time, but we could not tell them how it would be accomplished. Mark Howard, typically, insisted on putting together a special meal to bid us farewell, and so we had tinned steak and onions followed by an excellent pudding made from ground-up biscuits, margarine, powdered milk and raisins.

'You lucky twits,' he muttered wistfully during our meal. 'I'll miss you both.' He meant it, and not for the first time I wished he was coming with us.

At 8pm we were dressed and ready to go, and a little before nine we made our way to hut 27. The two ladder assemblies were handed down from the ceiling and then, with an alert team of stooges watching out for us, we carried them the short distance to hut 20. Here we greased the wooden runners with dripping and then waited for zero hour, which was 9.30pm.

The compound 'controllers' were outside, ostensibly walking around before turning in for 'lights-out' at eleven o'clock. The Germans allowed such walks up until this hour, so the officers did not appear suspicious as they strolled around having a smoke.

Next we blackened our faces with soot from the stove, and pulled balaclavas over our heads. We then became fidgety, making minute adjustments to our clothing and packs, and though there was some desultory conversation most men were lost in their own private thoughts. Even Rex was quiet – he sat like a statue on the end of a bench plucking microscopic bits of lint from his trousers. The minutes ticked by.

The pit of my stomach was cold and felt peculiarly empty because of the tension I was trying to combat. I looked across at Albert Arkwright, who was team leader on the second ladder. He too was tense, his eyes darting around the room, but always returning to the silent sentinel gazing steadfastly out into the compound. He reached down and retied his shoelaces.

I tried to think of home, that small yet wondrous part of the vast continent of Australia that I knew so well. I closed my eyes and a dark image of Corio Bay danced into my mind. The scene lightened, and the water turned an azure blue as the image spread before me. There, that was it – the colours were right, and I could even feel a slight swaying as I gently swung the small yacht into a sweet breeze, which swept lightly over me. Bright reflections of the sun danced gaily across the glassy surface, breaking and sparkling at each tiny swell. Gentle waves slapped laughingly at the bow, and overhead I could hear the harsh caw-cawing of a lone seagull wheeling around above the mast.

Someone in the hut suddenly spluttered into a suppressed cough, and the gentle image in my mind greyed over and disappeared, but it had given me a new peace, and evoked a determination to enjoy such earthly pleasures again. Some of the emptiness had left me. I felt warmer and more relaxed, and my resolve hardened. I clenched my fists and waited.

At 9.25 Rex and I, Tom and Dick moved over to our assembly and assumed our positions by the ladders. The other six stood behind us. The room was gripped in a tight cord of emotion as the time approached. We were now well and truly in the hands of the controllers, and were like coiled springs. By my watch it was 9.30; why weren't we going? What was the delay? Oh God, don't let it be called off now!

Suddenly the camp was plunged into darkness, and I was jumping out of my skin. Anxious moments passed, and then Captain Johnstone gave the all clear signal from the compound. Our controller bellowed 'Go!'

This was it! Rex and I grasped the apparatus and shoved it out the window where Stallard and Page were now waiting. They grabbed the front end and hauled it out as we ran out into the compound, seizing our end of the apparatus again. Our team of ten black-faced escapers then raced towards our spot on the wire. The other team from our hut had followed suit, and we could only guess that the two teams from the other hut had done likewise, but we were concentrating solely on our own effort. We came to the trip-wire (which had been secretly whitewashed earlier) and it stood out well enough to ensure we didn't run into it.

Having crossed the wire Stallard and Page pushed their end up high and we rammed our end onto the ground beside the inner fence. All around us bedlam had erupted, and the promised diversions were causing complete pandemonium for the guards. They had no idea what was going on in the darkness, nor where to go, although most of their attention was attracted to the noisier diversions – a long way from our operation. The two sentries in the closest towers were busy shouting at the dark shapes of men who had thrown up the dummy ladders, and were now scurrying back to their quarters, while these men for their part were shouting back in German, ordering the sentries not to take their eyes off the ladders!

Rex leapt onto our ladder with the ends of the platform firmly grasped in his hands, and the three of us held him steady as he ascended a couple of steps. With his great strength he then extended the brutally heavy platform upwards and outwards. As it clicked into place he was up and over like a flash. The platform effectively straddled the wire, and Rex swung deftly through the hole using the trapeze bar, hit the ground and was off.

I was all of three feet behind Rex getting onto the ladder. From a few yards away in the darkness someone let loose with a loud obscenity in a familiar Australian accent, indicating trouble with one of the ladders. But my training was paying off and I did not hesitate as I repeated Rex's smooth actions, crossing the wires, grasping the bar, and swinging to the ground outside the camp. I then began sprinting after Rex. Behind me the diversions were in full swing, and the wire twanged loudly as it was tweaked back and forth through the holes in the posts. The hysterical shouts of the Germans indicated their complete confusion.

I was about 20 yards clear when the first shot rang out. Adrenalin coursed through my body as I ran for my life, eventually catching up with Rex. I slowed to his pace as we charged through a field of turnips, while the shooting and shouting behind us rose in intensity. We could hear the machine guns in the towers rattle into action as the sentries blindly ripped away at the ant-like army of men scurrying away from the camp.

We sped on into the stooked hay field, bullets occasionally whining past us, and began to slow to a canter. A surge of elation coursed through me as I looked over at the running figure of my friend. We were free for the first time in eighteen months. Free from Warburg and the shackles of imprisonment. I was exultant!

When we were about a thousand yards from the camp we slowed to an easy jog. I felt good; our fitness campaign had certainly paid dividends.

Then suddenly, disaster struck. A group of armed Germans appeared from behind a stack of hay right in front of us and screamed at us to put our hands up. Of all the rotten luck, we had run smack-dab into the standing patrol.

Within seconds we had been surrounded by our highly excited captors, caught inexorably in a trap we had known to exist. Rifles and pistols were jabbed into our backs and stomachs, while our breath was choked with exertion, fear, and frustration. We stood there gasping, and a few moments later two more escapers were thrust into the middle of our small circle.

The German sergeant in charge was furious, but despite our bitter disappointment we knew we now had a job to do – we had to hold him and his men here, giving others a chance to make some distance. Three minutes; it seemed an eternity.

'How many have escaped?' the sergeant screamed. 'How many away?'

We stalled, pretending we were still winded by the run, and he barked out even louder. 'Answer me, or you will be shot!'

Rex handled the situation beautifully. 'Four men,' he blurted out. 'Four men is all. You have us all!'

The German thrust his face to within inches of Rex. 'How did you get out? How did you get past the wire?'

Rex breathed deeply a few more times. 'We jumped over it,' he said. 'It was easy!'

'You lie!' yelled the sergeant. 'That is impossible.'

We stood there mutely as he raved on about the impossibility of what Rex had told him, but we were satisfied we had done our job as the guards just idly stood around listening in and waiting for further orders. Finally the sergeant had finished his tirade; we were marched back to the camp with our hands in the air and taken to the guard house. Soon after two others joined us; six in all had been captured.

The guards then ordered us to strip naked, after which we were lined up in the passageway, standing well away from the wall and an arm's length apart. Talking was absolutely forbidden. Six wary, armed guards stood in front of us, obviously excited and jumpy, so we kept still and quiet. The camp lights were still out, and two hurricane lamps flickered eerily on the wall in front of us.

After a while, Deputy Kommandant Sturzkopf stormed in. Early on, the prisoners had christened him 'Bulk Issue' due to his rotund figure, and the name had stuck. He was paunchy and pompous in his massive greatcoat with the flamboyant velvet collars, and his face was dark with rage as he walked slowly along our line-up, glaring at each of us in turn. He looked very demonic in the dim light of the lamps, throwing shadows around the walls, and it was quite a relief when he finally strode out once again, cursing loudly.

We remained standing in the passageway for about two hours, cold, weary and thirsty, but we were also quite elated. Guards continually rushed in and out in a state of confusion; we could hear orders being barked everywhere, and the sounds of motor vehicles setting off out of the camp. Around midnight things settled down a little. I was beginning to tremble, not only with the cold, but also the after-effects of our escape bid. A guard came into the corridor, pointed at Rex and me, and ordered us to go with him into a small, dimly lit room. The contents of our packs were laid out on a small table, behind which sat Rademacher, his face bloated and red with rage. Our precious hoard of chocolate, our maps and compass all sat in orderly fashion in front of him. He looked as if he could cheerfully strangle us, then took in our discomfort and nakedness. He actually relaxed and sat back.

'You have been brought here for interrogation,' he began. 'I am sure you will cooperate, just as I am sure you know the consequences of your stupid escape attempt. You have read the notices warning you what might happen, so you have nothing to lose by answering a few questions. It may even save your lives!' He picked up one of our maps. 'We have already examined your escape equipment, and we know how you got out. Where did you get the ladders, and how many of you were there? Where did you get these maps, and how did you plan to get to Holland?'

Rex stared straight ahead. 'My name is Captain R. R. Baxter,' he said, slowly and deliberately. 'My army number is VX136.'

I chimed in. 'My name is Lieutenant J. W. K. Champ; my army number is VX707.'

Rademacher glared at us. 'You are being very foolish. Why not answer my questions? We will soon know it all anyway, so let us save some time. Come along gentlemen, if you give me some details now it will be a lot easier for you when we have to decide the punishment, and I am sure you know what this punishment may be. You are facing some very serious charges, so you must cooperate.'

Rex was unmoved. 'My name is Captain R. R. Baxter; my army number is VX136.'

Once again I followed suit. 'My name is Lieutenant J. W. K. Champ; my army number is VX707.'

At this, Rademacher exploded. He went berserk, yelling and screaming in unintelligible German, and it was a frightening sight. He jumped up from his chair and slammed his fists repeatedly onto the table, making everything fly into the air. When he was like this he was an absolute lunatic, and I was definitely frightened that he would draw his revolver and start shooting. Instead he picked up Rex's precious Dunhill pipe, threw it on the floor, and stamped on it in rage. The beautiful pipe, sent to Rex all the way from England by Mark's mother, was shattered.

'Raus!' he screamed. *'Raus!'* We needed no further encouragement and fled out of the door to the sanctuary of the corridor. One by one

our companions were taken away to undergo similar treatment, but Rademacher came up empty.

The long night dragged on, and I was being swept by a dreadful tiredness. Our guards relaxed a little, and one by one we were permitted to go to the toilet. At six o'clock in the morning the lights suddenly came back on, and an hour later we were given back our clothes. We dressed quickly, and half an hour later were escorted to the main camp gate, where to our surprise we were told to return to our quarters. Rex and I couldn't believe our good fortune as we hurried along towards our hut, laughing and going over the events of the night. We were eager to talk to some of the others, to find out what had gone on, and how many had escaped.

A little further along the road we came across a great sight. Still in position against the wire were our four ladders, watched over by a dejected-looking sentry. Outside, another German was recording the scene on film. The ladders and duckboards were a symbol of a great triumph.

We quickly learned that two of the teams had been successful – ours and Number 2. All twenty men on those ladders had made it over the wire. Number 4, the hastily put-together RAF team, had only managed to get two of their number away, while on Number 3 Doug Crawford, Jack Hand and four others had managed to scramble over before the order to return was given by Johnny Johnstone. Twenty-eight men in all out of a possible forty – not a bad effort at all. Six of us had been taken, so it now appeared we had twenty-two 'gone-aways'.

The only casualty was an officer who had sustained a slight bullet wound to the heel. Bobby Barr, Bill Rawlings and Alan Kirkwood, the fellows who had acted as the anchor men for the three successful ladders, had done a splendid and courageous job. They had stood their ground valiantly as the guards began shooting at them, and had only abandoned their task when the order to do so was given.

Two days later, all remaining officers in the camp began entraining for the new camp at Eichstätt in northern Bavaria. It was there that we found out about most of the others, as they were brought in by ones and twos. David Walker and Pat Campbell-Preston were picked up the very next morning when they passed a local railway station. Tom Stallard and Dick Page were caught on the Dutch frontier. Martin Gilliat and Phil Pardoe were caught nearly 200 miles north of Warburg.

Doug Crawford had an interesting story to tell. His team had rushed the wire from hut 21 and thrown the assembly up against the wire. Unfortunately it wasn't positioned correctly, and when Crawford launched the duckboard section it had hit the overhead power lines and rebounded. It was Doug's loud profanity I had heard as I scaled the ladder, and it was only his Number 2's quick action in shoving his hand against Doug's backside that prevented him from falling back into the compound. The man's name, appropriately, was Jack Hand.

Now steadied, Crawford managed to push the platform up and out – this time correctly – and he scrambled across the unsteady assembly followed by Jack Hand and four others. Several seconds had been taken up in the double launching, and the controller ordered the rest of the team to abandon the effort and get back to their quarters.

Doug and Jack were among the last away, and came in for a good deal of attention from the Germans. They ran hard, weaving and ducking, and split up to confuse their pursuers. Jack swerved into the hayfield, and ran smack into some members of the patrol. He ended up in our small group of six, which also included the two RAF fellows.

Now alone, Crawford ran until he had put a fair distance between himself and the camp. He then slowed to a walk, and took his bearings. His plan was to head for the Black Forest area and Frankfurt-am-Main to the south, and he was going to 'boy scout' it – travelling by night and hiding up by day. A small wood provided some shelter that night, although he only slept a little. He remained hidden in the wood all day and crept out when it got dark.

Doug headed steadily south-west through the remainder of the night, and as the first pastel streaks of dawn began to paint the sky he started looking around for a suitable place to hide. A haystack in a nearby field caught his eye, and he veered off towards it. He'd never slept in a haystack, and thought it would be quite comfortable. And so it seemed as he fell into a deep, dreamless sleep. Two hours later he woke with a start to find himself crawling with lice. He dozed fitfully and unhappily throughout the rest of the day, and resolved he would never sleep in a haystack again.

As dusk fell Doug gratefully left his hide and continued his way south. A couple of hours before dawn he made another disastrous discovery – his water bottle was missing. Realising that it would be difficult to go on without it he cursed his luck and turned back to a stream where he had filled the bottle two hours earlier. Fortunately he was able to retrace his steps, and when he arrived at the stream he found the precious bottle lying beside a small bush where he had dropped it. As it was nearly dawn he spent a frustrating day beside the stream and set off again that night.

Just after midnight he found himself approaching the village of Wilhelms, situated ten kilometres east of Kassel. He was exhausted by his long walk and settled down in the centre of a small clump of trees and slept until five o'clock, at which time he was woken by some vigorous industrial noises quite nearby. His cover was not very good and Doug decided to skirt around the village, hoping to find a more secure place to spend the daylight hours. He set off, and eventually found a thick wood a couple of miles south of Wilhelms where he spent another agonisingly slow day waiting for night to fall.

Three uneventful nights of moving south followed. On the following night, nearing the outlying area of Frankfurt-am-Main, he turned under a railway bridge and found himself walking into a large town. A young woman walking the streets smiled at him, and he decided it was safer to keep away from populated areas as much as possible. He retraced his steps, and after carefully skirting around the town soon found himself walking up a steep, bare hill. The stars were beginning to pale with the approaching dawn and Doug could see very little in the way of cover. He tried to break into a small brick structure at the side of the road, but it was too well padlocked. Needing somewhere to go to hide up during the day Doug looked further up the road. Very little cover was evident, except for a few scattered mounds of kale, and he decided that this would have to do. He made his way towards the nearest heap of kale and ran around the back of it. To his complete surprise he ran straight into an equally astonished German corporal, who quickly raised his rifle and jammed it into Crawford's midriff. He had apparently run straight into a dug-out in which the sleepy sentry had been whiling away the hours until he was replaced. Doug could do very little but raise his hands in surrender. He felt like a complete idiot.

When he had recovered from his surprise the German indicated to Crawford that he was to accompany him, and then marched him along a dusty dirt road back into the town, following at a safe distance with his rifle at the ready. There was great excitement in the town gaol when they arrived, and he was quickly thrust into an empty cell. The Germans kept a close watch on their new captive, and the telephone was soon running hot. He was eventually given a slice of dry black bread and a little dripping to chew on, along with a cold cup of weak but bitter coffee.

Early the next afternoon Crawford heard a screech of brakes outside the gaol, and he was soon being driven back to Kassel with a silent brace of guards sitting either side of him in the back seat of a car. On arrival at Kassel he was taken into a crowded gaol and thrown into another cell. Left alone, he soon fell asleep on the lice-infested bunk.

The following afternoon some security police arrived and began firing questions at him in rapid German. He picked up very little of what they were saying, but could make out that they were trying to pin a charge of espionage on him. He said nothing apart from the fact that he was an escaped prisoner of war, and would not give any information except his name, rank and service number. This was jotted down. They also examined the dog-tags around his neck, and then they left him alone.

Early next morning the questioning started once again, and this time he was told in English that he was no longer classified as a POW, as he had been captured in a classified military area. The penalty for this was death. Doug was asked to make a statement, but he gave his name, rank and number as a young officer took notes. He also told them he had escaped six days earlier from Oflag VIB at nearby Warburg. This, he said, could easily be checked and verified. After a while they left him alone again.

An hour later the head security man, accompanied by a large Alsatian dog, came into the cell and began questioning him in German. Doug just looked blank and repeated that he did not speak German. The officer grumbled something, then ordered his dog to keep watch while he left the cell for a few moments. When he returned, he was horrified to find the beast quietly nuzzling up to Doug, with its head in his lap. The unfortunate animal got a hefty kick to the ribs for its incompetence, and was dragged away.

Later on, the German who had transcribed Doug's statement came into the cell and politely asked if he would sign it. Doug took one look and refused. It was typed in German.

'But this is exactly what you said,' the young officer explained. 'I am a school teacher – at least I was – and I can promise you that this is an exact translation of your very words. Sign this, and you will be returned to Warburg. Your men are moving soon to a new camp, and you must join them. The espionage charges against you have been dropped – you have my word on this.'

He seemed sincere, so Doug skimmed through the statement. He could pick out a few words, and it seemed to run pretty true. 'Very well, I'll sign it,' he finally said. 'But with one proviso. I wish to write at the end that I do not understand German at all.'

'Agreed,' the German replied, and handed Doug the pen. He signed the statement and added his footnote.

A few days later he joined us in Eichstätt. He never did hear anything more about the charge of espionage, but eventually discovered the reason for the Germans' anxiety; the area he had been caught in was a top-secret zone, close to an underground

Messerschmitt factory. This was the source of the industrial noises he had heard, which had woken him at Wilmshelm. He had almost unwittingly stumbled into it, which would not have amused the Germans one bit. Like the rest of those recaptured he served three weeks in solitary confinement.

Six months later David Walker received a seemingly harmless card from England. It read in part: 'Darling David, I have just returned from a most interesting journey. Your two cousins send their kind regards. I trust you are well. Your affectionate aunt, Henrietta.' The card was from Henry Coombe-Tennant. Together with Robert Fuller and Albert Arkwright he had made a 'home run' all the way to England. Their plan, the same as ours, had worked perfectly. They had reached Holland, contacted the Dutch Underground, and stayed in a sympathetic farmer's barn for nine days before being passed along the famous Comet escape line through Belgium and France, and finally back to England.

Thus the Warburg Wire Job, as it became known, went down as one of the most brilliantly conceived, audacious, and successfully accomplished mass escapes of the war.

4

Eichstätt: The Second Escape

IT WOULD BE DIFFICULT to envisage a more desperate or dangerous means of escape than leaping out of the window of a train travelling at high speed with absolutely no protection, and in the full knowledge that one could easily jump straight into an oncoming pole, tunnel, or one of the many railway utilities that border a track. It takes a peculiar breed of person, one whom I would classify somewhere between an incredibly brave opportunist and a foolhardy gambler. I could never do it, but many did, and were for the most part successful. On the other hand several were killed in the attempt. The odds would be apparent to anyone who has ever travelled on a train. The risks would be enormous, and desperation would be the only possible motive. It was this desperation that led to the intrepid breed of prisoner who fell into the category of 'train-jumper'.

Lieutenant Clive Dieppe, another Australian destined for Colditz, was a train-jumper, and he travelled with us on the train from Warburg to Eichstätt. That is to say, he travelled part of the way!

South Australian-born Dieppe, of the New South Wales 2/1st Infantry Battalion, had been captured in Crete on 30 May 1941. Right from the moment of his capture he was determined that he would not remain a prisoner long, and had even tried to break away from a column of prisoners proceeding to Maleme, but was retaken.

Clive Dieppe was also in Salonika, and had worked out a plan with Lieutenant Boyce from New Zealand for scaling the wire and wall opposite the barber shop. The night before the attempt, in an incident similar to the killing of the Cypriot officers, some Maltese prisoners made an abortive assault on the wire in the same place as Dieppe and Boyce were going to make their break. The Maltese were mown down in cold blood by the guards.

Lübeck was Dieppe's next stop, and then he arrived at Warburg two days before our contingent. In Warburg he worked on two tunnels, both of which were found by ferrets. Although suffering from jaundice he and a Major Hooper devised a scheme in which they would leave the camp in a laundry cart. In the end his illness prevented him from taking part and the scheme was later used successfully by two other men. In another plan submitted to the Escape Committee he was going to hide inside a sanitary truck, but the committee wisely decided the plan was too dangerous, especially in light of his recent illness.

By this time Clive had submitted several plans to a number of committees with a singular lack of success, and he was becoming frustrated. He vowed that he would escape by himself using a scheme which did not need the approval of a committee – a daring leap from a moving train. That story is now told in his own words.

The news of a move from Warburg at short notice circulated through the camp, and immediately my thoughts flew to an attempt to escape from the train. As I thought about it the idea appeared more and more attractive. In the first place train escapes and the like did not have to be approved by our own Escape Committee; secondly, at this time I was engaged with others on a tunnel escape, and therefore had already been given and acquired a full escape kit (papers, compass, maps, etc.). The next strong point was that the Germans, with their characteristic method, would move us alphabetically, and I knew that being a 'D' I must be in the first batch, which would enhance my chances.

The main difficulty with individual escapes of this nature was of course that you couldn't plan your moves to any great extent, and had to meet emergencies as they happened. One such emergency occurred almost immediately when I discovered that a very thorough search, to the extent of stripping, was being carried out before we marched to the train. As my escape kit was in my trousers I thought I was a 'gone duck' there and then, but as my batch of ten went in to be searched I whispered word to the next in line, which was enough for him to arrange a noisy diversion while I was being searched. This he did, and while the guards rushed over to him I managed to slip away with only a half search and my gear intact.

After we were marched onto the train and things settled down, I had to plan the next step of my escape, which involved such things as timing of the guard patrols, selection of windows to be used, etc., and this all had to be done during the early part of the journey. None of this was easy because we were crowded forty to a carriage, plus guards, and the German escort was in the first car. We had been warned before we boarded the train that there was a fully armed guards' van complete with searchlights and machine guns at the rear of the train, so although my escape maps were to France and the train was travelling further away from what I hoped would be my destination, a daylight attempt was quite out of the question, The train travelled at what I think was its maximum speed, and during the whole of the day stopped only once. This added to my difficulties, but following more than a year of imprisonment and repeated frustrated attempts to escape, I had reached one of the all-time lows that marked a POW's existence, and I was determined to give it a go, come what may.

It was of course necessary to discuss my plans with those who shared my compartment as I naturally had to have someone to give the signal when the guards were turned away, and also to throw my kit out and cover up for me as long as they could afterwards. Also it was the thing to do to put them in the picture, as they may have to put up with some form of reprisal when the escape was discovered.

When my plans became known one of the officers, an Englishman called Bill Ashton, asked to join me. He had no escape gear, but a 'throw-in' around the carriage provided him with the necessary kit and food. The arrangement was that if I got out of the train without being discovered and there was sufficient time he would follow, and I was glad of the thought of having his company. It was arranged that four of us – myself, Bill, and our two stooges – should occupy the same compartment. The plan was that Bill and I sat near the windows, and the two sitting next to us would give a signal by tap when the right moment arrived.

By observation I had discovered that there were only about four or five seconds during which the guards were blind to our compartment, so the time factor was tight. On signal, I had to quickly open the window and throw myself out; Bill would throw out my haversack and then if given the 'all clear' by our stooge, follow immediately. His gear would be chucked out after him and then the window closed.

Ten o'clock was tentatively agreed upon as 'zero hour', and the only thing left to do was loosen the wire guard on the window and then sit and wait whilst the other lads settled down and the carriage became quieter. The tension was terrific as I sat and stared out of the window, watching the telegraph poles flash by, and trying to calculate my chances of missing them and the wheels.

Suddenly, at about 9.45, the tap came, and from then on I seemed to act automatically; wire off, the window down, and a quick dive through. I didn't even seem to think. I landed heavily on my right side, hitting my head, right arm and elbow. My fall, fortunately, was cushioned by landing mainly on blue-metal ballast on a slight clay bank.

I lay there, hugging the rails as near as possible, and waiting for what seemed an eternity for the rear guard van light to go by. The train passed, and I waited in a cold sweat for the alarm and the firing to commence, but the train just continued on and miraculously it became quiet. I picked myself up and discovered that there were no bones broken, and suddenly I realised I was free. For the first time in 14 months I was on my own – no guards, no wire, no restrictions. It was a glorious feeling.

A second or two of that beautiful solitude and I started searching for Bill. He was only about 100 feet or so away, and had had an even better landing than me. Our haversacks were also nearby, so it was obvious that the getaway from the train had worked as planned. Months later I was to discover that about fifteen minutes elapsed before our escape was discovered, our stooges having done an excellent job of camouflaging our vacant seats.

Our first thought was to find out where we were, so we walked back along the rails for about a quarter of a mile until we found a station named Burgthann (about ten miles south of Nuremberg). We then decided to go to ground for the rest of the night, as we were completely done through the strain, and the jolting from the falls.

We moved away from the station into the open country and soon came to a small running creek. Here Bill bathed my head and elbow and fixed me up as best he could; again we got that wonderful feeling of being free, so we sat and had a cigarette and chatted like schoolboys. We moved again a little further up the slope and chose what appeared at night to be a good 'hide' for the remainder of the night and the next day. The morning proved that our copse was a poor one as the surrounding area was mostly wheat country, and being harvest time all the workers were quite near to us. This meant that all day we were unable to sleep as we both had to keep constant watch of the workers. Later on I was to become much more experienced in selecting my hideouts for the day.

We planned to walk at least twenty miles each night, and to do that we had to commence at dusk. This meant that our most dangerous period was from 7–9pm. We also rationed out our food, realising that if we were lucky and escaped recapture, we would still have to live off the country for a good many days. I later got to loathe the sight of apples and raw potatoes. So began our long trek heading due west, which was mainly hard, monotonous walking; always on the alert, with just minor excitements, such as passing cyclists who could not be avoided and whose greetings of 'Heil Hitler!' had to be returned. There were of course the highlights, such as our first night when we narrowly escaped falling into a huge quarry which wasn't marked on our maps, and the night when, at dusk, a terrific thunderstorm began and we stood for shelter beneath a tree, only to see with horror a tree no more than 35 feet away split into two by lightning and burst into flames!

We had been avoiding large towns and villages up to this time, but by the fourth night we found that we would have to pass through a fairly large one named Rothenburg, as to avoid this town would have meant a long and hard detour up steep hills, and we decided to take a chance. On entering the town about midnight we found the main street was cobbled stone and our own footsteps echoed loudly. There was no one about, for the Germans are an early-to-bed race. About halfway through, and with what seemed like every dog in town barking, a light suddenly went on in the darkened street and a door opened. Probably foolishly, we took to our heels. Shouts followed us, and there were sounds of pursuit. We dodged into a side lane and at the end through a backyard up a steep incline to a path that led us up and around the town. Once again we had been lucky.

After eight nights of walking, Bill's heels and feet were shockingly blistered and infected, so we had a talk and he decided that he would have to rest up for a full day and night; but he insisted that as I was still in good shape I must go on alone. I hated leaving him, as he had proved to be a good companion and we were firm friends, but it was common sense that if I was to succeed at all I must continue. We shook hands, and I began my lone trek. Later I learned that he was recaptured the following night moving through a village. Forty years later we still keep in touch.

The days went past and I had a number of very narrow squeaks, such as the morning I woke up to find my hide for the day was overlooking a training field for infantry! Watching this training was actually quite absorbing at first, until I suddenly noticed one patrol of eight men heading my way. Luckily, they passed within a few yards of me, but the rest of that day was spent on the constant *qui vive.*

After about the eighth day my rations were completely exhausted, so I had to start living off the country; my food consisted mainly of apples and raw potatoes. All of these things, including the fact that I had no cigarettes or matches left (which to an inveterate smoker like myself was sheer hell) combined with the loneliness, the lack of sleep from having to watch on days when I had chosen a bad hideout, were beginning to tell on me. Mainly, I think I missed companionship most of all, as I had become used to living with lots of men, and suddenly to have no one to talk to, to laugh over the narrow escapes with and to say 'well, let's continue to give it a go', was the worst of all. However the days went by and I was still 'at large'. The cards were stacking up against me though, and I got wet through on two successive days.

On the first wet night I was just plugging along some rail tracks with the hope of jumping a train when I came across a small, lighted signal box. I watched for a while and decided I would go and ask for a smoke and a chance to rest out of the rain by the small brazier fire the occupant had there. The signalman was an old man of about 75 years. He gave me a cigarette and I chatted with him in somewhat halting German on my part. I don't know whether he guessed that his uninvited guest was a POW escapee or (as I tried to be) a foreign worker, but as I had noticed that there was no telephone there, I was not all that worried.

On what proved to be my last night's walking, and with a further repetition of the previous night's rain, I started to feel off-colour, and began to get that 'don't care' feeling. It was now into the 16th day since I had jumped from the train, and I had covered about 200 miles.

After crossing the Neckar River at a shallow point I followed a road heading westwards for approximately 12 miles and then found I had to go through another town. I was about halfway through when suddenly two policemen walked out of a darkened street, right into me. They shone torches, asked who I was and for my papers, and immediately became suspicious. They took me along to the police station for a further interrogation and the game was up. I learned next day that the town in which I had been recaptured was Meckenheim, south of Heidelberg – just ten miles short of the river Rhine and my objective, Alsace–Lorraine. Once there I had intended seeking sanctuary from a priest who, I hoped, would cover me until I could contact the Underground. The date of my recapture was 16 September.

From Meckenheim I was eventually taken to the police station at Mannheim for further questioning and another night in the cells. The next day, under police escort, I boarded a train for Frankfurt. During the trip I asked to go to the toilet, and while the train was chugging through a lengthy tunnel I managed to lever the window down, clamber out and drop down onto gravel. The train was travelling more slowly than the last one, so this was a simple matter. Once more I lay still until the train had passed, and then ran out of the tunnel into the countryside.

This time, I was on the loose for a further one and a half days in a heavy forest area, but was picked up by some farmers and taken to the police station at Russelsheim, and from there into a prison cell at a French POW Stalag camp north of Frankfurt. From there, I was escorted onto a train by a very watchful German sergeant, who did not take his eyes or gun off me until we reached the station, and ultimately camp, at Eichstätt, where I was thrown into the prison cells.

From these nefarious wanderings my health suffered very badly; I had to endure long hospitalisations in Eichstätt suffering from pleurisy and anaemia, and I continued to suffer chronically bad health right through my POW days in Eichstätt and Colditz. I would still assist in the planning and staging of some escapes, and even found myself with a place in the mass break-out of sixty-five officers from Eichstätt, but for the most part I was too ill to consider yet another solo effort.

Oflag VIIB, our new camp at Eichstätt where we arrived on 2 September, was situated in a wide valley, the northern boundary being practically at the foot of a bare hillside which comprised the north side of the valley. To the south was the small river Altmühle, and about half a mile beyond that lay the wooded slope of the southern side. The camp was rectangular in shape, about 600 by 300 yards in area.

The camp road or Lagerstrasse ran in a straight line along the front of a row of six three-storeyed brick buildings on the north side, while there were five single-storeyed concrete blocks in the south-east corner. Eventually there were about 2000 officers and ORs at VIIB, and we were accommodated in brick buildings with the usual allowance of space in our rooms. We now had a full-sized soccer pitch and several basketball courts, as well as two very rough dirt tennis courts. Later we constructed two five-a-side hockey fields.

The defences of the camp were strong. A double barbed wire fence comprised the boundary, and there were the usual sentry towers at intervals around the fence. These towers, however, were not situated right over the wire but were set about 30 yards outside. This gave the sentry a much clearer view of the perimeter, and a scheme such as the one put over at Warburg, when the line of fence posts was used as a cover, was out of the question. Everyone had to be in the buildings at dusk which was signalled by a bugle call, and at night the grounds were patrolled by sentries who had orders to shoot anyone caught outside. These patrols were accompanied by large, savage dogs.

The main gate of the camp opened into the grounds in which the German quarters were located, and a second gate led from there to the road outside. Another gate was placed at the east end of the camp, but very little traffic went that way.

Tunnelling looked the best way out, but even then there were severe natural obstacles to overcome. As already mentioned the north boundary faced a steep hill, and the other three boundary fences were on the top of a sharp downwards slope. To tunnel, therefore, it would be necessary to either dig up or down.

Shortly after we moved in the Germans announced that we were to have a weekly beer ration, and sure enough a few days later in came a large lorry carrying about a hundred gallons of beer. We had to queue up, and I think everyone in the camp was in the line. After waiting two hours I finally reached the bar and received my litre of beer. I took it into a corner and prepared to enjoy my first drink of beer for a very long time, but I was disappointed. It looked like beer, it tasted like beer, but somehow it lacked something. This 'something' I soon discovered was alcohol, and the next time the beer was on there were a lot less starters willing to wait two hours for a drink of lolly beer.

Ten days after we arrived from Warburg the Germans called a parade and informed us that about 150 officers, whose names they read out, were to be moved to Block 2. Rex and I were sent to a room on the third storey of Block 2, while Mark was sent to Block 8 at the other end of the camp, in an area which later became known as the 'Garden City'. Rex and I shared a rather large room with about twenty other officers, and slept in three-tiered bunks with the usual paillasse covered in a check-patterned cotton sheet.

It soon became apparent that the Germans had placed all prisoners with an escaping record in Block 2. The reason was obvious; Block 2 backed onto the northern boundary of the camp, from which the rugged, boulder and rock-strewn hillside rose steeply for a distance of almost 300 yards. To all intents and purposes it appeared an impossible area to either tunnel from, or to assault the wire.

The following day we met up with Mark and, by arrangement with another officer in our room who did not have an escaping record, we were able to have him transferred to our room, and the three of us now shared the one three-tiered bunk.

Food was a problem for a while as the customary argument about unopened tin cans took place, but after a week of haggling we were allowed to have our first Red Cross parcel with opened tins, and from then on we could trade an empty tin for an opened full one. We also arranged to have an issue of half a parcel a week to avoid other foodstuffs going bad, and this worked out quite well.

Our dull routine began; two check parades a day, lousy German food and ersatz (acorn substitute) coffee, and the only daily bright spot being the evening meal, compliments of our Red Cross parcels. We read books, we mooched around the camp and occasionally we played sport. Hockey and soccer were popular, and softball was the rage with the Canadians, some 100 of whom were there when we arrived, having been in captivity for only a week following the abortive attack by combined Canadian and commando forces on Dieppe. These recent prisoners were able to tell us about conditions in England and how the Allied forces in Great Britain were being trained and equipped for the final assault on the continent.

October passed and November came with the cold increasing as we entered winter. One day a special parade was called, and all the officers captured at Dieppe were ordered to fall out. The guard strength was twice the usual, so we knew something was going on. After a while the Dieppe chaps were marched out of the gate, and it wasn't until later that afternoon we found out they had been taken to the ancient castle at Willibaldsburg on the other side of the village. It was also reported that their hands had been tied with rope as a reprisal for the alleged action taken by our forces at Dieppe in tying the hands of captured Germans until such time as they could be escorted to the barges which would take them to England. The Germans had in fact captured a British order instructing our troops to do this, and photographs of the order were posted throughout the camp.

As a consequence, everyone was delighted when we heard through our secret radio that the Brits had ordered a corresponding number of German POWs in England to be handcuffed. Next day there was another special parade, and the last ten of each company to arrive were marched off to Block 1. Rex, Mark and I, who were habitually late on parade, were amongst them. When we got to the block we were told we would be moving in, and to return to our own quarters to fetch our bedding and food. Once we arrived back at Block 1, and the displaced tenants had taken their belongings to other quarters, we were allocated rooms. But that was not the end of it. In each room stood some goons with a pile of handcuffs, and they proceeded to manacle us like criminals. Fortunately our sense of humour came to the fore, and we nearly laughed ourselves sick, much to the chagrin of the guards. Once we were all manacled we were told (as expected) that our handcuffing was in reprisal for the British action, and the Germans had now handcuffed twice as many POWs as the British. We treated it as a huge joke, and soon after the guards had left our room a few of the chaps managed to slip their hands out of the cuffs.

That evening a team of goons arrived with keys to unlock us for the night, but when they departed it was minus a set of keys which had been purloined by one of the men. At eight o'clock the next morning, as required, we filed down the stairs to have the handcuffs put on once again by the guards. We then went back upstairs, where the cuffs were unlocked and removed! A continuous lookout was kept during the day, and if any Germans came close it was a simple matter to put the cuffs back on. At midday we would put the handcuffs back on, go downstairs, and a smirking guard would unlock them so we could have our lunchtime soup. It really was quite farcical.

Walks on the football field were now permitted for two hours daily, and with winter setting in we really looked forward to this exercise as a means of keeping warm.

After a few days the Dieppe officers were returned to the camp and confined to our block. They had endured a miserable stay in the castle at Willibaldsburg, and were glad to be back. All of us were completely isolated from the rest of the camp, and our little trio decided to find a way to get back into our old block again.

Anyone requiring medical treatment was required to parade before the doctor in the morning, so I did this and told him through an interpreter that I was suffering badly with a toothache, and needed to see a British dentist in the main part of the camp. He had no problems with this, although he said that I could not return to Block 1 and would have to find someone who would not only take my place, but wear the handcuffs for me. None of this was news to me and I had already arranged for an old mate, Captain Dick Davis, to take my place. He was happy to get back to Block 1 and be reunited with all his books and other belongings. It was a good thing for me that the doctor didn't check the veracity of my complaint; the last of my teeth had been removed twelve months before, and I was equipped with two full dentures. Shortly after Mark and Rex managed to pull the same stunt before it became overworked, and so we were back once again in Block 2.

Thankfully we had only worn the handcuffs for two weeks, but some of the chaps spent over 12 months in them. At one stage the Germans proudly brought new manacles into Block 1, which had an 18-inch chain to allow greater freedom of movement. An English naval officer was the block's SBO; when one of the Germans asked what he thought of the new handcuffs he gave the man a long, stony stare and replied, 'When I require lessons in progressive barbarity I shall ask for them!' It was a ridiculous and shameful affair which should never have been inflicted on men who were already suffering from the vicissitudes of being a prisoner of war.

It was early in December, with the snow thick upon the ground, that we were paid a little visit by Captain Frank Weldon of the Royal Horse Artillery. He told Rex and me that a decision had been made by the central Escape Committee to allow just one tunnel at a time to be dug from the camp. There had been so much tunnelling activity at Warburg that the ferrets had become far too alert and industrious, and in this camp one of the priorities was to lull them into a false sense of security. The committee hoped to achieve this by concentrating on just one tunnel with maximum security an absolute necessity.

The first tunnel, he revealed, would start beneath a lavatory compartment on the ground floor of our block, with a trap built into the tiled floor beside the toilet seat. This toilet projected from the rear of the building, and it was planned to drive the tunnel uphill to a small chicken coop in an enclosed allotment 120 feet away.

'You two have been selected to form part of a team of thirty-four,' said Weldon. 'There will be a management team of four, and six digging teams of five. What do you say?' We agreed, but only on the proviso that Mark Howard was also on our team. He promised to check with the committee, and the next day told us that presented no problems.

On 8 December, with our team acting as stooges, Frank Weldon and Jock Hamilton-Baillie began constructing the trap, a painstaking and difficult task. Using a hammer and chisel they carefully chipped away at the grouting between the floor tiles until, one at a time, they were able to lift them. At the finish of each day's work they would carefully replace the tiles and fill the gaps with dirt and dust. This work continued for six days until all nine tiles had been removed. Now a trap was made by cementing the tiles together into a solid unit, using some stolen work-site cement. A thin rod was set through the trap with an eighth of an inch protruding at each end. Two 'lifters' made of thin steel with a hook at each end could then be inserted in the sides of the trap, making removal and replacement a simple matter.

Now came the problem of soil disposal. It was decided to transport the earth and rocks to the other end of the camp and stow it beneath the floor of Room 3 in Block 6 in the Garden City. There was a four-foot space below the floor, and a simple trap made from short floorboards screwed together provided easy access. To carry the soil, dozens of small sacks were made from the legs of battledress trousers. Each bag was fastened at the neck by a loop of string, which would go over a hook at the end of a pair of braces worn back-to-front around the carrier's neck. The bags would then hang comfortably in front of the stomach and were easily disguised beneath a greatcoat.

With the concealing trap now ready, work could begin on digging the shaft, and this was begun on 28 December. On the first day Weldon and H. B. drove a shaft straight down for a distance of three feet. We now had some spoil to get rid of, and this was our old friend David Walker's department. He draped some braces around my neck, hooked on a full bag of dirt, and I set off on a trial run to Block 6 with my hands deep in the pockets of my greatcoat. I had no trouble as I walked like so many others down the Lagerstrasse, and after dumping the dirt through the open trap in Room 3 I returned and handed in the empty sack.

'How was it?' David asked anxiously.

'No problems,' I replied. 'An absolute cakewalk.'

After digging down to six feet, the two men spent the next eight days chipping a hole through the foundation wall of the lavatory, and once they'd broken through constructed a large chamber about four feet square and six feet high. The trap could now be closed while digging was in progress, and the long boring days of continuous stooging were over. Now it was our turn to dig.

George Drew, a strapping lieutenant in the Northumberland Rifles, was our team leader. Lieutenant Pat Fergusson (Royal Tank Regiment) together with Rex, Mark and I comprised the remainder of the team.

On our first day of digging duty George and I reported to the lavatory. We watched fascinated as Frank Weldon slipped in the two steel lifting tools and hauled the trap from its position, revealing a hole two feet square. We had already stripped off our clothes and handed them to David Walker, and now I followed George down into the shaft, eerily lit by the hissing carbide lamp Weldon had handed him. As I slithered down the hole I heard the trap clunk into place above my head. We were well and truly sealed in – a very strange sensation.

'Come on, Champy,' George finally said. 'Let's get cracking!'

We donned our working clothes – long underpants and a damp, muddy pullover – and picked up our digging tools. These were two fifteen-inch iron prangers, made from bed ends, and padded at the holding end. Sealed in the tomb-like atmosphere, I was surprised at how good the air was. The ground beneath the block was covered with a three-inch layer of concrete and a shaft had been driven upwards to the surface with a number of small holes punched through the concrete. This provided a perfect air inlet, and as the tunnel progressed another shaft was dug through to the base of the chimney in the adjoining room. A length of stovepipe was placed through this shaft and cemented to a hole made in the chimney, and a fire was kept burning in this room while digging was in progress. This caused a strong updraught which dragged the foul air from the working area. As the tunnel grew longer the stovepipe was extended through the chamber right up to the face. It was a most ingenious arrangement, and certainly made working conditions much better than I had known in previous tunnels. In fact the air was so good it was possible to enjoy a cigarette at the face during a break.

The carbide lamp continued to hiss merrily as George and I worked away at enlarging the chamber. The soft clay came away easily and by midday we had filled eighteen sacks ready for disposal.

Our team dug about three times a week, rotating in pairs for the shifts. We were also rostered for stooging duties when the trap was being opened and when the carrying sacks were being collected. Every evening we carried the sacks of spoil to Block 6. It was exhilarating to be doing something constructive instead of just reading in bed or brooding about the future, and there was always the prospect that the tunnel might carry us to freedom. Our progress was so good that we soon began to believe this dream would become a reality.

With the chamber now completed it was time to drive the tunnel forward. On 28 January Weldon and H. B. dug the initial two feet and next day put in the first wooden support frame. Timber for these frames came from beneath the floor of the attic in Block 3, and the boards varied in width from four to ten inches. They were just the right length, and perfect for shoring up the tunnel. It was comforting to work knowing that the risk of a fall from the tunnel's walls and roof was minimal, and every night new timber shoring would be inserted right up to the face as work progressed. I often remember a hut in Warburg, which used to have a large sign at the entrance saying: *'Don't slam the bloody door!'* Not because the noise was a nuisance, but we had stripped the hut of so much timber framing for tunnels that it was in constant danger of collapse!

By the end of January eight feet of the tunnel had been excavated and three days later we were at the 14-foot mark. George Drew decided it was time to press ahead full bore and added two men to each shift.

Two would work at the face, with one digging and the other loading the spoil into a box on a trolley fitted with rollers and pull-ropes at either end. When a box was full the second man would tug on a string running along the side of the tunnel, and the two men in the large chamber would haul the little trolley back, fill some bags, and then signal that the empty trolley could return to the workface. After an hour's work the two teams would change places. Rapid progress was now being made, and by 9 February the tunnel was 34 feet long.

The snow was melting on the ground, rain came, and though it was still bitterly cold it was evident that winter was on the wane. Late spring would be the ideal time to escape, so in order to further speed up the operation a night shift was introduced. Our team did the first night shift, entering the shaft just after the evening Appell. We maintained the same routine – two in the chamber, and two at the face. The time passed quickly, with a welcome break for sandwiches and a hot drink from a thermos around midnight. When we emerged at 7am we had advanced the tunnel by another four feet. After the morning Appell an hour later we climbed gratefully into our bunks and slept soundly until lunchtime.

Several large boulders temporarily hindered our path, but we dug underneath them and our progress was not impeded. One, at the 15-foot mark, protruded down from the roof for a distance of five feet and was known as 'The Coffin'.

At the 44-foot mark we commenced digging upwards at an 18 degree gradient to follow the slope of the hill behind the camp. This gradient was maintained by the use of a simple but effective measuring board with a plumb line moving over a scale of degrees, the edge of which was placed on the roof when a check was needed.

By now, despite our progress and enthusiasm, we were all becoming a little jaded with the long hours spent digging and then having to carry the heavy sacks of dirt over to Block 6. It was decided to engage another twenty men solely as spoil carriers, and if the tunnel was successful they would draw for escape positions after the working party.

Another large boulder was encountered at the 51-foot mark which in itself was not a problem, but another protruding from the roof just beyond it combined with a further rock bulging from the tunnel floor made things a little difficult. However it was possible to wriggle through the space between them with arms outstretched in front, while the trolley and box could just get through. This area was aptly named 'The Belly Crawl'.

With the tunnel forging ahead so well it was time to organise our escape paraphernalia, and David Walker suggested the three of us should now visit Hector Christie to discuss our plans and tell him what we needed. We had first met Hector in Biberach, and now he was in charge of coordinating the supply of maps, compasses and other escape gear. He and his group of 'backroom boys' manufactured an incredible assortment of items for the Escape Committee.

One of those 'backroom boys' involved in the making of maps was Lieutenant J. R. (Jack) Millett from Perth in Western Australia. Up until the time we found ourselves together in Colditz I only knew Jack in passing, but I was later to realise that he was one of those remarkable men who combine an eager and ingeniously practical mind with a fine sense of humour.

Jack was born on 19 February 1912, and as a youth had a variety of occupations – motor mechanic, welder, panel beater, and a tough stint as a gold miner. He was in the 11th Battalion militia at the outbreak of war, and when the 11th was formed into a new fighting unit he was quick to join up for overseas duty. Jack saw action in the Western Desert, in the first attack on Tobruk, and then at Derna and Gazi, before moving down to the Tripolitanian Front. From there he was shipped to Crete, where he took part in the bloody events of May 1941.

The island of Crete had been occupied in November 1940 by the British at the request of the Greek government, in order to prevent it falling into the hands of the Italians. The island was by no means heavily garrisoned, and the influx of evacuated troops from the Greek campaign did little to solve the problem of effectively making Crete the well-defended fortress that General Wavell desired. The men from Greece were not a formed army, and though most still had their rifles, they lacked other forms of weaponry. They had been bombed and shelled to blazes, not only in Greece, but on the sea passage to Crete. No artillery had been saved from Greece, no transport, and more than anything else there were hardly any aircraft on Crete. The soldiers, from the United Kingdom, Australia and New Zealand, had little but their stout hearts to try to defend Crete. At the end of April there were around 28 000 men on the island, excluding the Greek battalions, and not all of them were actual combat troops.

At eight o'clock on the morning of 20 May the first wave of German aircraft came sweeping in from the sea, some releasing gliders which they had towed in over Maleme airport. In all there were fifty of these gliders, each containing twelve men. By the end of the day the Germans had landed over 3500 troops in the area, but everywhere the paratroopers were dropped they suffered crippling losses before reaching the ground. In some places they lost four-fifths of their men.

Weary troops on the ground blazed away at the paratroopers, but even as they tried to stop the overwhelming assault from the skies the Germans were landing their troop carriers all over the island.

Eventually it was not the paratroopers who decided the issue, but the men who came in the troops carriers. About 650 of these large machines, each carrying between twenty and thirty men, were used – regardless of losses. The troops they brought in were met by a most resolute defence. During the nine days' fighting our men delivered no fewer than twenty bayonet attacks, and never lost their cohesion under the strain of a bombardment from the air which was practically continuous during daylight.

Enemy losses during the campaign were staggering; at least 6000 killed or drowned, and 11 000 wounded – and these were all crack troops. They also used 1500 aircraft, and a good number of these were shot down by minimal defences. While in Colditz Jack Millett wrote some notes about his own involvement in the savage fighting.

> Our battalion, after much cursing, digging and wearing out of boot leather, finished up with the job of helping defend the Rethymo aerodrome which is situated on the narrow coastal strip on the north of the island. The force in this area consisted of two AIF battalions, both of which were in rather poor fighting condition after their Greek show, and two Greek battalions that were not too keen. Our positions were on the hillside overlooking the narrow east–west airstrip. We had a front of roughly one mile.
>
> At ten o'clock on the morning of 20 May 1941, the first signs of the expected attack appeared in the shape of about a dozen Junkers

52s flying low over the ocean and heading straight for us. Everyone went to earth in a hurry but it was a false alarm as the planes turned off and headed for Canea, which is the main harbour and near which is the biggest 'drome on the island. These planes were all towing from one to four gliders and made rather a novel sight.

The first flight was closely followed by another couple of groups towing gliders and then at about fifteen-minute intervals larger gliderless flights were seen, mostly turning off for Canea but a few turning west to the only other 'drome on the island at Herakleon. This went on till about three o'clock when we were bombed for an hour. At the end of this an armada of Junkers, about 140 strong, and escorted by 40 or 50 Me 109s, and 110s, hove into sight.

Flying in perfect formation, they made for the shore line to the right of our positions and, on reaching the coastal strip, turned sharp east and commenced to spill their cargoes right along in front of us. The first planes unloaded slightly wide of our right flank and the last ones just clear of our left flank. Their timing and judgement was excellent but a slight cross-wind drifted some of the chutes, and their load, right into our positions, bad luck for the load.

A paratroop attack is no time for sightseeing, but busy as we all were pumping up lead, I think everyone there managed to snatch a look while yanking the old bolt back. A couple of hundred planes about 300 feet up, the air just full of multi-coloured parachutes, planes crashing right and left, ourselves pumping lead up just as fast as we could, the planes shooting back – all packed into about ten minutes.

Our fire was paying good dividends in the shape of crashing planes and limp bodies – I saw seven or eight planes heading earthwards in a hurry – two of them crashed 50 yards from me and made a hell of a mess. As the paratroopers neared the ground their tommy-guns were used to spray lead at us but didn't do much good against the old 303. The bayonet was used to good effect to clean up anything landing on top of us.

Some chutes were caught up on wings and tails and the people hanging in the straps must have had a most unpleasant ride back to Greece – or perhaps a swim in the Med. The Junkers 52 which crashed near me unloaded six bodies from about 60 feet up – three had chutes which opened satisfactorily but three of them must have been trying to fly – they hopped out without chutes and hit the deck pretty hard. Later on, when things quietened down, I had the job of burying these six and the crew of three who stayed on board. Another 52 crashed into the ocean – just one big splash and she was gone. On top of the crashes we saw quite a few planes that must have failed to reach Greece as some of them were well on fire before leaving us.

Although we could see some of the effects of our fire we were all surprised at the number of men still harnessed in their chutes when we started in to do some burying. Judging from what I saw in the area I would say that close to 500 were dead, or near enough, before hitting the ground and another 200 killed soon after landing. Add to this another couple of hundred killed in the ten days between the landing and when we packed it in and it makes about 900 killed out of a landing force of approximately 1800. We also had 200 prisoners and quite a number of their wounded. Our own casualties were roughly 100 killed, 300 wounded and the rest in the bag.

By sundown on the day of the landing we had the coastal strip in front of us cleaned up and the remaining paratroops were split into groups – one on each of our flanks. These groups could not be attacked in daylight – their air support was too hot – so we had to hammer them at night, and house to house fighting in the dark is no joke, believe me.

After ten days of these night shows the enemy were reinforced with troops, guns and tanks from Maleme and, as the rest of the island was in the bag, we were ordered to pack it in – and here I am.

From Crete, Jack Millett found himself on a Junkers 52 taking him to Athens, in company with several other fellow prisoners. Once there they were loaded onto trains and taken up through Greece to Salonika, sometimes marching to connect with various rail trucks. Jack spent three weeks in Salonika, during which time he and a friend named Fred Roberts hatched a plan to escape over the wire. However they quickly changed their minds when the five Cypriots tried to assault the wire the night before Jack and Fred were due to go, and were mercilessly shot down.

Eventually some men were evacuated up through Austria to Leipzig, and then on to Lübeck. Conditions here were bad, and food scarce. Jack and Fred hit on a scheme in which they would pretend to faint on parade, and be given food in the camp hospital, which they knew to be far better than their ordinary rations. When the time came Jack fell down, but Fred decided two at once would seem suspicious. Jack was taken to hospital, but soon after the Allies bombed the nearby town, and dropped incendiaries on the Lübeck flak defences. Some actually fell in the POW camp, destroying the German officers' mess; one landed directly outside Jack's window, and another landed in the next room, on the bed of an English major, which resulted in the poor man having to undergo a leg amputation.

From Lübeck Jack was eventually transferred to Warburg, where he helped in a couple of tunnels. One involved digging a tunnel out of his own hut with a Major Peters, but German sound detectors picked up the sounds of digging and the tunnel was discovered.

Curiously enough another attempt involved a wooden vaulting horse, inside which two men dug a shallow tunnel while others, including Jack, vaulted over the horse above. Not many months later three officers from Stalag Luft III – Eric Williams, Michael Codner and Oliver Philpot – hit upon the same idea and carried it through to fruition, with all three making it back to England. The Warburg attempt did not last very long before the ruse was discovered, but it is interesting to note that a 'Wooden Horse' escape was tried long before the successful one, which in the opinion of many is the most famous escape story of any war.

Jack Millett was not involved in the Warburg Wire Job, and as security on the scheme was very tight only knew of it once the mass escape had occurred. He was then transferred with the rest of us to Eichstätt and found himself billeted with some French Canadians.

It was in Eichstätt that Jack began his map-making exploits. He would painstakingly reverse etch sectional maps onto a hard gelatine surface, and using an ink made from indelible pencils would run off several copies. Then it was a matter of going over the faint maps with pen and ink and coloured pencils to produce superbly detailed 1:500 000 maps, which would then be given to those planning a break. Each map took hours to produce and it was tedious, often boring work, but Jack didn't mind – it kept him occupied. He was married and had a young son back in Australia, and needed some useful occupation to prevent melancholy setting in.

Millett was always terribly optimistic about the outcome of the war and even in Colditz he told me that Hitler could never win. He had studied military strategy years before in Australia, and was convinced it was just a matter of time before we would all be free men. Being perfectly confident that the Allies would win the war he never busted his guts trying to escape, but he certainly aided many others through his skills and willingness to help.

Time was marching on, but so too was the tunnel. We celebrated the end of February by digging to 92 feet, but we also struck trouble in the form of solid rock, first at floor level then rising until the whole face was covered. This was undoubtedly part of the hill, unlike the loose boulders encountered previously. However it was only solid at the base, the upper part having a well-cracked surface. The next night our team, now five of us, spent our entire 12-hour shift levering away the soft and cracked rock. It was tedious and slow work, but we managed to advance a further two feet.

Then another substantial boulder was met, right on our line. We dug to the right, same problem, so our engineers dug under it and two days later we were able to split it using a hammer and chisel.

Our luck finally seemed to have turned against us when some snooping ferrets discovered the earth under Block 6. However all was not lost; we had sufficient space to stow any further soil in the chamber. I later found out this had always been part of the strategy, cleverly planned by H. B. when conceiving the tunnel.

The Germans, in typical fashion, became very excited over the discovery of the freshly dug earth. They now knew for certain that a tunnel was in existence and, as predicted, were quite certain it was in the Garden City area. We watched with great satisfaction as they dug trenches in likely areas inside and outside the camp, hoping to cut across the non-existent hole. This wasted effort continued for several weeks, and they never appeared to suspect any block on the Lagerstrasse.

The next day, 5 March, a ledge of solid rock appeared at the face. After carefully checking the cover height and finding it to be over three feet above the top of the face, a start was made to go over the ledge with a reduced boring. With the rock ledge now the floor of the tunnel the height was reduced to 18 inches, making working conditions rather difficult. However the same width was maintained and we were able to press on to 102 feet. Then we struck yet another massive rock rising vertically across the face …

Branch tunnels were dug in each direction but the same problem of the rock face existed. Eventually these branch tunnels were extended around the rock and met a few feet further on, and this area became known as 'Piccadilly Circus'.

Our engineers continued to dig upwards with the slope of the hill. The earth cover was now less than a foot and extreme care had to be exercised when removing the earth. The voices of children could be clearly heard as they walked along the road above our heads. Grass roots appeared, hanging from the ceiling, and the entire working area was solidly shored with timber to prevent any fall of earth. Progress slowed appreciably, but by 24 March we had reached 104 feet – about fourteen feet short of the enclosed chicken coop.

More rock was encountered and the only way to continue was by using a hammer and chisel to painstakingly chip away at the hard face. The resultant noise was appalling and could be heard from the attic window of Block 2, some 30 yards away. To counter this problem, a stooging system was devised to warn the diggers of anyone coming along the road. A stooge would watch from an attic skylight in Block 2, and signals were relayed to a man at the ventilation chimney. He in turn operated a signal string that entered the top of the chimney through a small door, passing right down to the chamber where another man sent the message to those at the face.

Progress had slowed to about six inches a day, and the night shift had long been discontinued. On 29 April, by the engineers' calculations, we were just two feet short of the coop. After some discussion it was decided that this objective just could not be reached; the rock had beaten us at last. By now, however, the tunnel should have passed beyond the wooden garden fence, which afforded a certain amount of cover, together with the spring foliage which was now bursting forth on the bushes nearby.

An area on the left of the tunnel where the break would occur was scooped out so that a man could sit facing the road with his feet down the hole clear of the main exit. Captain Brian Evers had volunteered to act as stooge at this location, to receive signals, observe the road, and control the exit while the tunnel was breaking. He was not in the escape party and would return to the camp via the tunnel when the operation was completed.

Now our share of the underground work was finished, but Frank Weldon and Jock Hamilton-Baillie set about improving the excavation for our eventual exit. They enlarged the tunnel to the left of the 'Belly Crawl' to allow room for a man dressed in a coat and his equipment to squeeze though. They also removed the air line and disposed of it (which would have ramifications later on), dug a new entrance on the right-hand side of the tunnel a few feet from the chamber, to a shaft under the trap. They dug recesses into the sides of the tunnel at intervals to take lamps that would light up the more awkward parts, and installed a 'torch globe' electrical signal.

All of this took up until the end of April. Eight newly arrived Canadian officers who had been captured in the raid on Dieppe were invited to participate, and they drew for positions with the digging team. Mark, Rex and I got positions 35, 36 and 37. The third of May was the first in a period of moonless nights, and the break would be made when a good stiff wind rose up to deaden the noise we would inevitably make.

Our packs were now ready, adhering to the maximum size permitted through the tunnel, and were stored in the attic of Block 2. They were all numbered in the order in which the break would take place.

During the afternoon of 4 May a slight wind came up and word was passed that we would operate that night. In line with a prearranged plan we all assembled in the attic except for the first ten, who, just after 8pm, entered the tunnel. The remainder would be fed into the entrance as the escape proceeded, so the tunnel would be fully occupied at all times.

Weldon and H. B. had just removed the first of the timbers at the exit point when a message came through that the wind had dropped completely. Reluctantly they cancelled the operation for that night. We all spent an uncomfortable and frustrating evening in the attic.

Two days later a bombshell dropped. A note had been found pinned to the door of a lavatory adjoining the SBO's quarters. Pencilled in capital letters on a fly-leaf from a book was a warning that German security staff knew all about the tunnel under the toilet in Block 2, warned of a possible loss of life, and was signed 'A German Friendly to British POWs'. The Escape Committee immediately decided to investigate before the escape could take place.

The following day a second note was found, saying much the same as before, but this time warning that an armed German patrol would be waiting on the hillside when the tunnel broke. Everyone in the escape party was notified and sworn to secrecy, while all our outgoing mail was carefully examined for writing similar to that on the notes.

This state of affairs continued until 22 May. During this period the weather remained fine, which would have lessened our chances for a successful break, and the moon began to fill, flooding the countryside with unwelcome light. Each night a close watch was kept on the hillside, but everything seemed normal. Nobody could work it out; German activity seemed to indicate they were still convinced our tunnel was in the Garden City, and they paid scant attention to the area around Block 2 and the hillside behind. It was finally decided that the break would go ahead, but at very short notice. This way the perpetrator of the notes, now assumed to be a fellow POW, would not have time to communicate with the Germans.

The third of June had been a lovely but somewhat tiring day. For some time it had been set aside for a triangular athletics meeting between England, Scotland and the Dominions, and I had unsuccessfully competed in three of the sprint events. The day had been fine and sunny, with no wind, and the moment I settled down on my bunk I began dozing off. But Rex and Mark soon put paid to that, when they stormed into the room and shook me out of my reverie.

'Come on, Champy,' Rex said urgently. 'Get up – the break's on. Let's go!'

I was still befuddled. 'But it can't be,' I muttered. 'There's been no wind all day.'

'Well there sure is now,' Mark responded. 'Come on – we have to be dressed and assembled in thirty minutes!'

I rolled off my bunk and joined the other two in pulling on my escape clothing. I had dyed my battledress trousers and acquired a shirt, pullover and raincoat, and I had a little woollen cap, which I stuffed into my trouser pocket. Our civilian caps were in our packs, with our boots strapped to the outside. Quickly we ate the remainder of our Red Cross food; a few biscuits, some bully beef scraped from the tin, and a mug of cocoa. At seven o'clock we joined the others up in the attic once again, sitting on the floor in numerical order. They must have thought I was a pretty calm sort of fellow; I stretched out and immediately fell asleep.

Weldon, H. B., Brian Evers and ten others were already in the tunnel. They had taken with them Lieutenant John Penman who, having drawn the last number, was to go out with the leaders, lie in the long grass close to the exit, and act as traffic cop. He would then wait until everyone had gone and then climb up the hill, rolling up the guide string as he went.

A firm dig in the ribs from Rex woke me. 'Okay,' he whispered, 'we're next.' Clutching my pack under my arm I silently climbed down the stairs. Captain Jackson, an English officer in charge of the whole operation, halted me briefly on the landing. I had a few puffs on a cigarette someone handed me and then I was motioned to move on to the lavatory. As I entered the toilet cubicle Hector Christie tied a string around my waist, to which he attached my pack, and I dropped into the tunnel for the last time. Rex was crawling up the tunnel ahead of me, and it was my job to help his pack past the difficult parts. Mark, following on, did the same for me.

We knew that Weldon and H. B. were out. They had broken the tunnel in fading daylight, crawled up and made an opening in the fence behind the yellow hut in the corner of the enclosure, and then laid a string up the hillside.

Just twenty minutes later I poked my head out of the exit. The night air was unbelievably good and the smell of the freshly dug earth and the damp grass tingled in my nostrils. 'Take it easy,' hissed Brian Evers. I squeezed his hand and crawled away, right into the arms of John Penman, who fed the guide string into my hand and I crouched in the grass for a moment before continuing on to the fence, about 20 yards away. Rex was there, and Mark soon joined us.

We were about halfway up the steep rocky hillside when a searchlight suddenly came on and swept the hillside. It lit up the area like daylight and we just dropped to the ground, trying our hardest to look like small boulders. The long white beam danced across the hillside before the sentry changed his arc and played it over the wire on the north boundary of the camp, and then swung it into the camp compound. He'd obviously not seen anything on the hillside to arouse his suspicions, and we continued climbing.

It was 12.15am when we reached the top of the hill, pausing briefly to look back down at the camp. The sensation of freedom was indescribable, and a wonderful feeling of triumph swept through us as we saw the camp lit by the perimeter lights dancing in the darkness and the searchlights methodically sweeping the camp and its surrounds. It was a magic moment, but this was no time for sightseeing.

We set off in an easterly direction, making sure we gave the camp a wide berth before we swung south towards the river. All was quiet, and we reached the banks of the Altmühl soon after, turning left to once again head east. At one stage we got a terrific fright when we tripped over someone in the long grass, but to our relief this turned out to be John Beaumont, who had gone to ground thinking we were a search party. John went his own way and the three of us continued on to a small village where we knew there was a bridge spanning the river. After surveying the area Rex dashed over the bridge and hid in the darkness of some trees, and I was a few steps behind him. Mark seemed to be a long time coming, and suddenly there was a tremendous commotion as all the dogs in the village started barking. Somehow he had taken a wrong turn and wound up in the backyard of a cottage, staring straight at a chained Alsatian. Mark hurriedly backed off, and after what seemed an eternity he found the bridge and scampered over to join us.

Now heading roughly south we set off at a rapid pace and were soon out of the valley and onto level ground. We paused briefly to pull on our boots, and the gym shoes got an unceremonious burial in German soil. It was about two o'clock and we only had three more hours of darkness, so we set off in single file, taking turns to lead and keeping about 10 yards apart. Suddenly Mark, who was leading, dived into a ditch beside the road and the two of us immediately followed suit. A lone pedestrian was heading our way, and we held our breath as he neared and then passed us. We clambered out of the ditch and pressed on, stopping before dawn in a small thicket about 400 yards in from the road. The cover was by no means ideal, but seemed to be the best we could find in the darkness. We dozed fitfully and were awakened when all the birds in the forest greeted the full dawn with a magnificent chorus.

In the drizzly grey light of early morning we were better able to examine our hiding place, and decided to move to a more secluded spot further into the woods where we changed our sweat-soaked underclothes. We tried to sleep but were too tense, so we munched on some of our oatmeal cake and had a few sips of water as we studied our proposed route for that night, deciding to skirt around several villages along the way, at least until after midnight. The day passed slowly.

Just after ten that night we set off along the road at a fast pace. We had about 40 miles to travel to the river Danube and planned to make it in two nights. While detouring around one of the villages we came across a stream and managed to replenish our precious water supplies. Just after midnight we were back on the road again and we fair belted along. As dawn approached we began looking for some more shelter, and saw what seemed to be a large forest a short distance off to our left. Making our way through the trees we came upon a small clearing and after pushing our way right into the bushes we settled down and were soon sleeping soundly. Around ten o'clock we woke to brilliant sunshine and took the opportunity to spread our damp clothing on some bushes, where it soon dried.

Except for a light aircraft which droned over at about midday there was no evidence of any German activity, and so with growing confidence we lit our tiny smokeless jam tin stove. Fuelled with small pieces of paper torn from an unwanted book it gave off a surprising amount of heat, and we were soon devouring a dish of lovely hot porridge. This, followed by some chocolate and a cup of delicious hot coffee, did wonders for our morale. The rest of the day passed uneventfully as we studied our maps and went over our route to the Swiss frontier. Still 200 miles to go.

Our spirits were nevertheless buoyant as we set off again that night. We were now on the main road to the large city of Donauworth, and as before we chose to leave the road and travel cross-country to avoid several villages. Our objective for the following day would be to get as close as possible to the river Danube, lie up, and attempt to cross this formidable barrier the following night, hopefully by finding a boat. We had been warned against using bridges as they were generally guarded, and with sixty-five escapees on the loose it was certain that extra patrols would be in place.

Just after one o'clock in the morning we paused for a brief discussion. There was a large village looming up, and we debated whether to slip straight through it or make a long by-pass.

'The point is,' said Rex, 'we still have a hell of a long way to go, and we simply have to get some miles under our belt. We're still about ten miles from the Danube and we've only got about three hours of darkness left. I think we should stick to the road.'

Mark and I didn't argue; Rex had made his point so off we went. We were soon encouraged by the fact that the road did not go right through the centre of the village.

We were striding along nicely and nearly through the village when it happened.

'Halt! Halt, or I shoot!' came a shout from the darkness as a squad of well-armed soldiers and civilians sprang from a ditch beside the road. The corporal in charge pointed his pistol at us and cocked the hammer, while shotguns and rifles were levelled at us from all directions. We were well and truly caught.

As our captors jabbered away in excitement we were marched to a small army headquarters in the back room of a local inn. The civilians were dismissed and some off-duty soldiers were roused from their improvised beds along the wall to watch us. The sergeant in charge had almost been expecting us, asking if we were from Eichstätt. We said nothing, so the corporal went through our packs, removing the maps and compasses. It was obvious who we were, but we chose to remain silent. After a while the sergeant sighed, made a telephone call, and told us we were on the move. With a heavily armed escort of six soldiers we were marched a few miles south to the next village where, at about four in the morning, we were handed over to the local policeman. A clean but solid cell awaited us, and we wasted no time in lying down on the bunks to grab some sleep.

The elderly policeman woke us later on, rattling his keys in the lock and opening the cell door. He was sporting a very large pistol, but was accompanied by his wife and two teenage daughters who stared at us in wide-eyed fascination. The three fugitives had obviously become a local tourist attraction! Rex was soon chatting away, and the ice was broken. He said we were all hungry and arranged to swap some of our chocolate for a hot breakfast. The family left, but returned soon after bearing steaming bowls of porridge made from our oatmeal. This was followed by a magnificent meal of scrambled eggs – the first we had tasted in over two years. The good Frau beamed as we tucked in, the two girls giggled, and the policeman remained kindly but correct, keeping a tight grip on his pistol. His two assistants at the gaol would also constantly check that things were in order.

Later we were allowed to exercise under guard in a small garden near the cell and were regarded with mingled curiosity by the local village folk, some of who paused on their way to church to chat with us over the fence. They were all amazed that we had travelled from Australia to fight with England, and though it was clear that they had been indoctrinated with Hitler's propaganda about the Third Reich, their overall knowledge of the war was actually quite limited.

That afternoon a truck from Eichstätt turned up, already containing a dozen or so of our fellow escapers, and we were bundled on board. After picking up a few more 'passengers' en route we arrived back at the camp just after 6pm, where we were given a very thorough strip search before being taken one by one for interrogation. The usual questions were asked about where we were heading, how we planned on getting there, where we got the maps, and so on. We gave our stock response of name, rank and service number, which did not seem to surprise them at all, and in fact our interrogators seemed quite bored with the whole procedure.

Clad in just our underpants, eight of us were shoved into a bare cell. We spent an uncomfortable night here before joining the majority of recaptured escapers in a wooden building outside the main camp. The Germans permitted us to send messages to friends inside the camp, and they in turn sent back bundles of our clothing.

The following day about sixty of us were marched under heavy guard to Willibaldsburg, about four miles away, and an old castle set high on a hill. This castle was quite magnificent when viewed from the camp below, but it was a very different story when we got inside and were shown to our dungeon-like quarters, where we would spend the next three weeks. During this period we were fed on meagre German rations for the first two weeks, after which we were permitted to receive small quantities of Red Cross food.

Even at this time some were still thinking of making a break. Fellow escapees Gordon Rolfe, Bill Millar and Douggie Moir arranged for some helpers to remove a few bars from one of the windows, and late that night, with the sentry in the room distracted and using a rope which had been smuggled in, slid down to the ground fifty feet below. Unfortunately Rolfe and Moir were injured in the last drop of about twenty feet, and they were all recaptured after a brief taste of freedom.

When the three weeks were up, we were informed that a move was under way – but not back to Eichstätt. I was in the first group of 30 to leave, under the command of Captain Charles Hopetoun (Charlie to us, and post-war succeeding to the title of 3rd Marquess of Linlithgow). After two days and half of the second night, spent sitting up on hard wooden seats in a jolting train, we finally reached our destination. After detraining onto the platform at about 11pm we were formed up and marched under heavy guard a short distance up a winding path. We encountered a solid wooden door which soon swung open, and were ushered into the small courtyard. Another door opened and we went upstairs to a small room.

After a short wait we had to form into line and were taken one by one into a second room where we were subjected to a thorough search followed by more questions. About one o'clock we were taken through yet another door into a much larger cobbled courtyard, surrounded on all four sides by towering buildings. Suddenly an English voice called out through the darkness from a window high up to our left.

'Who the devil are you?'

'We're English officers from Eichstätt. I'm Charlie Hopetoun!' roared our good leader. 'Just where the hell are we?'

'Good God, Charlie, is that really you? Colin MacKenzie at your service. Welcome to Colditz Castle!'

And so we had arrived at Colditz where we were destined to spend the next two years of our lives.

But what of the Eichstätt tunnel and our fellow escapers? As time went by we were able to piece together the story, some of which led to our downfall, some of an amusing nature, and some with a flavour of tragedy.

It appears that several comic events happened during the break. Long after our threesome had clambered out of the tunnel there were quite a few lengthy delays, and the air became really stuffy with all the warm bodies breathing heavily, combined with the carbide lamps burning up the oxygen and a lack of ventilation. Lieutenant Roger Marchand, a French Canadian of rather bulky build passed out and also appeared to be stuck. Captain 'Screwy' Wright, who was two behind Marchand, called to the man in front, Sergeant Major Perry. 'What's the matter up there, Sergeant Major?' he demanded to know. 'What the hell's the hold up?'

'Officer up in front appears to be stuck, sir!' came the reply in Perry's best parade-ground voice.

'Well prod him in the arse, Sergeant Major, prod him in the arse!' said Screwy.

'Sorry sir, can't sir – out of range!' replied Perry.

As the night wore on, the now putrid air had its effect. Some of the escapers who had been subjected to the bad air and the fumes staggered around like drunken men when they hit the fresh air. One person, who observed the scene from an attic window in Block 2, likened the commotion as men ran up the hillside to the charge of a herd of demented elephants. This noise evidently attracted the attention of a sentry patrolling the road, and he notified the corporal in charge of the guard. Together they came close to the exit and practically staring Brian Evers in the face gazed at the hillside. Just then, by chance, an early rising farmer in a neighbouring house started chopping wood. The two guards relaxed and moved off again, believing this to be the cause of the sounds they had heard.

Once the mass break-out had been discovered at the early morning Appell a huge number of soldiers and civilians were deployed around the area to cordon it off. The total number in the field came to 60 000, or nearly a thousand searchers for every escapee. They were stationed on roads, tracks, bridges, and in fields. Using our escape as an anti-parachutist exercise they absolutely saturated the countryside. Little wonder we were all rounded up. Knowing this, the three of us were actually amazed that we had managed to get so far before we were caught.

Clive Dieppe, despite his illness, had teamed up with George Bolding in the break. They managed to travel about sixty miles, but after two nights encountered a small, deserted-looking bridge across the Danube. George had the idea of throwing a couple of stones into the water to see if there were any sentries around, but when there was no reaction to the noise they made their way onto the bridge, and walked straight into the arms of two armed sentries. Apparently these guards had been a wake-up to the stone ruse, and had simply waited for the culprits to walk straight into their clutches.

Doug Crawford and Pat McLaren were captured on a timber track by five armed German civilians who, quite indifferent to who they might have been, simply handed the two men over to the police. They just about had the local police convinced that they were two Serbs on their way to visit Pat's 'sister' near the Swiss border when the Gestapo arrived, searched their clothing, and found all their maps and money. The game was up.

Of the seven Australians who made the break from Eichstätt, the longest out was Jack Millett. Jack and his running companion Hamish Hamilton had worked out that almost all the escapers were going to head directly for Switzerland, and most of the search would therefore be concentrated to the south of Eichstätt. Millett suggested they head due north for two or three days, then veer east to Regensburg before heading south, skirting a wide path around Munich and then on to Switzerland. Their plans were sound – in fact most of the escapees heading straight for the Swiss border were picked up within 24 hours.

On the night of the escape Millett, who was one of those forced to wear handcuffs, removed his manacles and laid them neatly on his pillow. He and Hamish were actually the last two men to go through the tunnel, so they had a long, agonising wait in front of them. The tunnelling committee had earlier decided to remove the air line to give the escapers more room in the tunnel, and by the time the last few had made it into the shaft the air was heavy and putrid. Jack was quite fit, but he nearly passed out.

The plan called for Lieutenant 'Sandy' Sandbach to seal the tunnel after Hamish, but as Jack Millett poked his head out, the ground in front of him looked as if a herd of cattle had passed through, and he knew it would be futile to try and disguise their departure point. They had also been told to crawl across the open ground, but as dawn was beginning to break and he could just see the guard he helped Hamish out with his pack and they walked quickly up the hill. Hamish tired quickly, so Jack helped him with his pack and they raced over the hill in their stockinged feet.

They only made about a quarter of a mile the first night, could hear shots coming from the camp, and see patrols below them. Millett had lived in the bush back in Australia, and knew quite a bit about survival in the open, so he decided they would hide up for that day. The hillside was covered in rocks and pine trees, and over the years a thick carpet of moss and pine needles had built up undisturbed, so the two men tore out an area each, carefully rolled it back and climbed in, then covered themselves with the mat of needles and moss. They heard several patrols that day but nobody came near them. Around midday Jack received a huge fright when he felt his upper arm being gripped tightly, and thought 'That's it!' He peeked out and to his immense relief the culprit turned out to be nothing more threatening than a cow that had settled down right beside him. That night they left their hide and began walking north.

Another scare occurred a little later when they almost ran headlong into a soldier and his girlfriend taking a stroll along a path near a cornfield. Millett and Hamilton leapt into the cornfield and pretended to be lovers which so astonished the couple they hurried off.

The two men had soon been out for five nights, and were just twenty miles from Regensburg. By now Hamilton's feet were blistered and raw, and he was having trouble making any distance. As a result they decided to cut straight through Regensburg instead of making a wide detour. It was dark, the road was wet, and they ran straight into two Hitler Youths with Alsatian dogs. One of them pulled a gun and the escape was at an end for Jack and Hamish. The police eventually arrived and took them away for questioning, after which they were sent straight to Willibaldsburg to join the rest of us. Every man had to serve fourteen days detention for his part in the escape, and then all sixty-five were transferred to Colditz in two batches a few days apart.

Reverting back to the 'poison pen' letters; the morning following our departure a third note, concealed in a tin, was found in the wire in an attempt to make it appear that the tin had been thrown over the fence from outside. It had no doubt been placed in position when it was found that we were to leave, but had not been found in time. It was later learned that the Germans had in fact received a note from someone in the camp, giving information about the tunnel and its exact location. The Security Officer, suspecting it to be a desperate attempt to divert attention from the Garden City search, had despatched two ferrets to the lavatory in Block 2, but fortunately they found nothing and the whole thing was dismissed as a ruse to put them off the scent. And there the whole matter rests; the identity of the note-writing Eichstätt traitor was never discovered.

Later we were informed that the German High Command were so furious at our break-out, an order was issued to the effect that if any more mass escapes took place, those rounded up were to be shot. History now records that in March 1944, seventy-six officers escaped through a massive tunnel from Stalag Luft III, and all but three were recaptured. Fifty of those caught were callously shot dead in cold blood. The conclusion is distressing but rather obvious; it was just our good fortune that we went first.

Finally, it may seem that we wasted our time digging this tunnel which hardly seemed to reach a successful conclusion, but the escape proved a tremendous nuisance to the Germans. We shifted over forty tons of dirt and rocks without their knowledge; we occupied 60 000 enemy personnel for more than a week, and caused the German Kommandant and his Security Officer to be sent to the dreaded Russian Front. At the same time we gave our own morale a huge boost, believing that in some small way we had contributed to the Allied war effort as a whole, and the eventual victory.

5

Colditz

Oflag IVC was a special camp set up by the Germans for prisoners of war who had proved themselves to be a nuisance at other camps, either because of repeated attempts to escape, or their general attitude towards the 'master race'.

In addition there were certain personnel who had been dropped as agents in occupied countries, and the 'Prominente' who were held at the camp because of their connection with the British royal family, or with members of the British or Allied governments. It was believed that the Germans intended to hold these men as hostages, to be used as bargaining commodities should the need arise. At the cessation of hostilities, and owing to the chaotic conditions prevailing, the plan was never put into effect.

The surrounding country was hilly, and the river valley of the Zwickauer Mulde was very steep-sided near the town, especially on the east bank to the north of the camp, where the ground rose to a height of 720 feet. This river joins the Freiberger Mulde about two miles north-west of the camp, and together with two large wooded areas of the Forest Colditz, forms the chief natural landmarks of the area.

The camp was built on the ruins of a castle which dates back to the 16th century, and is situated in the Saalhous/Colditz area, about 25 miles south-east of Leipzig and 40 miles west of Dresden. The castle is on the east side of the small town of Colditz. The castle was originally the hunting lodge of Augustus the Strong, King of Poland. Owing to the nature of its construction the Germans believed the camp to be escape-proof. There was a dry moat with a high outer wall surrounding the castle. On the outer side of this wall there was a drop of nearly thirty feet to the terraced gardens below, which were built above a fairly high perpendicular wall.

The castle was divided into two main sections built round two small courtyards. The German officers occupied the southern section in which there were two main gates, one leading to the town, the other leading into the park. The other slightly larger courtyard was known as the prisoners' yard, with a guardroom adjacent to a doorway in a large double gate.

In both the German and prisoners' yards the surrounding buildings rose to three storeys high, with double attics at the top of the 90-foot walls. There were round towers on each corner of the prisoners' courtyard, and in these narrow spiral staircases wound their way upward, giving access to the upper three levels.

Prior to our arrival on 22 June, from a British contingent which fluctuated between sixty and ninety officers, eight had already made good their exit from Colditz – including an Australian airman – and reached England or some neutral country.

In Eichstätt we had a German guard company of nearly four hundred officers and other ranks to look after more than 2000 prisoners. In Colditz we had a similar number of guards, but this time to look after less than their own number! In all our time at Colditz there were always more guards than prisoners.

With such a massive influx of numbers from Eichstätt (all who took part in the tunnel break were sent to Colditz) the Germans would soon evacuate the Dutch from the Schloss to make way for us, and a few weeks later they also removed the other nationals. This left us virtually an all-British camp with a total strength of 228, plus a small Gaullist company of paratroopers from North Africa.

Our Senior British Officer at Eichstätt, Lieutenant-Colonel 'Tubby' Broomhall, arrived a few days after us and took over as the SBO at Colditz from Colonel Guy German – an ironic name under the circumstances.

It was in the early hours of the morning that we were escorted to our quarters on the second floor of the east wing off the northern inner courtyard. We were quite exhausted, but pleased to find that the rooms to which we were shown were quite spacious, in contrast to those in other camps. Gratefully we flopped onto the double-tiered bunks and were soon sound asleep. It seemed that I had hardly closed my eyes when we were rudely wakened by the loud mournful wailing of a siren located high above the courtyard outside our barred window. One of the longer-serving residents of the castle appeared at the doorway.

'Better get up, chaps,' he said. 'That's the five-minute warning to be in the courtyard for early morning Appell. There'll be another siren in five minutes. Don't be late or you'll find yourselves in the cells.'

I looked at my watch and groaned; it was only 6.25 in the morning. Everyone was clambering groggily to their feet and reluctantly pulling on some clothes, and then we made our way down the spiral stairs to the courtyard. Here we were formed up into threes with our senior officer from Eichstätt, Captain Charles Lord Hopetoun, out in front. Apart from us there were five other groups formed up around the small cobbled courtyard – the Dutch, Polish and French, and two other groups of British officers.

The SBO, Colonel German, stood in the middle of the courtyard with his adjutant. He formally called the British section of the parade to attention, greeted the German officer and stood us at ease.

I noticed that a sentry had moved in front of each doorway leading into the courtyard, facing the assembly with their rifles held horizontally behind them to prevent any latecomers from joining the Appell. After the count the other formations were dismissed, but our party of newcomers was ordered to stand fast by Colonel German.

'You are to be addressed by a Russian general,' he said sonorously. 'He is always counted in his quarters, but wishes to welcome you to Colditz. He won't be long.' With that he saluted and strode off. Forty long and cold minutes later a tall, elegant figure resplendent in a black and red cloak with a magnificent cap choking under braid and a chest laden with flamboyant medals emerged from a doorway. He was accompanied by a British naval officer, Lieutenant Mike Harvey, who was to act as interpreter. Charlie Hopetoun called us to attention and smartly saluted the general. Waving at us to stand easy, the general spoke out crisply in a resonant Slavonic tongue. Mike Harvey translated for us.

'Welcome to Colditz! Here we are all comrades with one common aim and that is to destroy the enemy. Perhaps we cannot destroy him physically, but we can destroy his morale. We must strive together with that common goal. Here we have the Dutch, the Poles, the French and the British, and of course me. Let us leave no stone unturned to accomplish our common aim, until that day – that great day – when our comrades in arms will burst through those doors with their guns blazing and flags waving, and destroy our miserable captors. Loud will be the cheering, great will be the rejoicing!'

I happened to be standing next to Laurie Pumphrey, who spoke and understood Russian well.

'He's a bloody fake!' he whispered. 'That's not Russian he's speaking. In fact it's not really anything.'

Quickly the word raced through our ranks, then heads began to appear at the windows above. Wave upon wave of raucous laughter echoed around the courtyard as we stood there like a bunch of twits, the victims of a practical joke.

Aware the prank had reached its climax the 'general' shed his coat and doffed his cap.

'Gentlemen!' announced Mike Harvey, his eyes twinkling. 'May I introduce to you Flight Lieutenant Peter van Rood – a damn nice fellow from the Netherlands serving in the Royal Air Force!'

A short time later, back in our quarters, we had a visitor. He introduced himself as Lieutenant Ralph Holroyd from Sydney. He said there were two other Australians already in Colditz, both from the RAF, whereas he was infantry like us, and had been captured in Greece after being wounded in 1941. Ralph sat down and filled us in on the information we needed to know about day-to-day life within our castle prison. There were four Appells each day, at 6.30am, 11.00am, 4.00pm and 8.00pm, and our 'Russian General' had been right about one thing; everyone, at all times, did their utmost to upset the German contingent.

The game, as we knew, was called 'goon baiting', and this was practiced at every possible opportunity. Unlike other camps where, to a degree, the British cooperated with the Germans in such matters as getting people out for Appells, in Colditz you were on your own. Should you fail to make it to the courtyard on time you were trapped behind the sentry, your name would be taken, and you would find yourself with five days in the castle's cells. This built up to a maximum twenty-eight days, which was served for any subsequent offences. The British Officers left it entirely up to the men under their command. In other words, it was up to you.

Our Kommandant here was Oberstleutnant Prawitt, a fellow who believed in order and discipline, but received little of either from his charges.

The only exercise areas available to us were the courtyard, which was only a little larger than a tennis court, and a small wooded park in the castle precincts, where we would be escorted twice daily if we so wished. There was no such thing as a parole walk, which was a privilege allowed in other camps, where escorted walks beyond the camp were permitted so long as the prisoner gave his solemn word not to escape. Theoretically, if a POW escaped on a parole walk having given his word not to do so and made it back to England, he could be returned to Germany for having failed to keep his word as an officer and a gentleman. I never heard of this happening, but at Colditz the Germans were not prepared to take any chances with our bunch of 'hardened criminals'.

After a pleasant chat with Ralph we felt much more at ease with our new home. But he had sounded a warning to us; Colditz was probably the end of the road for us as far as escaping was concerned. Not that we couldn't try to get out, and good luck to us if we succeeded, but following several ingenious attempts over the years, some of them successful, the Germans had the place sealed up tight as a drum, with listening devices implanted in the stone walls of the castle, incredibly good security, four Appells daily, and spot Appells called whenever they chose to do so, just to break any apparent routine. Floodlights illuminated every area of the courtyards (the only POW camp to be floodlit permanently by night), and the guard company was highly disciplined. Everything, he said, had been tried, and every area of the castle explored with a view to getting away.

This was disappointing news, but we had to accept the fact that we were here because the Germans believed us to be habitual escapers, and they were going to keep a close watch on us. On the positive side, Ralph also told us we were in a relatively good camp, and our fellow prisoners were a first-rate bunch.

Once Ralph had left us, Mark and I sat on the bottom bunk of our bed and had a bit of a chat about what we'd been told. We each had a cup of ersatz coffee, a rather bitter by-product of acorns.

'My God, this is ghastly stuff,' Mark growled, grimacing down into his cup. 'Thought I might have gotten used to it by now, but it just seems to get worse. What I wouldn't give right now for a mug of real coffee, or better yet a cup of billy tea.' Billy tea was made back in the Australian bush by tipping tea leaves into a boiling container of water resting on a campfire, adding two gum leaves off a eucalyptus tree, and finally brewed by grasping the tin's handle and swinging the whole lot around and around in a vast windmill action. It was then poured, and the result really is bloody marvellous.

We were silent for a time. Mark was obviously back under a starlit Australian sky, the smell of wood smoke and brewing tea once again evoking the special yearning we all carried in our hearts. I watched him as he looked up around the solid walls of our new quarters. Nothing had to be said. Sighing deeply he polished off his coffee in a single draught, grimaced again, and said he was going to stretch out for a bit. I was still quite tired and decided to do likewise.

As I began to drift off a particularly noisy German corporal burst into the room and began shouting at us. '*Achtung!* You will all be photographed for our security records. Come with me now!'

A mass of tired groans met this order, as well as some very succinct suggestions as to what the corporal could do with his security photos. Bloody hell, I thought, doesn't anyone get a chance to sleep around here? Nevertheless I decided to go downstairs straight away so I could get this latest nonsense out of the way quickly and return to my bunk.

I was the first of the new arrivals behind the corporal, and we wound our way anti-clockwise down the stairs to the courtyard, which was now devoid of prisoners. Those behind me were halted and told to wait their turn. A huge black camera stood near one wall, complete with tripod and black hood, while the photographer turned out to be a rather flustered civilian in a tired suit. The guard checked my name and directed me to stand with my back to the wall, behind a wooden structure resembling a miniature goal post. On the front of the horizontal bar he inserted a number into a frame which was at chest level. The photographer took off his lens cap, placed his head under the hood, and began focussing.

Then, without any warning, three water bombs came sailing through the air, apparently tossed from a window high above the courtyard. Splosh, splosh, splosh! One hit the sentry on his foot, another scored a beautifully direct hit on the photographer's covered head, and the third hit the cobblestones near me. The furious photographer began shaking his fist and cursing up at the now-empty windows. He pushed the slow-moving corporal in the back and demanded he catch the culprits. They both dashed up the stairway shouting and swearing, pushing the highly amused prisoners out of the way. I was left in the courtyard, a little bewildered and also slightly wet from the water bombs.

Immediately the coast was clear, two figures in RAF uniforms charged out of the next stairway along, swept up the camera and shot back the way they had come, carrying their prize aloft. Once again I found myself alone and a little uneasy. Later, I found out that the two culprits were Vincent 'Bush' Parker, an Australian Spitfire pilot in the RAF, and bomber pilot Peter Tunstall. Discretion being the better part of valour, I decided that I had better make myself scarce as well, and hotfooted it back to my room, along with the others who had been waiting on the staircase.

The reaction of the photographer and the corporal when they returned after a fruitless search to find the camera gone can only be imagined. Within minutes the Appell siren had blared out, and a squad of guards marched into our quarters headed by Hauptmann Eggers, who was later to become the camp Security Officer, and the photographer, who was frantically mopping his brow with a large handkerchief.

'Gentlemen,' Eggers announced. 'A very serious offence has just been committed, involving the theft of a camera. This is to be returned at once, or you will remain in this room until it has been recovered.' He barked out some orders, and while two guards stood by the door the rest began a systematic search of the wing.

Eventually they discovered the camera under an empty bunk. It was really of no use to the prisoners because of its size, but the disruption caused by its theft had been worth it. After the photographer had fawned over his prodigal machine and deemed it to be both intact and functional, the atmosphere became a little less electric. Eggers was still fuming, the photographer unhappy but relieved, and the prisoners quite pleased with the all the commotion caused by the incident. Bush Parker, grinning happily, looked at me and winked.

Once the Germans had cleared off he came over and introduced himself. 'Sorry about the water you copped, old boy,' he said. 'But I expect it could have been worse.'

'Don't mention it,' I replied. 'I thought it was great fun. But please tell me, does this sort of thing go on all the bloody time? I would like to get some rest occasionally.'

'Well,' he said, consulting his watch, 'you're lucky, Jack – you've got a whole forty minutes until the eleven o'clock Appell!'

I groaned.

We quickly settled into the routine. Generally speaking, despite the four Appells each day (which were reduced to just two a day once we became an all-British camp), we found life to be comparatively agreeable. Our quarters, although rather gloomy, were really more acceptable than those at Eichstätt. We had more room and a large stove, with a reasonable supply of fuel to do our cooking.

Soon we were issued with our own Red Cross parcels, which supplemented the usual German rations of soup, a few potatoes and black bread. This enabled us to indulge in some mild exercises in the courtyard and the nearby park area, where we were taken under guard. After our deprivations in Willibaldsburg we were soon reasonably fit and able to maintain a satisfactory weight level.

There was little goon baiting for a while, due mainly to the lack of opportunity, although on one parade the French, seemingly by accident, managed to drop a volley ball net over an unsuspecting guard. Not long after our arrival we heard that the rest of the Eichstätt mob were joining us, and we looked forward to seeing them.

On Saturday evening, 26 June, just four days after our arrival, the balance of the Eichstätt tunnellers turned up. Like us they had been marched out of Willibaldsburg and had endured the long, uncomfortable train journey to Colditz. They were dirty, dispirited and hungry. Numbly they submitted themselves to the inevitable and thorough search by the guards, were photographed, and then led to their new quarters where they all collapsed gratefully onto their bunks. Complete exhaustion overcame any thoughts of exploring their new surroundings or looking up old chums. All of them were soon sound asleep. Little did they know (or us for that matter) of the surprise that was in store for them.

By 6.45am the early morning Appell was over, and the 'new boys' flocked back to their quarters, hoping to pick up another couple of hours sleep. Then at 10.15am the door crashed open and in swept what was obviously the German doctor, with a nervous-looking orderly in tow.

'*Achtung! Aufstehen!*' screamed the doctor, who was immaculately dressed in a long white coat and German uniform trousers, with a gleaming stethoscope hanging around his neck. The orderly, in similar attire apart from the stethoscope, wore an ill-fitting forage cap. The doctor handed his medical bag to the orderly, cast a stern eye around the room, and then began to scream abuse in German at the perplexed occupants. He issued an order to his meek offsider, who began to read out the names of the officers who had arrived the night before. Sluggishly they roused themselves from their bunks, but not quickly enough. The doctor raised his fists and shouted even more invective at an ever-increasing pitch.

Phil Pardoe, who had arrived in our group, interceded by telling the new guys that he would translate for them. Best to maintain a bit of British discipline he said, and keep their tempers despite the ravings of this lunatic medico. After consulting with the orderly, Pardoe said all the new arrivals from Eichstätt had to undergo a medical examination, and were to proceed to a vacant room nearby.

In the middle of this room was a trestle table. Some of the other prisoners, curious as always, drifted in unimpeded to see what was going on. I went in too, and found it all very curious. We certainly hadn't undergone anything like this when we'd arrived.

All the while the doctor kept up a stream of abuse and threats, which was beginning to frighten the pants off some of the prisoners. Pardoe arranged them in a line in alphabetical order as directed by the orderly, and continued to translate the torrent of abuse from the doctor, who walked up and down the line, only stopping to wrinkle his nose in obvious disgust.

'You British are all filthy!' he shouted. 'You all smell like pigs, and are undoubtedly covered in lice. You will therefore take off your disgusting clothing when ordered, and my assistant here will treat you one at a time. You will lie on your back on that table over there, and if any of you does not obey my orders he will be treated by force and then thrown into the cells for two weeks, where I hope he will rot in his own filth!'

I noticed that some of the longer-serving inmates of the castle were watching the proceedings with barely concealed amusement. I considered this to be grossly unfair, and only served to compound the misery of the new guys. The doctor, amazingly ignoring the growing crowd of spectators, carried on.

'You!' he shouted to the first officer in line. 'Undress and come here. *Schnell*!' This done, he pinched and prodded at the unfortunate man's hair, pulled his ears, forced his mouth wide open to examine his teeth, slapped the back of his neck, and checked his heartbeat with the stethoscope. 'You will now lie on the table!' he ordered, moving on to his next victim.

The thoroughly miserable officer lay on his back across the table, and watched with mounting horror as the orderly opened the doctor's bag, from which he removed two large jars and a paintbrush. Opening one of the jars he stuck in his whole hand and then proceeded to smear some horrible glutinous mess over the poor fellow's stomach and neck. This done, he opened the other jar and dipped in the paintbrush which emerged covered in a thin purple-coloured liquid, which was then liberally applied to the man's armpits and genital area.

The discoloured and humiliated fellow was then allowed to roll off the table and hastily retrieve his clothing, furious at the indignities performed on him, and further enraged by the chortles coming from the gathering crowd of delighted onlookers.

The doctor, still raving away, had soon examined nearly thirty patients, and six of these had been subjected to the revolting smear treatment. Next in line was Lieutenant Ed Hannay of the Seaforth Highlanders who decided he would not be a party to such shabby goings-on. At about the same time as the doctor reached Ed, a hand appeared from nowhere in the background and filched the momentarily unguarded stethoscope. Some of the onlookers, seeing this happen, muttered silent approval, and the 'new boys' went up one notch in their estimation. The doctor, meanwhile, was facing Hannay and began to scream at him. Now it happened that Ed spoke quite good German, and his response promptly cut the doctor off in mid-sentence.

'Get stuffed!' he said stiffly, and all eyes turned to him. 'How dare you treat British officers in this disgusting manner! You and that little prick with you have absolutely no idea of military behaviour, nor even common human decency. Do whatever you want, but you can go to hell for all I care!' He folded his arms and glared.

The doctor turned purple with rage, and began to shake. 'Call out the guards!' he bellowed. 'This man has defied me, and he is to be shot! I order you to get undressed or be shot!'

'Up your arse!' Ed replied firmly in German.

The doctor took a deep breath, opened his mouth to speak, and dissolved into guffaws of laughter! He shrieked and slapped his thigh, and the tears ran down his face as he fought for breath. The whole room was now in complete uproar, and the poor half-dressed wretches in the middle could only stand stunned and open-mouthed.

The 'doctor' regained his composure somewhat, and then Harry Elliott, a well-known practical joker who had been in Colditz for two years, strode over to join him.

'Gentlemen,' he announced. 'My name is Harry Elliott. May I introduce your doctor, Howard Gee, a civilian prisoner here, and his "orderly" Bos'n Chrisp of the Royal Navy. We welcome you to Oflag IVC and trust you enjoy your stay with us – however short or long that may be. By the way, the jelly you were treated with is a harmless blend of decayed barley and mildewed cornflour, while the lice paint was derived from indelible pencils. This should wash off in a week or two!'

'Oh, and by the way,' cut in Howard Gee, in a rich Etonian accent, 'I would be grateful if the clever bastard who pinched my stethoscope could hand it back. It belongs to the Poles, and they want it back in one piece.'

The 'new boys' had been welcomed to Colditz!

6

Some Intrepid Internationals

WITHIN A FEW WEEKS of our arrival at Colditz the French, Poles, and the remainder of the Dutch contingent left. But the French had left us a legacy; they had been working on a scheme to use the underground drains as a means of escape. Frank Weldon paid us a visit and asked if we would be interested in joining a party from Eichstätt to work on it. We said we would, and asked what it entailed. Apparently it was considered possible that a tunnel could be dug from the drain in the courtyard across to another drain, the existence of which was known, and this might go clear to the outside of the castle. It was quite a long shot, but worth a look.

A few days later I found myself in the drain with Weldon. It was dirty, stinking work, and I was not sorry when the time came to surface. I only went down that drain three times, and a few weeks later, after it was firmly established that the plan was not feasible, the scheme was abandoned. This rather forlorn effort was my only attempt at any form of escaping from Colditz.

With the departure of the other Nationals from Colditz we were moved over to the west wing of the castle, which was to be our home for the remainder of our time there.

Located on the second floor, we had quite good facilities. We even had a separate room in which to eat, as well as a separate kitchen with a large stove. Here the three of us joined up with Douggie Moir (Royal Tank Regiment), Bruce MacAskie (Queen's Own Royal West Kent Regiment), Mike Wittet (Royal Scots), Alan McCall (Cameron Highlanders) and Micky Farr (Durham Light Infantry). The eight of us, including Mark and Rex, messed together for the next eighteen months – quite a feat in Colditz, where petty disagreements usually caused a mess to break up after only a few months.

Despite our experience of earlier prison camps there was obviously a lot we had to learn about life within the walls of Colditz. The ancient castle undoubtedly had a long and involved history, but most of our interest involved finding ways of getting beyond those forbidding walls. As a topic of conversation, it beat griping about meagre rations, cold showers and constant searches. Therefore it was not too long before we were being treated to sessions of entertaining stories concerning earlier attempts by the departing Frenchmen and other nationals to break out from the supposedly 'escape-proof' fortress prison. Some were brilliantly conceived and executed while others ended in dismal failure. A few proved to be amazingly successful.

The first person to escape and make it all the way home was French Lieutenant Alain LeRay. In April 1941, as a group of French prisoners were being marched back into the castle from an outside exercise area, LeRay hurriedly concealed himself in a doorway at the base of a building known as the terraced house. The guards did not notice his disappearance and a headcount back at the castle was rigged to cover his absence. As soon as the coast was clear, LeRay scooted back to the empty exercise area, clambered over the wall, and made his escape, which ended when he reached neutral Switzerland and safety.

Sheer bad luck ended yet another carefully planned escape that June. Over several months, French Lieutenant Boulay had been secretly sewing a mid-length skirt and ladies' jacket and manufacturing a fashionable, decorated wide-brimmed hat and handbag. Somehow his wife back in France had managed to send him a wig. On the chosen day, 5 June, Boulay joined a group of prisoners being escorted under guard for some exercise in a nearby park. As the group straggled down a steep path to the park, Boulay was at the front and wearing a long overcoat buttoned over his disguise. At the right moment, as they reached a blind bend in the path, his co-conspirators suddenly whipped off the overcoat, Boulay slapped the wig and hat on his head, turned around and began walking nonchalantly the other way. The guards took little notice of the woman passing by, but one of the prisoners who was sadly not aware of the escape scheme noticed that her watch had fallen unnoticed off her wrist. The chivalrous Frenchman picked up the watch, and began calling out to the retreating figure, 'Fraulein! Fraulein!'

The NCO in charge sent one of the guards sprinting after Boulay with the watch. On hearing the German bearing down on him, Boulay decided the game was up, turned and put his hands up and surrendered to a very surprised guard.

The following month, on 1 July, a French cavalry officer named Pierre Mairesse-Lebrun made another heart-stopping escape and successful 'home run'. Dressed only in a singlet, shorts and sneakers, he was part of a French group exercising in a fenced-off area of the park. Once the guards escorting the prisoners out of the park had been distracted according to plan, Mairesse-Lebrun and Lieutenant Pierre Odry ran to the back of the park, where Odry braced himself with his back to the high barbed wire fence, cupping his hands tightly together. Mairesse-Lebrun then ran at Odry, planting one of his feet in the man's outstretched hands. In a wonderful gymnastic display, Odry used Mairesse-Lebrun's momentum, tossing him upwards and over the fence. Landing and rolling without injury, the Frenchman then sprinted away in a weaving run while the shocked guards raced over to the fence and began firing at his disappearing back. Despite initially departing clad in only his sports attire, Mairesse-Lebrun made his way into Switzerland and eventually returned home to France.

People may rightfully ask why the Germans allowed their prisoners to utilise the exterior park when it provided so many opportunities to escape that were near impossible inside the fortified castle walls. Although reluctant, Kommandant Schmitt had to obey orders from the High Command in Berlin allowing POWs fresh air and exercise under the strictures of the Geneva Convention. Then things became grim when it was found that two Dutch officers had gone missing, followed soon after by two more. The security officers were perplexed, as the head count back at the camp gates after the exercise period was correct. What they didn't realise was that during games of football in the park, rucks of men would form over a supposedly sealed manhole cover above a water conduit. Fake bolts secured in place on an earlier game were quickly broken as the men crowded and jostled around the cover. Two men then slipped into the manhole and a new set of fake bolts were screwed into place. To cover their absence, 'Max' and 'Moritz' took their place at the subsequent roll-call to make the count correct.

In a perfectly clever ruse, the Dutch had employed the talents of a Polish officer who was an amateur sculptor. Using some stolen plaster he manufactured two heads which were then painted with human features. The heads, now named Max and Moritz, could then be fixed to makeshift frames. It was an easy task carrying the heads, frames, coats, boots and hats to the park, concealed beneath the long coats the Dutch officers normally wore. Once the escapers had been hidden and secured in the manhole, the prisoners would form up for their return to the castle, now accompanied by Max and Moritz, resplendent in their coats and caps, and held up by a man on either side. At the roll-call, a pair of boots completed the deception. Security was tightened even more, especially when an observant guard saw two men sliding into the manhole cover. They were quickly detained and the game was up. Nevertheless the dummy heads went undiscovered, ready to assist in later escape attempts. Then, when two more Dutchmen went missing, an alert guard at roll-call became suspicious of one curiously unmoving officer and Max fell into German hands. Later, during a random search in February 1942, the disembodied head of Moritz was also discovered. The great deception was finally over, but it ultimately resulted in four Dutch officers safely returning home.

By November 1941, a German electrician from Colditz town by the name of Willi Pöhnert had become a familiar sight around the castle. Any time there was a problem Willi was called in to fix it. His tool bag in hand, he would be checked in and issued with a yellow arm band bearing the number 54 and a picture of the German eagle before proceeding to the job at hand. Although slightly taller than Pöhnert, French Lieutenant André Perodeau resembled the labourer in many ways. By the end of the month, duplicates had been made of Pöhnert's clothes scarf and cloth cap, a yellow arm band fashioned, and a similar pair of spectacles completed the outfit. A false pass was manufactured, although no one knew exactly what it was supposed to look like. On the selected evening, while Willi Pöhnert was completing a job in the French quarters, Perodeau waited until the sentry in the prisoner's compound was occupied checking a fellow French officer's parole card. He quickly hustled by the two men with a tool bag in his hand, waving his pass at the guard. Distracted, the guard only gave the pass a cursory glance before waving him through into the German compound. Once there, he approached the final obstacle – a sentry stationed at the outer gateway. Although Willi was a very familiar visitor to the castle, the guard nevertheless asked to see his pass, which he scrutinised carefully. However it was not very well made and bore the wrong sort of stamp. The guard then began to question him in German. Perodeau did not speak the language and could only stare blankly at the man. All too soon the sentry had raised his rifle and the escape was at an end. It was later revealed that the guard's initial suspicions had been raised as the scarf the fake Willi was wearing was a different colour to the one Pöhnert always wore. Shortly after the ruse had been discovered the camp Kommandant had a photograph taken of Perodeau standing alongside a very surprised Pöhnert, at one stage jokingly remarking to the bespectacled electrician, 'It looks as if you have a new-found brother!'

* * *

In January 1942, Lieutenant Airey Neave made the first British 'home run' when he escaped disguised as a German guard along with Dutchman Tony Luteyn. In October that same year, Pat Reid and three fellow prisoners made their escape from Colditz. The four men spent several days hiding in a potato cellar before shedding their clothes and painstakingly squeezing out backwards through an extremely narrow air vent into a dry castle moat. Then, splitting into two pairs and disguised as Flemish workmen, they headed off. All four finally made it to Switzerland, creating great excitement back in Colditz when news of their successful escape was confirmed.

Inevitably, there were tales of a few innovative but ultimately unsuccessful bids for freedom that had us hooting with laughter despite recording an unfortunate ending. One such escape in May 1942 involved one of the great characters held in Colditz, Anthony Murray Allan, better known to us all as 'Peter'.

Scottish-born Peter was a lieutenant with the 51st Division of the Queens Own Cameron Highlanders when he was captured during the fall of France in 1940. A small, rather slight man – helpfully fluent in the German language – he would often be seen wandering the courtyard cobblestones wearing his beloved kilt. Peter was one of a group of prisoners known as the 'Laufen Six', after the prison camp from which they had made what is regarded as the first escape of the war by British officers. Following their recapture, the six officers were packed off to Colditz. He was always on the lookout for some way to end his unwanted captivity and in 10 May 1942 an unexpected opportunity came his way. 'It was what we called a snap escape,' he would later say. 'A spur-of-the-moment opportunity to get out of Colditz that I took immediately.'

It all began that morning when a horse-drawn cart containing a work detail of disinterested French army POWs clattered into the castle courtyard. The prisoners on board were tasked with loading dozens of unwanted straw-filled mattresses, stored in an attic, into the back of the cart. Within minutes a plan had evolved, devised by some quick-witted British officers, to place someone into one of the mattresses, sew it up, and then ask a sturdy-looking Frenchman to carry the mattress down the stairs and load it into the cart. With his light build and excellent knowledge of the German language it was quickly decided that Peter Allan was the obvious choice. He was given a passable change of clothing and 50 Reichmarks, while Pat Reid was finally able to persuade a far-from-convinced Frenchman that the scheme could work. To everyone's delight the mattress finally made it down the stairs and was tossed into the back of the cart without arousing the suspicion of the German guards supervising the loading. An uncomfortable, stifling and claustrophobic time lay ahead for Peter as other mattresses were thrown on top of his, until finally the French contingent and their guards clambered back in. He was worried that he might sneeze and give the game away, but more terrified of the fact that the guards could have stuck their bayonets into the mattresses to thwart any possible escapes. To his relief, the cart began to move and passed through the castle gates without stopping.

Fortunately it was not a long journey, although Peter had no idea when the cart would pull up, or where. Eventually all movement ceased and he was relieved to feel the mattresses being unloaded. All of them were dumped inside a deserted house in the village of Colditz and still no one had raised the alarm. Once the cart had moved away he managed to cut a slit in the mattress, allowing some fresh air in while he waited to see what happened next. After a couple of hours had passed he tore the gap wide open and crawled out, dusting himself down. Taking note of where he was, he then slipped through a window into a small derelict garden. Peter's long journey to freedom now began. Ahead of him lay the perilous task of crossing hundreds of miles of enemy-occupied territory and scrounging for food in order to reach a neutral embassy in Vienna. Once there, he hoped to seek the consulate's help in passing him along to then-neutral Hungary. At one stage in his eight-day journey – mostly on foot – he managed to flag down a passing car, hoping for a lift. When the door swung open he realised to his shock that it contained two Gestapo officers. He knew there was no choice; he either got in the car or gave himself away. Over the next hour his German underwent a tough test as he chatted to the officers, trying to sound normal while explaining that he was an engineering student. When – to his relief – he was finally dropped off, he gave the Germans his best Hitler salute and tried to look untroubled and casual as he walked away on rubbery legs.

By the time Peter reached the outskirts of Vienna he was starving and exhausted to the point of collapse. Desperately hungry, he asked a passer-by where he could get some assistance. The man helpfully pointed out a nearby building, but when Peter entered he realised it was the local police station. Physically unable to continue, dirty, dishevelled and with no identity papers, he knew the game was finally up. He had no choice but to reveal that he was an escaped prisoner of war. The duty policeman placed a call to the Security Officer at Colditz and a brilliantly conceived escape was at an end. The Scotsman was escorted back to Colditz where he was placed in solitary confinement for three weeks as punishment for his audacious escape.

A similar attempt featured yet another diminutive character, British Pilot Officer Dominic Bruce, who had been shot down over

Belgium in June 1941. A persistent and determined escaper, he had been sent to Colditz after a number of masterful but ultimately unsuccessful attempts. In September 1942 the Germans decided that far too many personal effects – particularly those in the British quarters – were badly cluttering up the place, which often impeded their searches for contraband material. Clothing, shoes, books, musical instruments and other items were scattered everywhere, so orders were issued that all excess paraphernalia must be gathered up and packed into large Red Cross tea chests, which would then be stored in an attic room in the castle. The opportunity was too good to miss, and once plans had been formulated, Dominic (known to his fellow prisoners as 'the medium-sized man') was nailed into one of the three-foot square boxes along with a number of bed sheets knotted together to form a 40-foot rope. The tea chest was among those carried up to the attic on the third floor of the German Kommandantur, following which the guards locked the room and left. Once they were gone and all was quiet, Dominic prized the lid off the chest and waited until an appropriate time for the next phase of his escape.

At around 3am Dominic opened the attic window and lowered the rope of sheets. He then made his way down hand-over-hand until he reached the ground. Once there he found a hiding place close to the castle, believing that when the escape was discovered the guards would be searching for him many miles away before finally giving up. Meanwhile he had left a cheeky note for his captors, which read, '*Die Luft in Colditz gefällt mir nicht mehr. Auf Wiedersehen!*' ('The air in Colditz no longer agrees with me. See you later!')

After two days of hiding and eating some of his rations he decided it was safe to move on. Disguised as a Belgian worker, armed with appropriate papers, he first stole a bicycle to begin his journey. He then caught a succession of trains as he made his way towards Danzig. Once he reached there, three weeks after his escape, Dominic made his way down to the harbour where he decided to hide in a small haystack until the morning. He would then look for a freighter bound for Sweden. Unfortunately a resident in a nearby house had noticed his furtive activities and alerted the harbour guards. Soon after, Dominic was arrested and taken away, later finding out to his chagrin that he had been trying to hide in a high-security submarine base. After being questioned for two days he was returned to Colditz and given three weeks in solitary confinement.

He may have been short in stature, but Dominic Bruce was not short on courage. Throughout his years of captivity he made a remarkable total of seventeen escape attempts. Like Peter Allan, however, he too would have to wait until the castle was liberated in April 1945 before he saw England's shores once again. Such was the determination, persistence and never-say-die attitude of just some of the gallant men with whom we would share the next two years in Colditz Castle.

April 1940: Lieutenants Jack Champ (left) and Bill Dexter in a contemplative mood aboard the troop ship *Neuralia*, heading for their first action in the Middle East. It would be another five years before Champ's days as a POW ended and he was able to return home. *(Courtesy of Jack Champ)*

Following his capture in Greece, Champ was sent to his first German prison camp, Oflag VB, Biberach. Here he met and befriended two men who would share all his days and adventures as a POW: Mark Howard and Rex Baxter. Front row, left to right: Jack Champ, Jack Paterson, Jack Young and Len Isherwood. Back row: Rex Baxter, Ab Gray, Mark Howard and Bert Morris. *(Courtesy of Ab Gray)*

The first escape was from Oflag VIB, Warburg. In all, twenty-eight prisoners used ladders cunningly disguised as shelving to straddle two parallel barbed wire fences under the cover of darkness. Champ was recaptured almost immediately but three escapees eventually made it back to London. These photographs were taken the following morning, displaying the ingenuity and audacity behind the mass escape. *(Courtesy of Jock Hamilton-Baillie)*

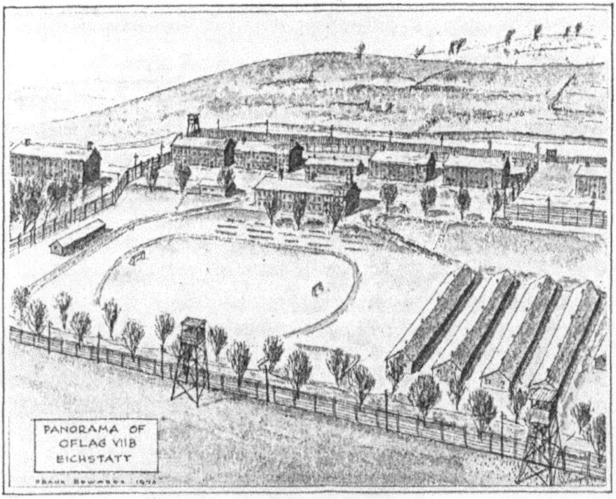

This panoramic sketch of Oflag VIIB, Eichstätt, shows a hill rising steeply behind the prisoners' quarters, which presented them with a difficult but novel means of tunnelling out of the camp completely undetected by the watchful German security guards. *(Helmut Reis,* Chronik der Jägerkaserne Eichstätt 1933–1952*)*

The Eichstätt tunnel began with a vertical shaft driven down through a ground floor lavatory in Block 2 (at the back, second building from left in the panoramic sketch above). Nine tiles were painstakingly removed from the concrete floor and cemented onto a removable slab to conceal the entrance. *(Courtesy of David Ray)*

Large obstructive boulders such as this often impeded and slowed down the difficult task of tunnelling, as they could not be excavated. These natural obstacles made life extremely difficult for the sixty-five fully dressed escapers involved on the night of the mass break.

Perched imposingly high atop a great rock promontory over the River Mulde, Colditz Castle, known as Oflag IVC, had been set up as a special officers' camp designed to hold the most difficult prisoners and inveterate escapers. With massive stone walls, a guard company outnumbering its inmates, and floodlit by night, the Germans had reason to call it 'escape-proof'. By the end of the war a record number of escapes and home runs had brought this haughty claim to ruin. *(Photo by Colin Burgess)*

Four months after his arrival in Oflag IVC, Champ was overjoyed when old mate Johnny Rawson turned up after two incredible but ultimately unsuccessful escapes from other camps. Always cocky and defiant, Rawson would not allow the castle and its formidable reputation to dampen his enthusiasm to break free from captivity. *(Courtesy of Jack Champ)*

The Diggers of Colditz, 29 February 1944. Top row, left to right: Privates Frank Brown, Harry Henley, Vic Jeffries, Claude Patterson and Eddie Walker. Middle row: Ralph Holroyd, 'Bush' Parker, Jack Millett, Johnny Rawson and George Bolding. Front row: Clive Dieppe, Rex Baxter, Malcolm McColm, Doug Crawford and Jack Champ. Lieutenant Mark Howard and Sapper Lionel Archer are absent from this photograph. Mark was in solitary after an escape attempt. Of the other Diggers, Bill Fowler had successfully escaped Colditz before this date, while Jack Goodwin and Private P. M. Ray had not yet arrived at the castle prison. Roger 'Doc' Playoust had been transferred from Colditz two years earlier. *(Courtesy of Australian War Memorial, P07203_001)*

Jack Millett hailed from Western Australia. Captured in Crete after fierce fighting, he became the Diggers' mapmaker. Millett painstakingly etched reverse details of the surrounding countryside (Colditz is top left in this one) into a plate made out of hardened jelly crystals from Red Cross packages. Ink made from indelible pencils was applied, and paper laid over the top, enabling multiple maps to be made from a single design. Millett would often colour his maps to emphasise certain details. *(Portrait courtesy of Australian War Memorial, P07203_008; map courtesy of Jack Millett)*

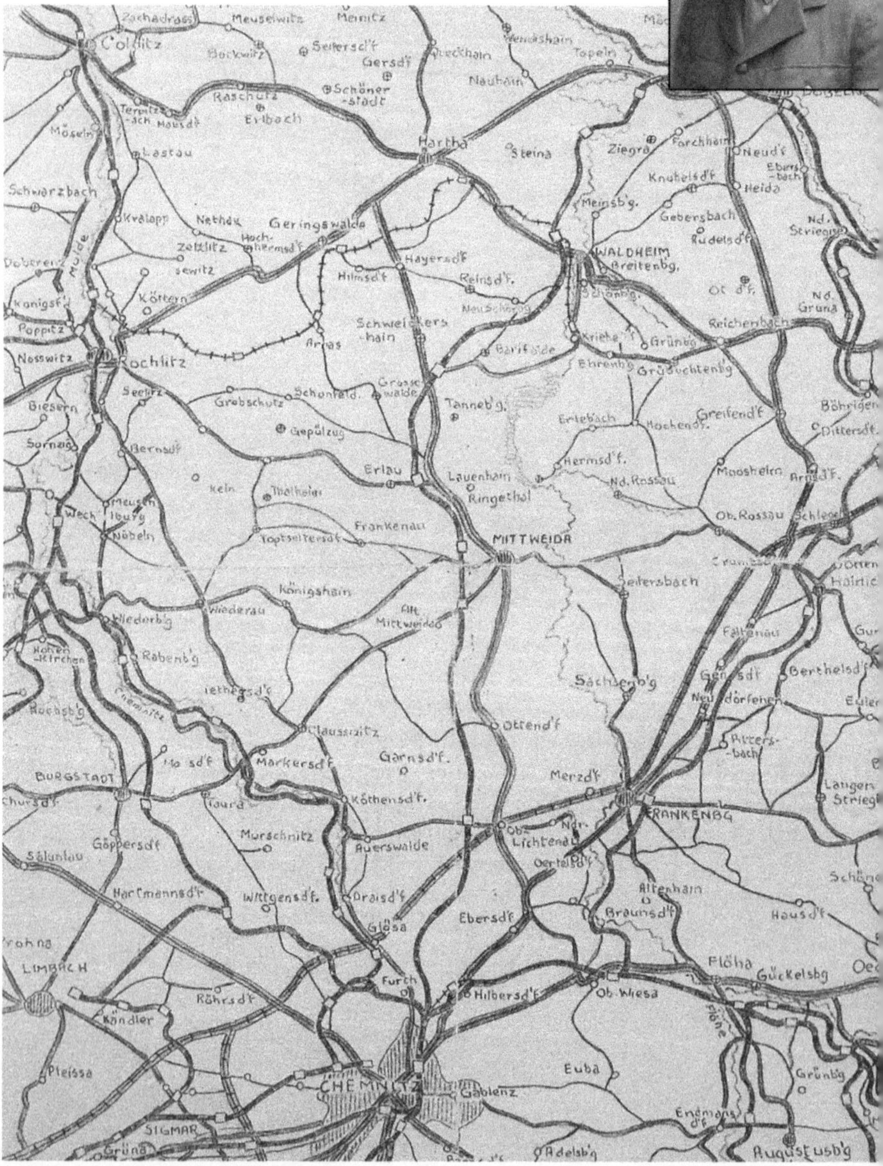

The extraordinary talents and sleight of hand employed by 'Bush' Parker featured in just about every escape attempt from Colditz. In his youth, 'Bush' had been a proficient juggler, magician and acrobat. He could pick every lock in the castle, allowing forbidden access to crucial areas for those contemplating or carrying out escape.

This photograph (and many others) was taken by Johannes Langer, a photographer who lived in the town of Colditz. Langer was recruited to take photos of any escape attempts from the castle for security files, but also took photos of POWs in exchange for cigarettes and food from their Red Cross parcels.

As indicated by his surly expression in this photo taken in Biberach, Champ's fellow Victorian Mark Howard despised his captors and the dull monotony of life as a prisoner of war. Coming from a long line of distinguished British servicemen, Mark was captured after being wounded in Athens. Always openly defiant to enemy personnel, he was often in the cells for disobeying direct German orders or neglecting to turn up for roll-calls in Colditz. *(Courtesy of Mark Howard)*

In October 1941 Squadron Leader Malcolm McColm had the dubious distinction of being the first Australian officer to arrive in Colditz. A persistent escaper in previous camps, he had once been on the verge of making a home run hiding aboard a ship, but fell asleep and alerted the crew by his snoring. Post-war, McColm became an outspoken and popular politician in Queensland. *(Courtesy of Michael Booker)*

Flight Lieutenant Bill Fowler, RAAF. In September 1942, he became the first (and only) Australian to escape from Colditz and successfully complete a home run back to England. Sadly, just a year and a half after his audacious escape, he was killed in a flying accident. He was awarded the Military Cross for the initiative and daring he displayed in escaping from the enemy. *(Courtesy of Imperial War Museum, CH11864)*

Medical practitioner Captain Roger 'Doc' Playoust was taken prisoner while caring for wounded soldiers in Crete, and his skills as a doctor were then employed in several POW camps. He arrived in Colditz in April 1942 but would only spend three months there before being transferred to treat prisoners in other camps. *(Photo and drawing courtesy of Denise Playoust. Drawing by Bill Prior.)*

This prized pastel portrait of Jack Champ was the work of the talented British artist Lieutenant John Watton, who created amazingly accurate drawings of many dozens of fellow POWs in Colditz. *(Portrait by John Watton, courtesy of Jack Champ)*

Although this looks like an approved photograph of Clive Dieppe and Ralph Holroyd (right) in Colditz, it was actually taken on Ralph's secretly constructed camera. Once, during Holroyd's many years in Colditz, his German mother was able to pay him a visit, personally approved by Adolf Hitler. It would make life extremely difficult for Ralph, as guards paid particular attention to his activities from then on. *(Courtesy of Ralph Holroyd)*

Giles Romilly (left) poses with Bush Parker in this official camp photo. As a civilian nephew of Winston Churchill, Romilly was one of a group of men known as the 'prominente' within Colditz. Due to their heritage or political importance they were closely guarded as hostages in the event of an Allied victory. Romilly was sent to Colditz after attempting to escape from an internment camp in Czechoslovakia, dressed as a woman. *(Courtesy of Michael Booker)*

Australian officers and orderlies celebrate an Anzac Day 'bash' with other international representatives, 25 April 1944. Seated front, left to right: George Bolding, Jack Patterson, Johnny Rawson, Harry Henley, Jack Champ, Vic Jeffries and Jack Millett. On the far side of the table, half-hidden behind Henley, is Ralph Holroyd; to his left is Frank Brown. Between Champ and Jeffries are Bush Parker and Lionel Archer; between Jeffries and Millett is Mark Howard. Seated far right is Rex Baxter. *(Courtesy of Jack Champ)*

Lieutenant Leo de Hartog poses for German photographer Johannes Lange with 'Moritz', one of two mannequins used to conceal several Dutch escapes from the camp park. Two heads, named Max and Moritz, were made and painted by a Polish sculptor. When dressed in a uniform coat and hat they fooled the German count at the castle gates. The ruse was eventually uncovered and the two dummies confiscated. *(Photo by Johannes Lange)*

Alleviating the boredom were some excellent plays, homemade musicals and comic farces, held in the theatre on the third floor of the castle. Often some German officers would attend to share in the fun. The production in this photo was *The Clog Dance*, set in Port Said. *(Courtesy of Mike Moran)*

Due to an obvious lack of female leads, the.prisoners would often wear wigs, dresses and make-up, and even shave their legs. In this photo, of a performance of *The Man Who Came to Dinner*, the 'medium-sized man' Dominic Bruce appears to have sacrificed his small moustache to take on the female role. *(Courtesy of Australian War Memorial, P07203_040)*

Several sports were played in the cobbled prisoner courtyard, including volleyball, cricket and soccer, as well as a vigorous game invented by the prisoners called 'stoolball' – a cross between soccer and football, using POWs perched on wooden stools as goals. *(Photo by Johannes Lange)*

Because Rex Baxter spoke fluent German, he was recruited by General Patton's Third Army to assist in advising village Bürgermeisters to lay down their arms and surrender to American troops as they moved through. He is dressed here in the uniform of an American captain. *(Courtesy of Rex Baxter)*

Celebrations erupted when American troops liberated Colditz on 16 April 1945. Prominent in this photo are the dark-haired legal man Alan 'Black' Campbell, standing at left behind the officer with arms folded, and Peter Allan, wearing his customary kilt. Bush Parker is two to Allan's left, wearing a dark sweater and raising his fists in triumph. *(Courtesy of Rex Baxter)*

The famed Colditz glider shown assembled in the attic room where it was secretly constructed. The glider was never used due to the impending liberation of the castle, but later tests proved it would have flown. Sadly, it was dismantled after the freed prisoners were evacuated from the castle. *(Photo by Lee Carson, courtesy of Michael Booker)*

Post-liberation, Champ, Rawson and Bolding met with Princess Mary, who wanted any news of her son, Viscount George Lascelles, who had also been held in Colditz. During the meeting, she learned to her amusement that he still owed some gambling money to Bolding – which she promised would be repaid. *(Sport & General Press Agency, London)*

Following the release of the original edition of *The Diggers of Colditz*, articles on the Australians involved in the story appeared in several newspapers and magazines. Champ and Rawson are here shaking hands during one interview for the *Geelong Advertiser*. *(Courtesy of* Geelong Advertiser*)*

During the interview process for this book, Champ and Howard were snapped while chatting on Howard's farm in Dunkeld, Victoria. *(Photo by Colin Burgess)*

In 1985, the co-authors posed for a photograph taken during their first book signing, held at Griffiths' bookstore in Champ's hometown of Geelong, Victoria. Rawson and Howard were also in attendance to help celebrate. *(Courtesy of* Geelong Advertiser*)*

7

The Old Boys

I HAVE ALREADY BRIEFLY INTRODUCED two of the Australians who were in Colditz prior to our arrival in June 1943, but as they were among the old boys in the castle, I think it only fair that I give all of them the respect of a proper introduction, and a chance to have their own remarkable stories told.

Malcolm McColm had the dubious distinction of being the first Australian officer to arrive in Colditz. He beat fellow airman Bill Fowler by two months, with Ralph Holroyd and Bush Parker arriving April and May of 1942.

Malcolm Llewellyn McColm enjoyed the type of boyhood which those who thrill to adventure can only wistfully imagine. His father, William E. McColm, was the skipper and part-owner of the mighty windjammer *Mount Stewart*, in which the weathered Scot and his wife, Adelaide, plied the freight trade between England and Australia. His was the last full-rigged ship to wear the Red Duster in the Australian trade.

On 25 June 1914, while *Mount Stewart* was docked in the Welsh port of Cardiff, Malcolm was born. Three months later he was baptised in Australia. His younger brother Don was born two years later in Peru, again while the windjammer was in dock. Young Malcolm was already walking the timber decks, albeit unsteadily. By the time 1926 rolled around, and his father reluctantly decided it was time to leave the seafaring life and settle on the land, the boy had already rounded the treacherous Horn of Africa on no less than three occasions.

Accompanied by his wife and two boisterous sons, Captain McColm sailed out to Australia for the last time, along with a good family friend, Charles Howard, who also happened to be the Earl of Suffolk and Berkshire. They had decided to throw their lot in together and buy up some good farming property, and finally found what they wanted in a large tract of land in North Toolburra, near Warwick in Queensland. The Captain and the Earl then fully engaged themselves in pastoral and farming pursuits for many years, but times were hard and prosperity did not come easily. They switched to growing tobacco but this too was unsuccessful, so the Earl decided he would return home to England.

Some years later the Earl of Suffolk's name jumped into prominence for several heroic deeds. Once back in England he married the actress Mimi Crawford, and during the early war years he was with the Ministry of Supply in France. Just prior to the fall of France he managed to smuggle some French scientists out of the country, as well as a fortune in industrial diamonds – invaluable for the British cause. Six months later he and two members of his bomb squad were delousing an unexploded German shell in London when it blew up, killing all three. The Earl was awarded a posthumous George Cross.

Long before these events, back in Australia, McColm Snr became a Member of Parliament, and Malcolm took his education at Scots College in Warwick, on the Darling Downs. In their exuberant youth, Malcolm and his brother Don often figured in rodeo and bronco riding competitions, which eventually led to their participation in Commonwealth buckjumping events.

For a short time Malcolm wandered into gold prospecting, but in 1936 he decided he would go across to England and join the RAF. He worked his passage over and wasted no time in signing up as a Pilot Officer. Not long after he met his future wife, Alberta. They married, and spent a few days in London before his wife returned to their home in Montrose, a village on the Scottish coast some miles north of Dundee.

Malcolm meantime took to the air force life with great vigour, and was posted to No. 139 Squadron in September 1937, flying two-engine Bristol Blenheims. With the outbreak of war he took part in bombing runs on petrol refineries, airfields and power stations in Germany, and was posted to No. 21 Bomber Squadron, stationed at Watton in Norfolk. Two days after Christmas in 1940, leading a patrol over Holland, his Blenheim was attacked during a raid on an airfield near Breda. He could not maintain control over the badly damaged aircraft, and when it began spinning out of control he gave the order for his crew to bale out. His wireless operator David Shepherd and observer Cecil Hann had already been killed in the attack.

Before jumping out of the Blenheim McColm managed to transmit a rather apologetic message to another aircraft in his formation. 'Tell my wife,' he said, 'that I'll be late home for dinner!' Little did he know that it would be another four and a half years before he could make that dinner date with Alberta.

McColm landed in a field near Breda and hid his parachute, harness and Mae West under some ice in a nearby dyke. He walked away from his wrecked aircraft, but ten minutes later was picked up by members of the German flak battery that had brought his bomber down. He was taken to a nearby airfield, then driven under guard to Amsterdam. On 28 December he was taken by car to Dulag Luft in Oberursel, arriving the next day. Following a tedious seven-week imprisonment at the Luftwaffe interrogation camp he was moved to Stalag Luft I at Barth. His post-war report reveals what happened during the train journey.

> At approximately 2030 hours on 16 February 1941, Flight Lieutenant Newman and I jumped off the train in which we were being transported from Dulag Luft to Stalag Luft I. The train was travelling at a speed of about fifteen or twenty miles per hour when we climbed through the carriage window near Prenslau. It was our intention to reach Stettin. Our escape equipment consisted of a very small-scale map of Germany, a compass, twenty Reichmarks and a quantity of food saved from Red Cross parcels.
>
> After jumping from the train we walked across country for about 12 miles. We then hid in a barn until dusk on 17 February. We then resumed walking until we arrived near Pasewalk, where we stayed in a barn until the morning of 18 February, when we were discovered by the farmer. We were handed over to the civil police at Pasewalk, and that evening we were taken by a Luftwaffe officer in a car to the aerodrome at Prenslau.
>
> On 21 February we were taken by train to Stalag Luft I where we were sentenced to eight days' solitary confinement. At the same time I was sentenced to a further eight days' solitary confinement

for having stolen a cap badge from Sonderführer Eberhardt at Dulag Luft.

Following McColm's arrival at Stalag Luft I, it didn't take him long to become involved in the construction of a tunnel. Twelve officers were working on the tunnel, and it was successfully completed on 19 August. It was hoped that as many as thirty men could escape through it. The next night McColm, Flying Officer Tim Newman from New Zealand and Squadron Leader Charlie Lockett were first into the tunnel, finally breaking through outside the camp.

McColm was dressed in a camp-made cap, navy blue roll-necked pullover, air force trousers and thick rope-soled shoes, and it was planned that the three of them would travel together to Lübeck. McColm went through the tunnel first, followed by Newman and Lockett. They had arranged to meet in a nearby field, and after an anxious wait Lockett finally emerged with shots ringing out behind him. He had been spotted emerging from the tunnel, a searchlight had picked out the exit, and the balloon had gone up. There was no sign of Newman, so the two men scampered away. They later found out that Newman had disappeared in another direction with the sound of shooting, and was picked up three days later.

Lockett and McColm walked south-west by night and hid in woods during the day until 26 August, when they boarded a goods train travelling towards Lübeck. On arrival at Schwaan they got off the train while it was stationary and hid in a swamp until evening. The two of them resumed walking and eventually boarded another goods train.

On arrival at Bad Kleinen a German got into the truck where they were hiding and heard their voices. He shone his torch on them, and the two men jumped out of the truck, fleeing into a wood where they hid up until nightfall. They spent that evening trying to find another train heading for Lübeck, using the method of examining destination labels on the trucks as they arrived at the marshalling yards at Schwaan, but their efforts were not successful.

At 6.45 the next morning Charlie Lockett, who could speak a little German, bought two third-class railway tickets to Lübeck. This time they boarded the tram as passengers, and arrived at the Baltic port two hours later, where they spent the rest of the day walking around the town. They hid their suitcases and other effects near the river, and that evening went to the docks in order to find a Swedish ship. They boarded one such vessel where they asked the cook and first mate if they would hide them. The two nervous Swedes went away to talk it over, and while they were gone McColm and Lockett hid in a coal bunker. They had only been there ten minutes when they were discovered by a stoker, who reported them to the chief engineer. He in turn told them to go ashore and said if they refused he would report them to the police. Reluctantly they disembarked and boarded several other ships, without being able to obtain help.

Eventually they found one Swedish seaman who agreed to help them stow away on his ship, but just when they were congratulating themselves on their good fortune Lockett noticed they were being observed through binoculars by a policeman on the docks. They decided it would be prudent to abandon their efforts for the night, and hurriedly left the dock area.

Cold and dispirited, they returned to the place where they had hidden their suitcases, and decided to separate and attempt to get on different ships. McColm returned to the docks where he seized an opportunity to board the SS *Tarnan*, and stowed away amongst some auxiliary steering gear in the stern. The subsequent events are described by McColm in the book *Detour*, recording possibly the most unfortunate capture ever to befall an escaped prisoner of war.

> Only the box-covering of the steering gear on the stern of a Swedish ship – but almost Heaven! I think of the thirteen days that have passed since the tunnel was opened and the camp lights left behind – days of glorious freedom and excitement before reaching Lübeck; of that never-to-be-forgotten moment when foot was first set on a neutral ship; of the search for a hiding place; of the days and nights spent crouched in the steering box before the ship sailed; of hard beating heart every time a footstep sounded nearby; of sailing and my efforts to avoid the ever moving steering quadrant as the ship negotiated the numerous river bends; of the disappearance of flat pine covered Baltic shores into the dimness of the dusk.
>
> And now the moment has arrived, the moment when captivity is to be nothing but a memory. Now I dare to dream – dreams of home; dreams kaleidoscopic in their content; dreams beyond description – fading gradually into sleep of exhaustion.
>
> Then noise – a voice – an awakening. Back to reality, to contact with a frightened Captain who insists on returning me to German hands. Back to Germany. Back to captivity.
>
> And why? Because I snored!

McColm's snoring had indeed alerted a deck hand, and he was taken to the Captain. Although the ship was eighty miles out to sea the Captain told him that he would be handed over to the German pilot when he came aboard in the morning. There were heavy penalties for neutrals who helped prisoners to escape. Swedish ships were under German pilotage and escort because of the minefields, and the Captain ordered that the ship be turned around and anchored near the German watch-ship. The next morning, 1 September, a German pilot came on board and McColm was duly handed over.

He was placed on the German watch-ship, but even then he tried to escape by stealing a motor boat moored to the ship. However he was caught in the act and closely guarded from then on. Later that day a supply boat came alongside and he was taken to Warnemünde and handed over to the Luftwaffe.

Two days later McColm was taken back to Stalag Luft I, where he was sentenced to 34 days in solitary confinement for his attempted escape. He found out that Charlie Lockett was also in the cells; he had been picked up before his ship had left the wharf at Lübeck. They had only served five days of their sentence when they were moved to Oflag XC, ironically located at Lübeck, where they were placed in the cells until 8 October 1941, when the two of them were taken by train to Oflag IVC, Colditz.

Once in Colditz McColm kept himself relatively fit playing volley ball, stool ball (a rugged game devised by Colditz POWs incorporating the rules of several sports) and rugby, and also exercised with a medicine ball. He was billeted with his escaping chum Charlie Lockett, Squadron Leader Geoffery Stephenson, and Major Wood of the Royal Engineers. In the evenings he loved playing bridge, and at other times he was busy teaching English to a French POW, Captain Andre Perrin, who in turn tutored McColm in French. He suffered a little from an ulcerated stomach, and was hospitalised in Colditz on several occasions.

In October 1942 McColm assisted Pat Reid, Hank Wardle, Billie

Stephens and Ron Littledale in the incredible escape which saw the foursome make successful 'home runs' into Switzerland.

Ralph Holroyd grew up in Sydney during the Depression with its attendant dearth of career opportunities. There was little money in the family coffers to encourage him while at school in the sports he loved – grade cricket and football – so he turned instead to athletics.

Leaving school, he was apprenticed to his local pharmacist, hoping to pursue a commercial course. He left this position when a vacancy occurred with a leading firm of commercial photographers, and started work with them as a junior in their darkroom. The experience would later prove very useful in Colditz. He combined study with his work and eventually became an accountant with the firm.

An adventurous youth with a passion for the great outdoors, Ralph was fond of sailing, skiff racing and offshore cruising in the summer months. He joined the army when war became imminent but got bogged down as an infantry instructor. After some difficulty he was finally given his 'NX' (New South Wales) number for overseas service, but had to drop rank back to sergeant in order to be posted overseas with the first reinforcements of the 2/2nd Battalion. He regained his commission soon after, as adjutant to a large body of men on the *Aquitania*.

Then followed months of training in Palestine and Egypt, almost to the point of becoming stale, but Ralph Holroyd was relieved to be among the first soldiers to go into North Africa's western desert. One day the famed war correspondent and photographer Frank Hurley snapped a photograph of Holroyd opening Lord Mayor's Comfort Fund parcels outside Solum and this photo became widely known back in Australia when it was used on posters encouraging greater contributions.

Holroyd was involved in the fighting in Bardia and Tobruk, and was Mentioned in Despatches for his part in the action. His battalion was then rekitted and crossed the Mediterranean to Piraeus, the port of Athens, where they entrained on 26 March 1941 and proceeded north to relieve positions held by the Greeks. They advanced as far as the mountains overlooking the Albanian border, which were partially covered in snow, sent their transport back and marched by night to take up a defensive position in the lee of Mount Olympus.

Here, within the Vale of Tempe, was a pass offering a way through the mountains from Larissa, the largest city of the Thessaly region, to the Aegean coast. On 17 April 1941, given the strategic importance of the pass, the 2/2nd Battalion was ordered to Tempe Gorge to confront a formidable enemy force. Under the command of Lieutenant-Colonel Fred Chilton, the battalion had orders to hold the western end of the gorge in an attempt to prevent German troops and armaments from outflanking Allied positions through the surrounding hills.

Meanwhile the 21st New Zealand Battalion, under Colonel Neil Lloyd Macky, had suffered substantial losses during German attacks at Platamon, on the coast of the Aegean Sea, and their line had been broken in fierce, close combat. Colonel Macky was ordered to retreat his battalion inland and regroup at Tempe Gorge to assist in defending the gorge and prevent German infantry troops and Panzer divisions from passing through to Larissa. As part of their strategy to stall the German advance, battalion engineers were charged with blocking a railway line on the northern side of the gorge, as well as a road on the southern side. They successfully blocked a railway tunnel by removing the wheels from a boxcar and blowing the rail tracks on either side of it, destroyed and mined sections of the road, and blew up a railway bridge crossing a narrow defile.

That night, in hopes of preventing a flanking attack by the German 6th Mountain Division, the 2/2nd Battalion had dug in near the exit of the gorge at Tempe Village, and further back near the village of Gonnos. Their position was somewhat strengthened at dawn by the arrival of soldiers from a battle-depleted 2/3rd Infantry Battalion. Now numbering around 1,500 men, the Australian and New Zealand troops were ordered to hold the gorge until at least 19 April to allow the ordered retreat of the 16th Brigade forces through Larissa. Under instructions to hold as long as they could 'if necessary to extinction' (according to later reports), their transport was driven away to ensure they did just that. That same evening the first German tank trundled up the gorge and was met with concentrated anti-tank and mortar fire.

Unfortunately the demolition work carried out by New Zealand engineers proved to be of minimal effect, as German and Austrian mountain troops began to surge over the top of the pass the following morning. Despite suffering a heavy number of casualties they soon overran the vanguard of gallant defenders in what has become known as the Battle of Tempe Gorge. Tanks from the 2nd Panzer Division found they could successfully ford the swollen river, albeit turret-deep, and were able to flank the gorge to the west of the Australians, followed by vast numbers of German infantry troops. Fighting then broke out at the village of Gonnos and quickly spread.

The Allies now started to take heavy fire, and their casualty count rose alarmingly. Although they managed to destroy three Panzer tanks, it rapidly became a one-sided battle, as the soldiers had no artillery or air support, and were only armed with rifles,

Bren guns and mortars, and 2-pound anti-tank guns. They were facing insurmountable odds, both in numbers and equipment. As well as outnumbering the Allied soldiers, the Germans employed a Panzer battalion of around 100 tanks, heavy machine guns, and a much larger and superior artillery force. They also had the added advantage of Stuka dive-bomber aircraft and Messerschmitt fighters, which continually bombed and strafed the Allied defence lines.

As the fighting continued, the 2/2nd Battalion's D Company reported that large enemy forces, about two battalions in strength, were moving towards the south-east and south-west of the Pinius River in a three-pronged advance. In response, Colonel Chilton despatched units to the area in an attempt to prevent these troops from crossing the river. In the ensuing exchange of fire, the battalion's Bren carrier commander was killed, along with his driver. Four others were wounded.

Two soldiers who maintained covering fire in another nearby action were later awarded the Military Medal for gallantry. A second platoon commander was wounded along with three others, one mortally. As the battalion's history records:

> Meanwhile on the far right, C [Company] under Platoon Commander Lt. Holroyd had been in action and had defeated several German attempts to cross the river. Further to the right, pressure was increasing on the front, held by the New Zealand 21st Battalion, who were under heavy mortar fire and were holding off enemy attempts to cross the river.

Despite heavy losses, an increasing number of enemy troops were able to make their way across the ruined rail bridge. The Allied defences soon began to crumble. Realising the hopelessness of the situation, and to prevent further losses in what was shaping up as a final assault on their defences, Colonel Chilton reluctantly gave the order to withdraw, and then it became a matter of every man for himself. While some groups and individuals managed to scramble to safety and make their way to the coast, initially chased by streams of German bullets, shells and mortar bombs, the remaining Australian and New Zealand defenders were eventually overwhelmed and taken prisoner.

While the Germans were victorious in the Battle of Tempe Gorge, their losses were huge. They had also failed in their strategic aim, which was to prevent the escape of some 10,000 British soldiers in the Olympus sector through Larissa, who would set up a new defensive line at Thermopylae. Their capture (or even slaughter) had been thwarted by the resistance of the Australian and New Zealand forces. Sadly, in the process, the 2/2nd Infantry Battalion was virtually wiped out as an organised fighting force.

Around four o'clock on the afternoon of 18 April, Ralph Holroyd was directing machine-gun fire during the bloody skirmish when he suffered a crippling wound to his right heel, caused by a stray and (fortunately) almost-spent machine-gun bullet that ricocheted off a rock, badly damaging the bone structure in his heel. Corporal John Cyril Gleeson saw Ralph fall and assisted him into some cover where he dressed the bloody foot as best he could before calling for a runner to help the wounded lieutenant hop back towards a gully some 100 yards behind. Ralph was unable to walk, let alone run, and all too soon he was one of those rounded up, becoming a reluctant prisoner of the enemy forces.

Once the battle was at an end, the wounded from both sides were moved to rudimentary field dressing stations, where German soldiers were being attended to first. By the time Allied troops were able to receive medical treatment the injuries of many had deteriorated even further, with potentially deadly septicaemia and other bacterial infections setting in for several of the more seriously injured.

Together with other wounded soldiers, Ralph was finally transported to a field dressing station where his heel was cursorily treated. Another ambulance then took a number of wounded prisoners to the nearby town of Katerini, where Ralph was transferred onto a crowded fishing vessel manned by German marines. The vessel carried him over five days to the port city of Salonika, known as the second city of Greece, situated on the Gulf of Themai. Once there, he was placed in a guarded ward in an overcrowded general hospital located on the campus of Anatolia College, the administration building of which now served as the headquarters of the German army. Here he was finally given some treatment to his badly injured foot. Each night, he witnessed dead bodies being carried out of the ward.

One of the examining doctors discovered that, as a result of his wound, Ralph was suffering the early stages of osteomyelitis – a potentially serious infection of the bone. The infection was slowly spreading into his leg, and though it was treatable, the standard procedure at this overworked hospital was to amputate the affected limb. Fortunately for him, a Greek doctor looking after the ward had studied in Vienna, so in desperation Ralph talked to him in German and managed to convince the man he should try draining the abscessed parts rather than just perfunctorily chopping off the whole right leg. This procedure was carried out and the primary infection was arrested before it took hold in the bones in his leg.

As Ralph slowly recovered from his wound, and with nothing but time on his hands, he began mulling over ways to shorten his captivity and escape. During weeks of exercise aimed at getting his shrunken tendon to work reasonably well, he also made contact with some of the local townspeople, most of whom were quite sympathetic to the Allies. They came to the hospital as staff, orderlies, nurses' aides and partly trained volunteers. His plans began to come together, and with the help of two courageous women he devised a scheme to simply walk out of the hospital. The women's father, George Sgouros, was a trained surgeon, and he agreed to look after Ralph if he could somehow find a way out of the hospital. Being classified as a bed patient the guards at the door of the ward were not as watchful as they might have been, which worked in Ralph's favour.

On the appointed day, the women smuggled in some civilian clothing which he donned over his uniform while a small diversion was taking place, and when the visitors left he boldly strolled out with them. Still hobbling, Ralph quickly made his way by prearrangement through the old town of Salonika to the apartment home of the George Sgouros and his family. As he remained hidden in an attic back room over the next two months the kindly surgeon would continue to tend his injured leg, keeping the wound clean and dressed and reducing the inflammation.

With the first part of Ralph's escape plan successfully completed, the next step entailed finding and commandeering a caique – a Greek fishing boat – and sailing by night from one island shelter to another until he reached the Turkish coast. Subtle enquiries were made on his behalf, but things became even more difficult for him and his helpers when it was discovered that the Germans were far from pleased with his disappearance from hospital, and placed a bounty of 200,000 drachmas on him, dead or alive. It was not long before an informant decided to claim the reward and gave the Germans the information they needed. A house-to-house search ensued in the street.

On 9 October 1941, as Ralph was in the middle of his morning shave, German troops burst into the apartment and he was surrounded. He tried to deny he was the wanted fugitive, but a search soon uncovered his Australian uniform, and the game was up. He was dragged out of the house and marched down the street, leaving a terrified family behind him.

Following his interrogation by the Gestapo, Ralph was taken to another hospital – this time not a civilian facility, by one run by the German army. By comparison, this hospital was damaged and in bad repair, with conditions that could only be described as filthy. Lice and bed bugs swarmed through the meagre beds in plague proportions. Despite this, one of his chief concerns was the immediate fate of the surgeon and his family who had kept him hidden and looked after him for all that time.

It would not be until after the war that Ralph learned what had happened to the family after he had been captured. It came in the form of a letter from Lysandre Sgouros, the son of the surgeon, who was following in his father's footsteps and studying medicine. In his letter, he told of the bitter hardships experienced in occupied Greece during the war, and was seeking Ralph's help in acting as a guarantor for him to come to Australia and pursue his medical career. He wrote that after Ralph had been taken away, his father George Sgouros had been sent to prison for aiding and sheltering a fugitive prisoner of war, while their home and all their possessions had been confiscated. The elderly man suffered badly in prison; he became deaf, and his health deteriorated badly. After 21 months of captivity he was finally released following repeated attacks of malaria, returning to a life of family poverty and suffering. Despite his best efforts, in his poor physical condition and deaf, he could no longer find work as a hospital surgeon. During his time as a POW, Ralph was able to send an occasional food parcel to the family who had risked so much to help and shelter him. Post-war, he explored various official channels to see if there was any possibility of securing some financial aid for the family, but none was forthcoming. He continued to send food parcels to the family, but as a man of modest means after the war, there was precious little he could afford to do, let alone go guarantor for Lysandre. It was an incredibly sad postscript to his war experiences.

On 10 October, much to their relief, Ralph and several other wounded prisoners were removed from the hospital and herded aboard a troop train heading north from Salonika to Upper Silesia in south-western Poland. It proved to be a nightmarish journey of ten days, subsisting on a meagre four-day ration of food, and occasional Red Cross handouts of bread and soup at wayside stations along the way. As recorded in his diary, the train journey took them through Romania, Yugoslavia, Croatia, Hungary and Austria, before crossing the border into Germany on 17 October at Regensburg. From there the train continued through Nuremburg, Chemnitz, Riesa, Breslau and Oppeln in southern Poland, before arriving at their final destination: the POW camp of Stalag VIIIB (later renamed Stalag 344) located near the small Silesian town of Lamsdorf.

At the same time Ralph was enduring the crowded rail trip to Lamsdorf, an official postcard he had sent to his father – possibly written whilst he was in hospital in Salonika – arrived at his parents' home in Mosman on 14 October. It was a pre-printed card stating that the sender was a prisoner of war in good health. The card was signed by

Ralph in his unmistakable handwriting over his hand-printed name, rank and the AIF designation. It arrived with his father Charles well before any official army notification of his status. That notice, in the form of a telegram, arrived two months later on Christmas Eve, 1941.

Following a period of interrogation, Ralph was admitted to the camp hospital (lazaretto), which comprised of eleven concrete buildings set apart from the main POW compound. Six of these buildings were self-contained wards, each capable of housing one hundred patients, and the hospital contained surprisingly adequate facilities and was fully equipped. Although headed by a German officer, the hospital staff was entirely made up of prisoners with skilled medical experience, including surgeons, radiologists and general physicians. Ralph was eventually admitted to the lazaretto on 4 November, where he received some thorough medical treatment four days later. After X-rays had been taken of his fractured heel, he would undergo an operation on 17 November, performed under anaesthetic by New Zealand surgeon Major Alfred Slater to clear localised bone infection, mend other damage, and restore normal function to his heel. Then the slow process of walking and rehabilitation could begin.

Although he was in the hands of a top-flight surgeon, Ralph knew that the man was extremely busy, carrying out an exhausting number of emergency operations that day. 'Expect instruments to be all gory and blunt by the time my turn comes,' Ralph noted in his diary. At 3pm he was given an injection of morphine in his bed, but remained conscious. Half an hour later he received an injection of the medication atropine in lieu of ether, and would only recall counting up to 18 before he fell unconscious. When he woke the following morning, slightly dizzy, he realised the operation had been a success. There was no longer any pain in his injured foot, and a pair of crutches stood by his bed. He soon began the slow process of rehabilitation and building up his strength once again through walking ever longer distances. Shortly after, his army papers finally caught up with him and he received a 14-day spell in solitary for his two escape bids.

Ralph Holroyd was of mixed parentage; his father was Australian and his mother German. She had been visiting relatives in Schleswig Holstein when Hitler invaded Poland, and had been forced to stay in Germany by the authorities. Eventually she found out through her husband back in Australia that her son was a POW in Germany, so she began to make enquiries. Someone took notice, and it was soon arranged for Ralph to be interviewed as a potential spy for the Fatherland.

He was put up in a comfortable apartment in Berlin along with a British artillery sergeant, treated to good food, and was allowed occasional guarded walks, accompanied by two NCOs and an unfriendly dog. After two weeks, on 16 March, the two of them had some visitors – two smooth civilians, accompanied by a Luftwaffe officer. Being slightly senior Holroyd was interviewed first, but after just twenty minutes he was dismissed as being uncooperative, having given false answers to all of the questions, and having no leanings at all towards collusion. He was sent back to his room, and his roommate was interviewed for two hours. He managed to string the interviewer along for a while, but in the end he too was dismissed as uncooperative. They later learned, much to their astonishment, that the smooth civilian was none other than 'Lord Haw Haw' William Joyce, later executed in England for his treasonable exploits.

Since Holroyd was not sufficiently appreciative of Berlin's hospitality he was escorted onto a train by an officer and an NCO, ready to resume his life as a POW. They stopped overnight at

Dresden, and in the morning resumed their travels. At the end of this particular train journey was Oflag IVC, Colditz.

Without any doubt the most enigmatic of the Australians to set foot in Colditz was Vincent 'Bush' Parker. A man of considerable mechanical talent, ingenuity and courage, it was Bush who played a leading role in almost all of the British escape attempts from the castle walls. His expertise in mastering even the most difficult of locks proved invaluable in giving passage where it was previously denied, and access where it was meant to be impossible. Bush Parker deserves a book of his own, for his escapades were many, his enterprise unequalled, and his lighter side, as a magician and cardsharp, still talked about with amazement. Jerry Wood in his Colditz book *Detour* accords Bush Parker the following tribute:

> His facility at picking locks had to be seen to be believed. He would get through any door irrespective of where it was or how heavily it seemed to be guarded. It was only necessary to divert the sentry's attention momentarily for Bush to noiselessly unlock the door and slip through. Usually he would first of all have to make a key of some old bit of metal. At one time or another his skill was needed on nearly all escape attempts. It enabled needed and as yet uncensored parcels to be stolen from the German Censor Office. Ever cheerful, he was one of the best athletes of the camp.

'Bush', as he would become known in the RAF, was born in Durham, England, on 11 February 1919, the youngest of three sons. A difficult birth left his mother in a weakened state and she died when he was only a few months old. His father, grief-stricken, did not know how he was going to bring up or support yet another youngster. However help was at hand, for his wife's older married sister Edith offered to adopt the boy and raise him. His father agreed after a time that it would be for the best, and the infant legally became the Parkers' only son at the age of 18 months.

In 1928 Vincent and his parents Jack and Edith emigrated to a new life in Australia, intending to live and work with his mother's other sister and her husband. This couple, the Biles, lived in a tiny fruit farming settlement called Bilyana, midway between Townsville and Cairns. But misfortune and ruin struck the area in the shape of a devastating cyclone while the Parkers were still sailing out from England, and when they arrived their dreams and new home were gone. Jack Parker was able to get work as a fettler on a line gang with the Queensland Railways and worked at nearby Rungoo. Meanwhile he sent his wife and young Vincent to a less primitive life in Townsville. Here, for a while, Edith took in washing and ironing and did domestic work to keep them in food and clothing. In 1929 she became station mistress at Purono, and Jack was able to transfer to be with his family at the small rail siding known as Nineteen Mile.

Young Vincent grew into a sturdy, robust and handsome youth, who adored the splendour and vastness of the land around him. He attended the Bohleville State School where he impressed the sole teacher, Jessie Hooper, with his agile mind. Combined with his scholarly accomplishments was a devilish sense of humour, an ability to perform amusing feats of magic, and a vast repertoire of card tricks. Much to the chagrin of Miss Hooper her prize student could also be the most frustrating and distractive, but it was hard to chide such a popular and hard-working youth.

Apart from an incredible agility on roller skates and a burgeoning interest in photography and acrobatics, Vincent loved animals. A pony given to him by his parents was shown attention rarely seen in those parts, and they became almost inseparable. Vincent would spend hours teaching Bluey to respond in different ways to a series of whistles, and the animal in turn would play to a rapt audience of local kids; turning, playing dead and stamping out numbers.

After leaving school Vincent moved down to the city of Townsville and took a job with Kodak. It was during this time that his flair for acrobatics set him on the road to a possible career in show business. A former friend, George Watson, recalls that one day a piece of invoice paper was caught in a gust of wind from an open door and blew out of the office window to the footpath, eight feet below. Vincent sprang out of the window, executed a perfect somersault and landing, and retrieved the document. A promoter from a nearby department store happened to witness this extraordinary action and called in to see the youth later that day. After watching Vincent readily perform some more of his acrobatics and sleight-of-hand tricks the promoter asked him to take on a job as a showman at his store, which he accepted.

While he was working at the store a visiting magician from New Zealand known as 'The Great Levante' caught his act, and saw great potential in the confident, cocky young entertainer. He asked Vincent to travel with him to New Zealand and join his company of travelling magicians after honing his skills a little. The lad was thrilled at the prospect, much more so than his parents when he told them, but they finally agreed that he could go. And so, at the age of eighteen, Vincent took leave of his family and travelled to New Zealand.

Once there he applied himself to learning the higher skills of the professional magicians, but after several months decided that it was not the life for him. Returning to Sydney he worked at a few jobs before successfully obtaining a billet as a steward on the passenger liner *Ontranto*. He journeyed to England in this capacity, then returned to Brisbane as linen-keeper aboard the same vessel. He then returned to England on the ship and travelled across to Durham and the home of his original family. He stayed with them from October 1938 to February the following year.

By now he had begun reading about the young men who were training as pilots with the RAF, and the more he read, the more determined he was to apply. His two older brothers, both fighter pilots, were the ultimate decider, so he cabled his mother in Townsville both to seek her permission and to ask her if she would send him the necessary money to put him through RAF flying school, to which she agreed. He entered a special air training school to undergo a three-month course which he passed in just six weeks. He was appointed Acting Pilot Officer in July of that year and posted to No. 234 Fighter Squadron.

On 15 August, now a full Pilot Officer, he took off in his Spitfire from Middle Wallop field to intercept some German Me 110s. He managed to destroy two of the bombers before he was shot down, and had to bale out 900 feet above the English Channel. The Germans ran a highly efficient sea rescue service, and within four hours he was picked up by speed boat and taken to Cherbourg. He had been wounded in the shoulder, and was given medical treatment before he was flown the next day to the Luftwaffe transit camp of Dulag Luft in a Junkers Ju 52. Here he was interrogated, and given the usual spurious Red Cross forms to complete, but he only filled out his name, rank and service number. He was kept in a cell for three days, and then allowed into the main camp.

Bush was only kept in Dulag Luft for five months, but in that time he was involved in digging two tunnels. His companions in these ventures were Lieutenant-Commander James Buckley and Lieutenant Peter Butterworth of the Royal Navy (who later became a well-known film comedian, appearing in several *Carry On* movies), Captain Griffiths (a flying Marine), and Squadron Leader Roger Bushell. A feisty and determined pilot from South Africa, Bushell was later sent to Stalag Luft III where he formed the massive 'X' organisation, overseeing the construction of three massive tunnels. In March 1944, seventy-six officers escaped through one of the tunnels and fifty were shot dead upon recapture. Bushell was one of the Great Escapers murdered by the Gestapo. But that was three years away at this time.

To his annoyance Parker was removed from Dulag Luft in February before the tunnels were completed, and he was transferred to Stalag Luft I, an air force camp in Barth, where once again he was involved in escaping plans. The tunnelling team was now headed by Buckley, together with Squadron Leader 'Pappy' Plant of the RAF, and Peter Fanshawe, RN. Bush was not only involved in tunnelling activities, but also busied himself making compasses for intending escapers. These were made from a magnetic razor and a magnet taken from the back of a German loudspeaker in the camp. He was caught digging in one of the tunnels and given fourteen days in the camp cells.

In June 1941 he became one of the camp 'ghosts'. This meant concealing himself inside the camp and remaining hidden for as long as possible. The Germans would assume that officers who disappeared in this way had escaped from the camp, and their records would be adjusted accordingly. The 'ghosts' could then be used at Appells to cover absences due to tunnelling, or even to conceal the escape of someone who had gotten free of the camp. Parker and his fellow 'ghost', Flight Lieutenant Dakeyne, made plans to slip away during a count, and after six weeks were all but ready. Unfortunately the ferrets caught them during a surprise search of their hut, trapping them in the roof where they were hidden. For this they were given ten days further detention in the cells. Not to be deterred, Parker (now with the rank of Flight Lieutenant) made another bold bid in January 1942, as he recounted in *Detour*.

> It was just another idea. The football field, which was in another compound next to ours, was covered with snow, two feet deep in places. The Camp Kommandant must have been rather surprised when we asked for permission to play rugger as it hadn't been used for several weeks. Permission was granted but the football hour was changed from 4pm–5pm to 2pm–3pm; quite an obstacle as you will see. Only players were allowed in the playing compound, 31 for rugger and 23 for soccer. Players were lined up, counted, then taken through three gates. The field itself was controlled by two towers and two guards who patrolled the wire. A Spitfire pilot had been shot and killed here three weeks before, having cut the wire from his compound and attempting to crawl across the playing field at night.
>
> Two games were necessary before a furrow was carefully made in the snow about the size of a man's body – then the big game arrived. I'd read about sheep buried under snow for three weeks and surviving, so decided that I could last six hours all right; you see it meant a wait from 2.30 until 8.30, when it was quite dark. We succeeded in faking the count, getting an extra man among

> the players, and the game started. I had two pairs of trousers, two jackets, four pairs of socks and numerous layers of underclothing on and hardly moved in the first half.
>
> Immediately after half time we got a scrum over the furrow, I slipped through the scrum, slipped a sort of white periscope gadget over my face and lay full length in the trench to be covered over with snow by the front row forwards. The scrum half followed the ball in and adjusted everything perfectly leaving my small periscope just clear of the snow; my only track of time was to count the changes of guards when they marched by. Those six hours were an eternity, my legs grew wet, ached and became numb; I couldn't move. As I broke to the surface the breaking of snow seemed like the crackling of artillery. I was still in the searchlight beam and made slow going to the wire as the searchlights swept over me several times. I reached the wire and lay very still, for the patrolling sentry approached, he paused, stopped, then suddenly screamed and ran towards me. He didn't shoot and I was taken to the cells.
>
> What we had not accounted for was the fact that I would steam, my warm and wet body was condensing in the cool night air. The guard told me afterwards that he couldn't make out where the 'smoke' was coming from.

By now Parker was determined to get away, and within a few days of being released from the cells he was at it once again, this time disguised as one of the ferrets named Charlie Piltz. He was dressed in a pair of dirty overalls similar to those worn by the security personnel, and carried a dummy torch made out of Red Cross tins. In his overalls pockets was a pass stating that he was an Italian worker, a camp-made compass, and a map he had traced. He managed to fool the sentries and easily passed out through the camp gates. Parker then headed off towards the woods, but his freedom was short-lived. He ran straight into Piltz – the man he was impersonating – was arrested, and given another fourteen days in the cells. Immediately upon release he was sent to Stalag Luft III at Sagan, from where the mass break-out known as the Great Escape would later take place. Here, true to form, he attempted yet another escape.

> I arrived at Stalag Luft III in March 1942, and started my own tunnel assisted by a large number of others, including Flight Lieutenants Casey, Panton and Dickinson, but it was discovered before completion. While serving ten days in cells after having been caught in the Vorlager while attempting to escape, I took a key from a door while exercising and altered it with a nail file to fit the lock of my cell. While Flight Lieutenant Dickinson, also in cells, diverted the guard's attention, I opened the door, jumped out of the window, and climbed over the wire. I was wearing RAF trousers and a grey sweater, but had no escape equipment or food with me.
>
> I walked to Sagan station and jumped onto a goods train as it was pulling out of the shunting yard, and got as far as a shunting yard in the suburbs of Chemnitz hidden in one of the wagons. There I jumped out as the train was stationary and hid in a wood all day. The next night I climbed onto another goods train stationary in the same yard, and travelled to Grünburg where I again got out in a shunting yard, about dawn, and stole a bicycle. I rode the bicycle for two nights towards Poland, hiding by day, and managed to steal a loaf of black bread from a farmhouse one night by climbing in through the kitchen window.
>
> I then discarded the cycle as it had a flat tyre and climbed onto another goods train in the yard at Zulichau on the Polish frontier,

> but while climbing from one truck to another to get into one going to Warsaw, where I intended to get help, I was seen and caught by the station police.
>
> I was taken back to Stalag Luft III where I was given twenty days in the cells. I was put in a cell with Dickinson and we managed to get two saws smuggled in by orderlies with which we started to cut the bars fitted to the cell window. Our work was discovered by German guards, and we were both sent to Oflag IVC (Colditz).
>
> While serving this sentence for my attempted escape I tried to bribe one of the guards to obtain some tools. He reported me, and I was given another ten days' confinement.

Ever persistent, Parker and Dickinson were straight into escaping activities as soon as they were released. This time they joined forces with some of the old Colditz hands, 'Rex' Harrison, Dick Howe, 'Lulu' Lawton and 'Scarlet' O'Hara, who were making an exploratory hole in the roof in one of the attics. One day, however, their stooges did not act quickly enough when some guards approached the area, and they were caught red-handed.

Once out of the cells for this attempt, Parker started to concentrate on lock-picking and the making of keys, until he had made one for every lock in the castle. His keys were made out of coal shovels, bed iron and coat hooks.

One of his side interests was as a director of the British Distillery Monopoly, which manufactured relatively drinkable alcohol from all manner of foodstuffs. The other directors were the Dutchman van Rood, and 'Bag' Dickinson. The three men operated bigger and better stills over the years, and even found a use for the awful dyed sugar beet waste which arrived in barrel-loads as our 'jam'. The trio distilled it, and distilled it again, and the result was described by Pat Reid in *The Latter Days.*

> The distillers transformed half a dozen casks into vats, where the 'jam' fermented, giving off a foul smell. The ferment was distilled to produce 'Jam-Alc'. It tasted of old rubber tyres. The Company conscientiously tried to improve its quality but, experiment how they would, even after three distillations, 'Jam-Alc' still tasted of rubber.
>
> In spite of this gastronomic disability it had a ready sale, at a low rate of exchange – for instance, three bottles of Jam-Alc for a bucket of coal – among a clientele who seemed to be able to stomach it without immediate undue ill effects.

One of Parker's closest friends in Colditz was Canadian RAF Flight Lieutenant Don 'Weasel' Donaldson, and he still recalls his Aussie chum with admiration and respect.

> We became close friends during our stay at Colditz, and got to know each other rather well. And still, for as well as I knew him and understood his character, I knew very little of his past …
>
> When I first saw him I thought how strikingly handsome he was in spite of his unkempt state. He was a rugged individual, quite tall with handsome features and thick black hair. His good looks and loud way of talking made him outstanding in a crowd. Bush liked to talk a lot and seized every opportunity to be the orator. He desperately needed companionship and was constantly seeking it.
>
> Between our living quarters and the attics in Colditz there were massive steel doors festooned with cruciform locks. Each lock

contained 27 tumblers. These attics were the perfect place to hide our forbidden articles, and it had been our burning desire to get to them. There were always those massive doors to stop us. The very first time Bush saw the locks he announced to one and all that they posed no problem. As this was a top priority job we eagerly encouraged him to unlock those barriers.

The scene was just like you have seen time and again in the movies; three desperate men up in a dusty old attic with very poor light; all concentrating on that door. A tube of toothpaste was the only equipment Bush had. With his ear pressed against the door he cautiously worked the locks. When a tumbler would lift he injected toothpaste to hold it in the open position. Finally he had manoeuvred all of the tumblers the right ways and the door swung open.

Excitement ran high when word of our success spread throughout the camp. We had numerous activities planned for the attics. However, there were more problems to deal with. The doors were in a restricted area and the guards often conducted surprise searches and counts. Our chief concern was not to be caught near those doors. Within a week Bush could master a lock in 30 seconds without using the toothpaste. From that time on, he was kept busy opening locks and letting us into our secret hideaway. From there we received and broadcast messages, and even worked on a glider. Bush informed us that the lock had never been made that he couldn't open. After watching his demonstration on the doors, we all heartily agreed.

Bush was not only a wizard with locks, he was also a sleight-of-hand artist. Whenever a few of us would get together for a bull session he would go into his act. One of his favourite tricks was to pull a cigarette from someone's ear. As cigarettes were very scarce it was considered clever to find one in the conventional way, let alone

> in the ear of one of the audience! Usually we were informed of an impending search through our underground services. However, one day the guards rushed in and made us stand against the wall, five feet apart. I was horrified to see Bush had a hand full of small tools, and all he had to cover them with was a towel. As he was being searched he kept moving the towel hiding the tools from one hand to another. To everyone's amazement the Germans didn't seem to notice; they finished searching him and went on to the next prisoner. It took exceptional composure to behave as Bush had.
>
> He was an outstanding hero among fellow prisoners. I feel fortunate indeed to have had Bush's friendship during those traumatic years at Colditz.

Bush had an incredible memory for intricate details – extremely useful when playing cards. He combined his memory and conjuring ability with mesmeric skills, and he had the most fascinating array of card tricks I have ever seen. The way he rigged a pack of cards during the shuffle was completely undetectable, seeming to create whatever hands he wished at will. But let me make one thing perfectly clear; despite these skills Bush never cheated anybody when money was on the table. On many occasions he would purposely rig a pack as part of an intricate joke on someone, but he never took advantage of his friends – it was just against his grain.

The one person he had tremendous admiration for was legless air ace Douglas Bader, who had been sent to Colditz following several escape attempts, and the two men really got on well. Both were Spitfire pilots and fiercely independent. At the same time they had a healthy respect for the other man's abilities. They would often be seen deep in conversation during walks around the courtyard, Bush waving his hands around as he talked, while Bader stumped along beside him with the rolling gait he had developed, a smile on his face and wreathed in smoke from the pipe firmly jammed into the side of his mouth. The only time there would be any conflict between the two was at the card table, over a game of bridge. Bush, with his phenomenally good memory was a hard man to beat. Sometimes when you played cards with him you would catch his eye, and a friendly smirk would tell you that the cards you were so carefully concealing were an open book to him. It was terribly disconcerting. Bader, on the other hand, simply hated losing at cards. He just couldn't accept defeat in anything – particularly a game of chance – and when he lost at bridge he would growl and mutter and get terribly upset; not at the others, but at himself.

On one occasion Bush was partnering Mike Wittet against the pairing of Bader and Guy German. It was a marathon game, and the latter team was slipping behind on points. Guy German was philosophical about it all, but Bader was getting quite annoyed with himself. It came Parker's turn to deal, and as he straightened the cards to shuffle he caught Wittet's eye across the table and gave him a sly wink. He took his time over the shuffle, while Bader huffed and puffed and drummed his fingers on the table with impatience. All eyes were on the deck of cards, as Bush always made shuffling into a masterful spectacle, fanning, dividing and layering the cards with remarkable dexterity. He dealt the bridge hands, and Bader picked up his cards with a grunt. The annoyance fled from his face and the game progressed much more satisfactorily from his (and everyone's) point of view. Every so often he would get a marvellous hand, and he became far more boisterous. 'Got you here, old boy!' he would thunder, slapping his hand down with unconcealed delight.

He was the only one at that table who did not realise that these phenomenally good hands only seem to come when Bush was dealing! He never woke up to the fact, but I'm sure if he had he would have cut Bush cold, and probably ignored him from that day on. Needless to say, they remained friends throughout.

Bush certainly was an enigmatic character. His persistence in trying to escape, his manipulative and mechanical skills, his consummate dexterity as a conjurer – all were an integral part of this amazing person. As Pat Reid once said, 'Colditz would not have been quite what it was if Bush had not been there.'

8

Home Run

THERE WAS ONE AUSTRALIAN OFFICER in Colditz I would never meet for the simple reason that he had successfully escaped from there nine months before our arrival, and made it back safely to England. Tragically, he would die test-flying an aircraft just three months later.

Hedley Nevile (Bill) Fowler was born in London on 8 June 1916. His father was a Paymaster-Commander in the Royal Navy, while his mother Florence was the grand-daughter of Sir Henry Ayers, a Premier of South Australia with the distinction of having Australia's monolithic landmark Ayers Rock (also known as Uluru) named after him.

The family moved to South Australia in 1920 and settled in Adelaide but temporarily returned to England in 1924 so Bill, their only child, could attend Rugby School. This done, they returned home to Australia in 1933. Flying was something Bill had yearned to do since childhood and in 1936 he enlisted in the Royal Australian Air Force. He was seconded for service in the RAF the following year.

Once in England, and following further training, Bill was assigned to No. 3 (Gladiator) Squadron. Like several others he was allowed to retain his dark-blue RAAF uniform. At gunnery school he struck up a friendship with fellow Australian Leslie Clisby, who would blaze a brief but spectacular trail of glory in the skies over France. Because they both wore the RAAF uniform the two friends quickly became known as 'the Diggers'. Clisby would later go on to shoot down sixteen enemy aircraft – thirteen of them in the last five days of his life – before he was killed after destroying two Me 110 fighters.

Coincidentally he was shot down on the same day as Bill Fowler.

In October 1939, Fowler was posted to No. 615 Auxiliary Squadron (Churchill's Own) and flew to France in mid-November. On the morning of 15 May 1940, he found himself flying 'tail-end Charlie' with five other pilots, providing high escort for bombers sent to destroy bridges over the Meuse River. Over the three previous days he had shot down two Me 109s and a Do 17.

Just before midday he noticed a pair of Me 109s hurtling at their formation out of the blinding sun. A hail of bullets and fiery tracers slammed into Fowler's Hurricane, and flames erupted beneath his shattered instrument panel. He also noticed his boots were on fire, so he tipped the doomed fighter over and allowed himself to fall out, landing under his parachute near a small stream in the forest of Ardennes.

After disposing of his parachute and tossing away the revolver he always carried he set off on foot to get clear of the area as quickly as possible. Eventually he teamed up with a group of French infantrymen who were trying to make their way back to their company. Four days later the ragged group was surrounded by German tanks and forced to surrender. Being an airman, Bill soon found himself on the way to the Luftwaffe's interrogation centre, Dulag Luft in Oberursel. In July he was moved to Stalag Luft I in Pomerania, and over the following year did very little to provoke his captors. He seemed to fall into the dull camp routine, and late in 1941 was made parcels officer for the camp – a position of some trust, which would indicate that his slate was acceptably clean to his captors.

But Flight Lieutenant Bill Fowler's seeming acceptance of life as a POW was a ruse; he always had an ace up his sleeve. He began making a bogus German uniform out of stray pieces of dyed clothing, and on 5 November walked out of Stalag Luft I disguised as a German guard. Once clear of the camp he stripped off the uniform to reveal civilian clothing underneath, and began walking. His plan was to make his way to the Baltic port of Sassnitz, where he would hide aboard a ship bound for Sweden. Unfortunately he was arrested on the docks, and returned under close guard to Luft I. For his efforts the German authorities decided they would send him off to their 'bad boys' camp, Oflag IVC.

Like those before him Bill Fowler found life in the castle prison insufferable, yet he quickly concluded that escaping from the fortress prison would be a very difficult proposition. He was heartened by the fact that, despite the odds, some had already succeeded. Then, just a month after his arrival, two more prisoners escaped and made it back to England. One was Airey Neave, the first British officer to make a 'home run' from Colditz. Years later he was callously murdered by an IRA bomb that blew up his car outside the British House of Commons. Neave's daring escape seemed to steel Fowler's resolve and give him fresh inspiration to seek a way out of the ancient castle. Meanwhile, he indulged himself in some of the lighter goings-on, which helped the prisoners to maintain a little sanity in those grim days.

Bill was the fellow who first took advantage of a plague of wasps infesting the creeper vine that grew over many of the interior walls of the castle. Always on the lookout for ways to intimidate the guards, Bill caught one of the wasps, tied a thin cotton thread round its waist, and attached it to a rolled-up cigarette paper. One of Colditz's great raconteurs, Jim Rogers, takes up the story.

> When released, the wasp buzzed like hell along the floor but could not quite take off. Eventually we found that a wasp can perform level flight with about two-thirds of a cigarette paper attached.
>
> Bill's idea was that, since leaflets were being dropped by the RAF all over Germany at that time (we had seen a few) it was up to us, with our commanding sight of the town, to play our part. Hundreds of wasps were caught and to each was attached a cigarette paper with a message: *'Deutschland Kapt!'* – 'Germany's had it!', which was all there was room for. Wasps bearing the message were released in streams for several days over the town. Whether they did any good we never discovered, but the idea kept us amused.

Bill Fowler decided against joining tunnelling teams. Instead, every waking hour was spent looking for some other way out, but he was in a crowded company: dozens of his fellow prisoners were also scanning the place, trying to find a weak spot or some means of exit so far undiscovered. Bill would often be seen standing against a courtyard wall gazing along the walls and roof lines looking for something everyone else had overlooked. While most of the Colditz 'kriegies' wore a mish-mash of clothing, Bill always stood out in his dark-blue RAAF uniform; he'd received it in a clothing parcel from home, and wore it all the time.

When Captain Bill 'Lulu' Lawton first devised a new escape plan, he took Fowler into his confidence. Lawton had noticed that on two or three mornings a week, a small contingent of Polish prisoners from the nearby Zachadrass camp marched up to the castle under the command of a German NCO and private, delivering equipment. When they left they carried two empty boxes on a length of rope between them.

Lawton's plan called for him, Fowler and some accomplices to dress themselves as orderlies and guards, and the escape would take place from the clothing store. Three British and three Dutch-speaking officers were selected as the escape team. A highly original and unlikely place from which to begin a short tunnel into the clothing store had already been suggested by Lawton – the office of the German RSM, named Gephard. The scheme meant ripping up the floor under his desk to work on the tunnel; the escapers would then make their way down into the clothing store, disguise themselves as the fatigue party, and then boldly walk out of the castle along the sentry path.

Gephard's office was secured by a padlock and a difficult cruciform lock, but one of the Dutch escapers – Lieutenant Damiaen van Doorninck – had already gained an enviable reputation for picking difficult locks. Van Doorninck took careful measurements, which Bill wrote down, and 24 hours later he had manufactured a four-sided cruciform key from a blank supplied by the British. He also made a set of skeleton keys suitable for the outer gates.

Meanwhile work was begun on the tunnel leading to the wall of the storeroom, the stones of which were fortunately secured by old and crumbly mortar. One of the tunnellers had to be locked in Gephard's office every night and let out in the morning after carefully camouflaging the hole.

By 8 September 1942 all was in readiness, and the escape team presented themselves at the evening Appell as usual. The six escapers plus two helpers (Pat Reid and Derek Gill) then stole into the sick bay and hid themselves under some beds until that section of the castle was locked off by the guards. The eight men then made their way to Gephard's office.

At midnight, the escapers had a huge fright when two guards stopped outside the door and one asked his senior officer if he should open it for inspection. As the guard rattled his keys the officer changed his mind and decided it was pointless checking the RSM's office, so they moved off, leaving the eight relieved prisoners mouthing prayers of thanks. The six who were to escape then clambered down through the tunnel and into the storeroom, where they finalised their plans. Fowler and van Doorninck had decided to travel together. Van Doorninck advised the others to walk as far away from the camp as they could along the rail tracks. Then they assembled the wooden boxes, placed their suitcases inside, and settled down to grab as much sleep as they could.

Right on 7am the guards changed. The new sentry would not know whether anyone was supposed to be in the storeroom or not. It was time to go. Dutch officers Donkers and van Doorninck were dressed respectively as the German NCO and private, while the others wore fatigue outfits. These four picked up the ropes and carried the wooden crate out of the storeroom between them, marching casually down the pathway leading out of the castle. As the six men reached the massive gate in the outer wall, van Doorninck immediately encountered a problem. The lock looked larger than he had anticipated, and all three skeleton keys failed to turn the tumblers. He turned to speak to fellow Dutchman Donkers, but instead found himself confronted by a nonplussed German NCO holding a set of keys. Van Doorninck decided to bluff it out.

'Have you got the keys?' he asked in a clipped voice.

'Yes,' the German replied. 'Didn't you know that?'

The Dutchman looked suitably humbled. 'No, we have only been a few days in Zachadrass.'

At this, the German smiled broadly; it wasn't often that he could prove himself superior to a stupid private. Despite the fact that they could be revealed as imposters at any moment, van Doorninck was inwardly relieved at the smug look on the guard's face – he would love to see the same man's face once the Kommandant realised how six men had exited the castle! Donkers meanwhile had remained silently aloof, and the four bogus Poles were wondering what was going on. In spite on their inward disquiet they managed to look impassive and bored.

Donkers then scowled impatiently at the guard, who hurriedly opened the gate. On the way down the path towards Zachadrass, van Doorninck looked back a few times, ostensibly to check that the orderlies were not falling behind, but in reality to keep tabs on the friendly guard. Once round a bend in the road the party dressed in the civilian clothes they had made back in camp. They then split up.

Van Doorninck and Fowler settled down to a stiff pace, reaching Penig around midday. It was a warm day, so when they spotted an inn with seats outside they sat down and ordered two half-litres of pilsener, which they thoroughly enjoyed. When they arrived at Penig railway station they bought tickets for Plauen using their false identity cards, which had also been meticulously forged in Colditz. Rather than expose themselves to any further scrutiny they spent the next two hours in the local cinema.

Meanwhile, back at Colditz, things had gone as planned. The 8.30 morning Appell had been carried out in a state of controlled confusion. Just before a second roll-call was mustered, a report came in that a woman had reported finding some German uniforms in the woods nearby. By eleven o'clock the Kommandant had confirmed that six prisoners were missing and the alarm was raised.

On the train to Plauen the two men spoke only when it was required. Their identities were standing up well, and with more than seven million foreign workers moving around Germany at the time, no one seemed curious about them. At Plauen they bought tickets for the evening train to Stuttgart, but there were constant delays. The two men bided their time, sitting at a small table in the waiting room together with several civilians and a Gestapo guard, who carefully scrutinised everyone in the room.

At 2am it was finally announced that the train had been cancelled, but that the morning train would depart as scheduled. Fowler and van Doorninck sat the time out patiently until morning.

Their train had been going for half an hour when the conductor, accompanied by a Gestapo agent, informed the two men that they had the wrong tickets; they were for the night train only. Fowler, who only had a smattering of German, pretended ignorance throughout the conversation, while van Doorninck sorted it all out by paying a few extra marks surcharge. To their relief they were then left alone. After many delays and a change of trains they finally reached Stuttgart at 8.30pm.

Fresh trouble now loomed. Two queues had formed in front of a pair of ticket collectors, and all passengers were coming under the close inspection of two Gestapo agents in civilian clothing. There was time for the two escapers to consider their next move, so they put their suitcases down and waited for a chance to slip through the barrier.

Soon after, with his colleague occupied elsewhere, the second Gestapo agent suddenly latched onto a suspicious-looking character, and the chance the two men had been waiting for was upon them. Fowler and van Doorninck immediately joined one of the queues and passed straight through the barrier. After this close call they decided against travelling back to the main station, and boarded a tram moving south through the suburbs.

Night was falling when van Doorninck spotted a lighted pub sign. Inside they found a friendly couple serving drinks and the Dutchman quickly established that a room was free for the evening. Following normal Gestapo procedures at all such guest houses, the two men handed their papers to the hotel keeper and retired to their room, after requesting to be woken at 6.30.

The following morning the hotel keeper woke his guests with a small breakfast tray – the first decent meal they'd enjoyed in many days, but when they trooped downstairs ready to depart they were asked for their ration coupons. Van Doorninck apologised and explained they did not have any because they had expected to be at their destination by this time. Fortunately the proprietor waived the whole matter with a smile and returned their papers.

Over the next two days, Fowler and van Doorninck moved slowly to Tuttlingen, near the Swiss border. From there they decided to walk to the frontier. Through careful briefing back at Colditz they knew the preferred escape route over the border by heart, and were reasonably confident they could make a safe crossing.

On the afternoon of 12 September the two men settled down in a thicket and managed to doze until sunset, when they heard the barking of sniffer dogs well to the south. Once darkness set in, they crept to the western edge of the wood and, removing their shoes, crawled through an adjoining cabbage field until they were within 30 metres of a known sentry position. It was a nerve-racking wait, with freedom so tantalisingly close. Just as they were beginning to wonder if they should chance a crossing a noisy motorcycle roared up and squealed to a halt by the distracted sentry. Seizing this opportunity the two men quickly dashed across the road. After running for half a kilometre they sat down, looked at each other and hooted with laughter. They were in Switzerland. Their journey had taken 87 hours.

Although the most harrowing part of the escape was now over for Bill Fowler, his return to England was still at the end of some difficult hurdles. Switzerland, being neutral, could not formally offer assistance to escaped prisoners of war, and he had to make his way to Gibraltar. A network of clandestine helpers had already been notified, however, and they helped Fowler and another Colditz escaper, Ron Littledale, cross France and move into Spain on 29 January 1943.

In Spain, their ordeal continued. Fowler and Littledale were arrested and taken to a military prison in Figueras, where they were placed in a filthy cell with two small bunks and fourteen other mournful occupants. On 1 February they were marched off to the central prison where they had their heads shaved, were inoculated under unhygienic circumstances, and placed in a tiny cell where they remained under the most appalling conditions for three weeks. 'Two died during our incarceration,' Bill later wrote to his parents, 'and their bodies were not removed for 48 hours.'

Eventually, they were visited by a representative from the British Consulate and taken to Barcelona, where they were given fresh civilian clothing and told to stay put, regaining their strength until 18 March. Six days after that Bill was transported to Madrid with six other RAF personnel then to Seville and finally Gibraltar.

Bill Fowler was later awarded the Military Cross for his audacious escape, and spent several months during 1943 instructing aircrew members on escape and evasion techniques.

On 26 March 1944, he was killed while testing a Typhoon dive-bomber aircraft. It was exactly a year to the day since he had phoned his parents to tell them he had escaped and was safe. Bill Fowler was buried with full military honours at Durrington cemetery in Wiltshire.

Perhaps he could have seen out the war as a POW, but that didn't seem to be a part of Fowler's make-up. He had risked his life to escape from his captors, and had risked it again as a test pilot.

The following year Maxwell and Florence Fowler were invited to Buckingham Palace, where they received their son's Military Cross from King George VI, given for 'the initiative and daring' he had displayed in escaping from the enemy, and for 'exceptional service'.

It's a pity I never got to know Bill Fowler; it would have been a great pleasure to meet him and shake his hand.

9

Austrian Escapade

October began on a despondent note. I loathed being a prisoner, and wanted desperately to go home. I found myself becoming morose and unreasonable; I snapped at people and withdrew into my books, wanting nothing more than to be by myself. My dreams had a savage intensity, and I would wake in a sweat, for more often than not I would find that I had subconsciously placed my loved ones in the middle of the filthy war being waged outside. I would stand and watch in horror as a ring of armed Germans closed in on them while they sat in my old living room at home, listening to the war news on the wireless. I would scream silently, and tug at invisible bars, trying to shout a warning as certain death crept inexorably towards them. I thrashed and squirmed, trying to get free, wanting to do something – anything. A muffled cry would break from my lips and I would sit bolt upright in my bunk, my trembling body soaked with perspiration.

I had to do something to shake myself out of this awful melancholy, for I had seen others cracking under the awful strain, and I feared for my sanity. But on the second day in October, like a breath of fresh air, an old chum came to stay, and it was only a couple of days later that I realised I was over my little spell. It began that afternoon when Rex Baxter came sweeping into the room and thumped me on the shoulder.

'Snap out of it, Champy – there's someone upstairs having a bath that you will want to meet!'

I wasn't in the best of moods. 'For goodness sakes Rex, will you just piss off. Who could be in this rotten, miserable dump that I'd be anywhere near pleased to see?'

'It's Johnny Rawson, Jack,' he replied. 'And he's just in the tub at the …' I had leaped off the bunk and was on my way!

It was great to see Johnny again, and I shook his hand with uncontrolled glee as he sat awkwardly in the small metal tub. I was so damned pleased he was back with us, but I also had a million questions to ask him. He said he would drop around later as he had been billeted in Ralph Holroyd's mess, and he wanted to get some new clothes off Ralph, our camp Quartermaster, before bringing us up to date with his activities. His mere presence in Colditz meant that he had been a pest to the goons again in Eichstätt, and we were dying to hear his story. He came around after evening Appell and in his own inimitable style told us of his remarkable, if unrewarded, escape across Germany.

Following the mass exodus from the tunnel at Eichstätt, German security was tightened considerably. New guard towers were erected in and outside the camp, searches were more frequent, and snap Appells were called throughout the day and night to prevent tunnels being dug between scheduled roll-calls, as was the case before. Tension was high, and many escape plans withered and died.

The Germans drew up a 'black list' of 120 prisoners who were considered undesirable and had them moved out with no prior notice on the morning of 1 July to another camp at Rotenburg. Johnny was annoyed to learn that his Ned Kelly colleague, Andy Benns, had been taken with them. The news of our successful tunnel had delighted him, for he did not know of its existence, and such an exercise in mass escape was a good old kick in the backsides of their captors. It made Johnny all the more determined to make good his own escape before he too was shifted to yet another camp from where escape might prove more difficult. He was keen to get away, and decided that now was the time to formulate some plans.

Tunnelling was definitely out, at least for the time being. Our little effort had seen to that. The snap Appells and increased search and security measures, including buried sound detectors, meant that other methods had to be devised.

While he was deliberating, the thirty-two Warrant Officers who had been in the camp for the past eight months received orders that they were shortly to be transferred to an NCOs camp somewhere in upper Bavaria. Johnny tucked the information away in his mind for possible use. Two days later he was taking a constitutional around the perimeter road with Jock McCulloch of the Black Watch and two of the Warrant Officers named Lewis and Owens. 'Don't know if we'll be here much longer ourselves once you've gone,' Rawson remarked to Lewis, a small dark-haired Welshman. 'One thing's for sure – I'd rather be going to your new camp. It would have to be a damn sight easier to get away from than this bloody place.'

Lewis laughed. 'Good Lord, Johnny, you can take my place and good luck to you, but the Jerries would soon tumble. They can spot a bloody Aussie bushranger a mile off!'

Rawson was pensive. 'I don't know; I think I could pull it off.'

Lewis stopped abruptly, and the other three pulled up. 'Hang on, Johnny,' he said. 'I do believe you're half serious about this.'

'Just something I'm working on at the moment,' Rawson mused, pulling a cigarette from his tunic jacket and lighting it.

Jock McCulloch looked puzzled. 'What is it, Johnny?'

'I was just thinking out loud about changing places with Lewis here when they go off to this NCOs camp,' he replied thoughtfully. 'Security would be a joke after this dump, and there's always the chance of getting away on a working party of some kind.'

'You're absolutely right of course,' said Lewis. 'There's just one small snag – you'd have to get past the identity check at the gate here. The blokes going have been here for quite a few months, and the Jerries know us all pretty well by sight. It's been tried before, you know, with only limited success.'

'Yes, you're probably right,' said Rawson, with a touch of resignation in his voice. 'It was just a thought.' They continued walking and the subject was dropped. After a while Rawson and McCulloch returned to their own block where they sat on the doorstep and nonchalantly watched a nearby game of softball. Jock spoke up.

'It could work you know, Johnny. The escape I mean. After you'd mentioned it I sized myself up against Owens. We're both pretty much the same build, with sandy hair and a moustache. But it's not only Lewis and Owens – if they're the two we try to impersonate. We'd need to get the help of the other NCOs to give us a bit of a smother while we try to get out with them. I honestly don't think we've got anything to lose by giving it a go.'

'Only fourteen days in the bunker,' Rawson reminded him

pensively, and then he slapped his knee. 'Let's go and see Lewis and Owens again!'

The two NCOs were not surprised when Rawson and McCulloch approached them again. They agreed to exchange identities, and to drill the two officers with details of their family and military backgrounds in order to parry any awkward questions from the Germans.

'Just one thing, Johnny,' said Lewis. 'About my mail from home. I don't know that I can go without it indefinitely.' The question hung in the air, and Rawson made a quick decision.

'If you care to nominate someone in the lot we go with, I'll make sure they hang onto it for you,' he promised. 'And furthermore, if Jock and I haven't made good our escape within three months we'll turn ourselves in to the goons and explain who we really are. Does that sound alright to you?'

This was agreeable to all four men and they shook hands. Rawson then returned to his quarters and spoke to Arthur Brown, the senior officer of his battalion. He explained the situation, and was assured that Lewis and Owens would be taken care of by the officers should the masquerade be successful, and that any mail for Rawson and McCulloch would be held by him until it could somehow be forwarded.

The following day, after an extensive evening briefing session with Lewis and Owens, it was decided that with the move imminent it would be best if the change-over took place without delay. That night the two officers moved in with the NCOs and vice versa, and all were heartily welcomed by their new mess mates, who were pleased to be part of the conspiracy.

A make-up man from the camp theatre spent an hour with Rawson the next day, trying to change his appearance to something like Lewis. He altered the hairstyle and narrowed the eyebrows, and finally declared himself finished. Rawson surveyed the result in a piece of mirror, but silently thought the disguise a long way from perfect. However it would have to do. McCulloch was a lot easier – the make-up man merely trimmed down his magnificent moustache to a more modest style and changed the part in his hair. He was certainly a lot nearer the mark than Rawson.

That day the two of them studied secret maps of the Swiss and Serbian areas, but could not agree on a mutually satisfactory plan. While McCulloch opted for the Swiss border, Rawson wanted to head in the latter direction. That evening they had a bit of a binge with their new mates, and got to know most of them by their first names.

At five o'clock the following morning, 8 July, the Germans did as expected and roused the hut, ordering the occupants to pack their gear for movement out of the camp within the hour. Rawson's assumption, that the evacuation would be sudden, had turned out to be correct. The actual move took longer than planned, and they waited in their quarters all day with the only movement being that of their bored guards, who changed shifts at four-hourly intervals. Rawson and McCulloch filled in some of the time questioning each other on their new identities: ages, wives' names, POW and service numbers and other relevant biographical details.

Finally, at ten that night, the evacuation began. They were all marched down the stairs and along the camp road, past the guard house and on to the Kommandantur, where they had their names checked off. They glibly answered the security guard's questions relating to their POW numbers, rank, name, age, marital status and nationality, and then waited for the photograph check, which was the last hurdle before being trooped out of the camp. At last it was Rawson's turn, and he was matched against the photograph of Lewis. Hauptmann Klau, the camp Security Officer, looked at Rawson and then at the photograph. He frowned, and looked again.

'Kommen Sie mit!' he ordered, and Rawson followed him into a small room. Klau swung around. 'You're not Lewis!' he spat out. 'Who are you?'

Rawson put on a tame expression. 'I beg your pardon?' he asked meekly.

'You're nothing like Lewis,' Klau repeated. 'You are a British officer.'

Rawson pretended to take umbrage at the accusation. 'Is that so?' he said belligerently. 'Could you please tell who I am then?'

'That I do not know,' was the response. 'But I do know you're not Lewis. Your fingerprints will soon clear up this matter.'

Rawson became a little dejected. Even a quick check of his prints would soon give away his little game, and he said nothing as a bald-headed corporal took his fingerprints and handed the card to Klau. The Security Officer tried to compare the fresh prints to those of Lewis, but even Johnny could see that the originals were badly smudged, and a definite comparison was almost impossible. Klau reluctantly gave up, and resorted once again to his bullying tactics.

'You know you are not Lewis. Tell me who you are!'

'You tell me!' Rawson replied curtly. 'It appears I've been under some sort of misapprehension for 28 years.'

'Don't talk to me like that!' said Klau, drawing himself up, 'Or I will send you to the bunker immediately. When was this photograph taken?'

'Nearly three years ago,' Rawson replied. 'Before the generous rations the German army gave us had the opportunity to show its effects.'

Klau did not know what to do, and shook his head. 'You British are all the same. You are all mad! Remember this – I do not believe you, and I will see you again, I am sure.'

Rawson couldn't believe it as he was shown out of the room and ordered to fall back into his place in the assembly of prisoners. Jock, meantime, had experienced no trouble at all, and the security guard had not even blinked when checking him against the photograph.

By now it was two in the morning, and everyone was getting impatient. They were counted and checked off twice more until finally, at seven o'clock, they were marched three abreast away from the Kommandantur and down the road to the town of Eichstätt.

At the station they were loaded onto a train with eight men and two guards to each compartment. For the next few hours Johnny enjoyed one of the most pleasant days since his capture on Crete, as the train slowly wended its way through the lovely Bavarian valleys. They reached their destination by mid-afternoon, and were ordered out onto the platform of Parsberg station. Once again they were counted and then moved off in trucks to their new camp, Stalag 383, Hohenfels, where to their delight they were simply counted again and then handed over in the camp Kommandantur to the Senior British Officer.

When he found a few moments Rawson asked one of the British staff if there were any Australians in the camp, and was pleased to hear that there were many NCOs from his old battalion, including RSM Bill Baxter whom he knew well. He asked if Baxter could be told he was there and come to the Kommandantur, but to greet him as Lewis. Baxter arrived a few minutes later, played his part perfectly, and soon Rawson and McCulloch were on their way to Baxter's hut. He was full of questions, and the two officers quickly explained their intentions of escaping, at which he promised any assistance necessary.

Baxter then rustled up a couple of extra bunks, and after the two new arrivals had greeted several old friends they retired for the night. Next morning after a breakfast of boiled eggs they went on a tour of the camp.

Stalag 383 was an enormous place, containing the greater part of British NCOs in Germany. The huts were small, holding between six and twelve men, and were quite old and drab, while the camp overall had a messy look about it. Most of the men simply wore shorts and boots, but appeared to be in good health and spirits.

The Kommandant was a rather pleasant fellow who had made conditions as tenable as possible. Baxter told them that the guards were quite tame, and things were relatively lax. Two tunnels were under way, and both of them had reached the perimeter wire. He also told them that a German infantry battalion almost completely surrounded the camp, and three miles along the Parsberg road was an artillery training post. Nearly every night both of these units would conduct exercises, and for this reason very few escapees ever made it out of the immediate area. Because of this the camp guards had become rather slack and decreasingly vigilant.

Jim Stirling, Rawson's old canteen sergeant, cooked up an excellent lunch after which they got down to business. It was decided that as they had about two months in which to escape they would conserve their food and keep their eyes open.

Two weeks later Baxter came into their hut with a small piece of news.

He'd been reorganising the Quartermaster's store, and on his way back to the hut he'd bumped into the fellow in charge of one of the tunnels, which by now was well past the wire and almost ready to break. Two of his digging team were not well, and he needed workers urgently. Rawson and McCulloch were more than willing, and the next day they were digging away underground.

The two men each took a two-hour shift at the face of the tunnel which snaked out from beneath a hut near the wire, and made good progress. They dug for another two hours the next day, and that evening packed their kit, food, water and maps. Jock still wanted to head for Switzerland, but Johnny was equally adamant they should head for the Serbian border.

They woke next morning to find it raining heavily, and were told that water had gotten into the tunnel, which would need a little repair work once the rain stopped. However it was still raining as heavily the next day, and just after lunch disaster struck. A convoy from the artillery depot had been passing along the road outside the camp when one of the trucks suddenly found itself bogged in a deep rut, which was caused when the roof of the tunnel collapsed under its weight. There was great excitement amongst the guards, and for the next couple of days security was tightened. Although disappointed, Rawson and McCulloch decided that further tunnelling was out for both of them, and would only be used as a last resort.

During his wanderings around the camp, Johnny had noticed that work fatigue parties went out of the camp at regular intervals, and that two in particular were away for quite a while. He checked this with Baxter who found out that a party went to Parsberg station twice weekly to pick up the camp's potato rations. Even though the same men were supposed to be in this group, substitutions were frequently made.

The corporal in charge of the party was quite cooperative when Baxter told him that two officers bent on escape were in the camp, and he promised that room would be found for them on the next trip. They planned this to be a purely reconnaissance trip; after one or two such trips they would make their getaway.

Two days later, at seven in the morning, they presented themselves with the other members of the fatigue party at the main gate. The German Feldwebel hardly gave them a glance, checked them off, and the two men climbed into the back of a truck with the NCOs and two guards and off they went. The country around the camp was agricultural and gently undulating, with woods scattered here and there. A few miles from Hohenfels they began to pass the training area, and were able to observe the German troops on manoeuvres.

As they drove on to the town of Parsberg the countryside grew quite hilly, the woods much thicker and closer together. Their truck drove straight to the rail siding, where a number of train trucks carrying potatoes were being unloaded by parties of POWs. Within a few minutes they were busy helping with the unloading. At noon they stopped work for lunch, moving across to a small group of trees, where two guards kept watch over them. Meanwhile the Feldwebel and a couple of his men departed for a tiny beer house which lay adjacent to the station.

Up to this time, neither Rawson nor McCulloch had picked up any interesting ideas for a break, but they kept a sharp eye on the station routine. During the afternoon several goods trains came their way heading south, and most stopped at Parsberg before continuing. On one such occasion the two hastily talked over jumping on board a recently arrived train, which they felt sure they could accomplish without being seen, but they decided to bide their time and wait for a better opportunity. They would almost certainly have been missed very quickly and picked up at the next station.

By four o'clock they had finished unloading the train and sat under the trees waiting for their transport back to Hohenfels. Rawson turned to look at the small rise behind them. 'What if we arranged a small distraction for the guards and slipped behind those trees and made our way over the rise?' he asked McCulloch.

'Worth a thought, Johnny,' was the reply. 'But I wish we knew what's over the crest. We might run straight into the middle of a village or something. A bit risky, mate.'

They decided to talk it over back at the camp. That night they tossed around a few prospects for their getaway with Baxter, and finally decided to try their luck with the plan of slipping over the hill at the goods yard. The chief advantage lay in the fact that if the break was made at lunch time, one of the two guards would have to stay with the other prisoners, leaving only one to pursue them. They assembled their escape kits, and each had good quantities of chocolate, powdered milk, oatmeal, sugar, and Jim Stirling's raisin and oatmeal cakes. Rawson had a compass, knife, ground sheet, cigarette lighter, two boxes of matches, water flask, three pairs of socks and a pair of rubber-soled boots. He somehow managed to squeeze all of this into his haversack.

The following morning they would make their first attempt, and Jim Stirling cooked up a splendid supper that night. After a cigarette or two they went to sleep.

At six o'clock they were woken and told it was time to move out with the fatigue party. Again there was no problem at the gate and they duly arrived at Parsberg. Leaving their coats and haversacks under the trees they set to work at once. At lunchtime the Feldwebel took off for the beer house with the two elderly NCOs in charge of the working party, leaving two guards to look after the prisoners.

Time passed slowly, then one of the guards told his companion he was going to the toilet. The two escapers pricked up their ears; this might be the chance they had been waiting for. A minute later a truck loaded with French prisoners pulled into the goods yard, and the occupants started pinching a few of the potatoes, filling their pockets. Seeing this, the second guard leapt to his feet shouting, and charged off in their direction. Providence had just given Rawson and McCulloch the opportunity they had been waiting for. They scooped up their gear, bolted around behind the trees and sprinted over the rise, relieved to see open fields before them. A distant shot from a pursuing guard caused the two men to split up, but they later met up again in some nearby woods.

Rawson's story of his next few days deserves more than the brief account to which this book is limited, but it is of days spent sleeping in woods and copses, and walking steadily southwards by night, sometimes in driving rain. He and Jock McCulloch had split up after two days as they'd planned, with McCulloch trying for Switzerland (only to be picked up soon after), and Rawson making a bee-line for Yugoslavia. After twelve days of interrupted sleeping, close calls, and nights of forging gamely ahead, he crossed the river Inn at Simbach and headed on into Austria.

Near Kircheim he encountered an unguarded group of French POWs on a working party, and though they were hostile, fearing reprisals, they gave him some biscuits to be rid of him. Rawson's rations had run out by now, and he had been living on a miserable diet of raw potatoes and sour apples.

On the road that night he noticed two suspicious characters also on the move, who were assuming the pattern adopted by army personnel on a long hike – resting ten minutes every hour. After watching them for three hours Rawson decided to take a gamble and approach the two men. Stepping out from behind some bushes he called out to them softly, saying he was an escaping POW. There was silence from the two men, and he repeated his salutation.

This done, one of them approached and held out his hand. *'Ich bin Ruskie!'* he said in genial reply.

The three men shook hands heartily, delighted to find someone else on the run from the Germans. The two Russians had escaped from a factory near Regensburg, and were also heading for Yugoslavia. They explained in German that capture for them would mean death, as Russia was not a signatory to the Geneva Convention; if caught they could expect to be shot without trial. Despite the fact they had been on the run for several days, hiding by day and walking by night, both men seemed quite happy and remarkably carefree. They decided to join forces, and here Johnny takes up the narrative.

> As it was nearing dawn we decided to walk to a wood; we found one about a mile away, and having made ourselves comfortable slept well into the morning. On waking we took stock of each other, and I was amazed at the light-hearted way they approached their perilous escape. One, the black-headed fellow, was about six feet, while the other, a redhead, was about five foot seven and very broad, and looked quite strong. They had only the clothes they slept in; not even a haversack or ground sheet, and they certainly looked a villainous pair. I'd brought a razor with me and a few razor blades, and we all scraped ourselves reasonably clean. I regretted that my

studies of German were confined mainly to the essentials, but I was pleased to hear that they knew of Australia, and they were very proud of being allies of Britain.

That night we walked three abreast through the villages and one quite large town. Nothing worried my friends. Around midnight we came across a farm set fifty yards back from the road. We approached carefully and Redhead, going ahead, opened a door into the barn. There were two cows and a horse and other farm creatures all making the usual animal noises, but in no way did they appear to be disturbed. Redhead tried another door and we were soon in the kitchen, with a fat lamp glowing. Within a few minutes my haversack was full of bread, butter, and all the sausage it could hold, as well as some better quality apples with which we filled our pockets. Looking about we discovered articles of clothing that we thought could be useful, and, I quote from my charge sheet of 2 December 1943: '*one brown coat, a purse containing 40 Reichmarks, a pair of shoes, another gentleman's coat, a black leather briefcase* (which we filled with anything edible), *various papers and an enamel pot*'. Feeling very pleased with ourselves we went outside and made our way back to the road.

As we turned left to continue on our way Blackhead whispered that there was a can of milk ahead, apparently waiting to be picked up in the morning. We were delighted and, filling the newly acquired enamel pot, drank our fill. Redhead thought it was too valuable to leave by the side of the road, and hoisted it on his shoulders – a five gallon milk can, three quarters full! He was a very strong lad indeed. For the next few hours our ten-minute rest breaks were most enjoyable: fresh bread and butter, sausage and plenty of milk. That day we slept well, and also ate well.

In the evening we went off very confidently, but realised that the milk can, although still a quarter full, would have to go. It was rather too obvious, being so close to its former owner. Also, I thought that we should shift away from the road, in a move to a less important one, which would take us slightly to the west of Ried. Around 9pm we were walking past a small pub in a village when Redhead decided he wanted a drink! The coats we had obtained were being worn by Redhead and Blackhead, and I was wearing my only shirt that I'd washed a couple of days before. With 40 Reichmarks burning a hole in my pocket we walked in like any foreign workers, and I plonked down a 5 Reichmark note and ordered *'Drei Steine, bitte!'* At the other end of the bar half a dozen ancient citizens continued to drink their beer, and took not the slightest notice of us. We had another three beers, and then feeling we might be pushing our luck a little we said *'Guten Nacht!'* and disappeared through the door. Blackhead picked up our pot, and we went off in very good spirits.

Towards morning we found a good hide, and spent the day eating and sleeping. There seemed to be no foresters in the area, and at dusk we went to the edge of the wood. We were in a lovely valley, with only farms and the occasional farmer to be seen.

That night nothing of interest occurred and we just kept walking, travelling a little over twelve miles. I was really lost but the compass showed we were heading almost directly south-east. Redhead thought we were wise to avoid the main road, even if it did take us a little longer. I agreed, and Blackhead simply smiled.

The following night, as we went through a village, I saw a couple of bikes outside a pub. Redhead was thirsty again, and we went in and had a stein each. Nobody took any notice, but I felt uncomfortable and we went out again. We'd gone about twenty yards when the pub door opened and a couple of locals came out and watched us until we were out of the village.

I convinced Redhead the pub game was too risky, and we didn't try it again. The next day we talked about how much sooner we would reach our destination if we were riding instead of walking. The trouble was that Blackhead had never ridden a bike.

I remember that day very well, as Redhead told us of life in his village, how he was conscripted on the outbreak of war, and how the officers and NCOs in their unit had complete control of their men – literally of life and death. He was fiercely patriotic, quite determined to return to Russia, and on the way would fight with Tito's partisans.

Quite early that night we passed through a large town – I had no idea which one, but it was the first time we had come across so many people after dark. There were many bikes in the town square, but it was too dangerous to touch them, so miles further on we passed through a village and outside a pub were three bikes. We grabbed them and were out of the village in minutes. As Blackhead couldn't ride, we made for the nearest cover, and tried to teach him. Fortunately it was moonlight, and within half an hour he became quite proficient. We started off; I was leading, Blackhead about twenty yards behind, and Redhead bringing up the rear. It was great riding along in the moonlight. We felt as free as a breeze, and until then I hadn't realised how hilly the countryside was. When hiking we took it as it came, but riding we found the hills heavy going, and generally ended up walking. Even so, in a few hours we had travelled further than in the previous three days.

We'd reached the top of a hill and were going well when the descent began. It got steeper and steeper, and I was glad to have good brakes. Suddenly Blackhead flashed past me, and was out of sight in seconds. He had a fixed wheel, and we'd forgotten to tell him how to stop the bike! I waited for Redhead to catch up, and all we could hope for was that our companion had reached the bottom without panicking. It was a winding road and right at the bottom was a rather sharp turn to the right over a narrow stone bridge. Below was a stream, and we couldn't see any sign of Blackhead or his bike. We eventually had to presume he'd missed the turn and gone over the side. It must have been about fifty feet, and it was certainly bad luck for him. He hadn't said much, but was always laughing.

We carried on, although our spirits were depressed somewhat, and travelled a good distance. That day Redhead was quite morose, for Blackhead had been with him since the day they were taken.

That night we waited till well after dark before starting. The country had flattened out a lot. We were riding down a valley and doing well, but getting hungry, and Redhead decided to get some food. We still had our pot, but our rations were reduced to dry bread and apples. I was the bike holder, and Redhead disappeared, coming back a few minutes later with bread, butter, sausage and a piece of cake. That day we slept and fed well, and Redhead's depression seemed to pass.

We started well that night, and the country became undulating. Towards dawn I was getting nervous, but nothing seemed to worry Redhead. In the distance I thought I saw some trees. As we neared the woods we passed quite a few workers off to the fields, and quite a few on bikes, but nobody took any notice, or so we thought! We reached the woods and rode straight in on a well-used track. About fifty yards in there was a large clump of bushes. We hid our bikes there, and moving further away from the track we found a satisfactory hide.

That evening I walked ten yards ahead of Redhead and reached the bikes to find them uncovered. I turned to warn Redhead, when a voice yelled, *'Hände hoch!'* I ran like hell, with Redhead a few yards in front of me. I was zigging and zagging, and a few shots went over our heads. I went off to the right as Redhead went to the left. The next thing I was flat on my face, having stumbled over a bush. I could hardly get up, and as I did so I heard a voice say, *'Mein Freund, kommen Sie mit!'* And that, apparently, was that!

Johnny Rawson was behind bars again, having been on the loose for twenty-two days. He later discovered he had made one glaring error in his choice of bicycles to steal, as the one he was riding bore a swastika and was identifiable as belonging to a village policeman.

The fate of his two Russian companions sadly remains a mystery.

10

Burning the Candle

LATE IN JANUARY 1944 Doug Crawford requested permission from the Kommandant to have some group photographs taken of the Australian contingent to send to our families. This was duly given, and after lunch on 29 February the ten officers were carefully posed and photographed. Another photograph was then taken, incorporating our Australian orderlies. The resultant photographs, one of which appears on the cover of this edition of the book, were quite splendid, but sadly incomplete: Mark Howard's face was missing. He was in the 'cooler' once again for failing to turn up on time at an Appell! Recently I have also noticed the absence of Sapper Lionel Archer from the orderly group, though I cannot recall why he was not with us that day.

We always tried to make ourselves useful, and we each used any of our particular skills to assist in making escape equipment. Ralph Holroyd, for instance, manufactured a very workable camera using spectacle lenses and some spare bits of wood and metal. It was most effective and was used to take snaps for use in fake passes and other documentation. The film came from those guards who were able to be bribed, usually with chocolate or cigarettes.

Jack Millett was now exceedingly busy as a map-maker, a very time-consuming and mentally taxing occupation, so he liked to relax by playing in several open-air sports. Perhaps his most singular claim to sporting fame is that he was the runner for the legless airman Douglas Bader at Colditz cricket matches. Bader would crack away at the tennis balls we used, and Millett would hurtle down to the crease at the far end while the irrepressible Bader would hoot with glee and urge him on in rather colourful terms. Jack didn't smoke before the war, but took it up in Crete. While map-making in Colditz he was never short of a smoke, as the Escape Committee gave him 120 cigarettes a week for his fine efforts.

On 5 March a most unusual and certainly unique meeting took place in the castle, when Ralph Holroyd's mother was actually granted permission to visit her son in Colditz. The permit was signed by none other than the Führer himself – Adolf Hitler.

Ralph's mother was of German extraction, having been born in Hamburg in July 1883. She arrived in Germany on an extended visit to friends and relatives towards the end of 1938, and had been trying to leave the country since the outbreak of war. Although permission was originally granted, Paula Holroyd could not raise enough money to leave the country by the many highly priced means of exit, and she was finally ordered to stay, despite repeated applications to the Swiss Consulate at Hamburg and Berlin. Her husband Charles back in Australia was powerless to help, and could not even send money. Their only communication was by a quarterly Red Cross message of twenty-five words.

When Paula found out that her son was a POW in Germany she sent several pleas to Berlin asking for permission to see him, but the Oberkommando der Wehrmacht repeatedly denied her requests. In desperation she wrote off a long heartfelt letter to the highest authority in the land, namely Adolf Hitler. Incredibly, on 18 February 1944, she received consent for a brief visit to Colditz, in an order personally signed by the Führer. A letter was sent to Ralph at once by his mother.

Paula Holroyd arrived in the township of Colditz on 4 March. It was arranged through the Kommandant that the visit take place between three and six o'clock the following evening. Hauptmann Eggers called in to see Ralph that night and gave him the final details, including a single condition of the visit: he would have to be present in the room with mother and son throughout the meeting.

Ralph spent the next morning slowly and deliberately preparing for the visit. Word had flashed around the camp and several of his friends had popped in to wish him luck, presenting him with chocolates, tea, milk, sugar and other food items, which he placed in a Red Cross box in preparation. Padre Dick Heard, who was in Ralph's mess, cooked up a magnificent cake.

Just before three o'clock Ralph was taken to a cosily furnished anteroom off the German officers' mess, carrying his Red Cross carton stuffed with afternoon tea goodies. His mother was already in the room, together with an uncomfortable-looking Eggers, who sat a discreet distance from the couple as they were reunited. Mother and son soon fell to talking about Ralph, his father, and the latest news from home. She was pleased to receive reassuring and substantial news of her husband, as their own Red Cross correspondence was more in the order of sending and receiving short telegram-like messages, unlike Ralph, who was able to receive long letters from home.

They had their tea, and Ralph even invited Hauptmann Eggers to join them. He was touched by this thoughtfulness, but regretted that as a German officer he had to decline on principle. Paula then extended her personal invitation and this time he was quite happy to accept. He shared some tea, cake and chocolate for a while before allowing them to continue their conversation.

Eventually the meeting was over, and following a tearful farewell they finally parted at six o'clock, after a highly unusual and poignant mother and son reunion. Happily, at the end of the war, the entire family was once more reunited back home. In the neatly written diaries he kept throughout the war, Ralph wrote that the only regrettable consequence of his mother's visit came when the Germans began to take an inordinate interest in him.

> From then onwards I was a marked man, my escape priority slipping to zero, and locked up at night in doubly guarded quarters, in which the 'Prominente' members of the English aristocracy (their import to the Germans being by now well documented) also had rooms. Being attached to the hospital and dental block, our lights were not turned off at 2200 hours, which was quite convenient for developing and printing photographs taken of practically all potential escapers, with which to adorn their phoney documents, passes and 'Ausweis'. I also turned my hand to tailoring, my specialty being German officers' uniform caps. It was here that I got to know

> Mugsie Moran, due to the Germans' methodical way of putting Camp Paymaster (Mike) and Quartermaster (me) together. My job in this respect was to issue food parcels and clothing when available, and when not, to take from the rich and give to the poor.

It was Ralph who told me about another Australian, a medical officer, who had been at Colditz when he arrived in April of '42. Captain Roger Playoust, known to everyone as 'Doc', had arrived in Colditz from Stalag XIIIC at Hammelburg ten days before him on 19 April to tend some of the French contingent. Ralph was delighted to learn that Playoust, then 42 years of age and a member of the 2/1st Australian Field Ambulance, had been a general practitioner before the war in Military Road, Cremorne. They quickly discovered they both lived in the northern Sydney suburb of Mosman, and were practically neighbours, Ralph had told me with a laugh.

Ralph, who recorded all such things in his diaries, told me that Playoust's parents had arrived in Australia in 1899 from northern France to set themselves up in a woolbroking firm. Roger, the youngest of ten children, was born on 14 January the following year. In the latter stages of the First World War he volunteered for service in the French Army, but arrived in Europe too late to see action. One of the first to enlist when war broke out again in 1939, Playoust and several other medical officers gallantly decided to stay behind to care for the wounded at the fall of Crete and were taken prisoner. Once in Germany his services as a doctor were put to use in several camps, and Colditz was just one of the many detours organised by his captors. He departed Oflag IVC three months later on 28 July, and post-war became good friends with Ralph Holroyd and his family.

* * *

It was one of those slow days in March 1944. I was lying on my bunk trying to digest some of the intricacies of economics, while Mark was fiddling with some bits of string, trying to tie a sheet bend knot which I had shown him that morning. Rex strolled over and sat on the foot of my bunk.

'You know, Champy,' he began, 'I've been talking to some of the Poms here, and they don't even know – haven't even got the faintest idea – what Anzac Day is all about.'

'Not surprising,' Mark interjected. 'Neither did I before I came out to Australia, and my father commanded a destroyer in the Dardanelles at the time of the Gallipoli landings! Never talked about it much though.'

'Bloody ignorant of the bunch here,' snorted Rex. 'And I reckon we should do something about it!'

'Like what?' I asked, putting my book aside. 'Holding classes on the colonial campaigns? Or perhaps we could get passes from the Kommandant so we could visit Anzac Beach?'

'Like ... holding a commemorative dinner,' said Rex, ignoring my sarcasm, 'and inviting a representative from every other country here to come along.'

'You're really serious about this, aren't you Rex?' I asked. The look on his face told me he was. 'But a dinner? What with? A dinner just isn't a dinner without food, and that's not exactly plentiful right now.'

Rex was really getting into the swing of it now. 'I know, I've thought about that. The countries we could invite would be England, Scotland, Wales, Ireland, New Zealand, Canada, South Africa, the United States, Holland, France, Poland and Czechoslovakia. That's ... twelve. There's seventeen Australians here, including the six orderlies, and that gives us a total of twenty-nine all up. The way I figure it, if all of us were to go without two evening meals over the next few weeks, and also get the orderlies to scrounge up some extra spuds from the kitchen, we would have enough food to put on what would at least look like a decent menu.' He looked at the two of us for encouragement. I looked at Mark and he shrugged. Why not?

'Okay Rex,' I said. 'But what about grog? You can't very well have a dinner – especially on Anzac Day – without something to drink, and we don't have any because our mess believes in eating our raisins rather than fermenting them.'

'Couldn't agree more,' said Rex, his eyes alight. 'But don't forget our old mate Bush Parker is well into the distilling business here, and I'm sure he would provide enough hooch for the purpose. I know it's bloody awful stuff – it smells like cat's piss and would burn a hole in a steel plate – but we'd only need a bottle or two, which we'd break down with a lot of water, and that should see us with enough to drink, and minimum casualties!'

Mark slapped his chest with his hands. 'Okay Rex,' he said with a smile. 'Just remind me to keep out of the clink on the twenty-fifth of April will you?' He had spent many weeks in the castle's basement cells for failing to make the courtyard in time for Appells.

'Let's have a meeting then,' I suggested. 'I reckon we could use McColm's room in the Saalhaus wing. There's only Mac and one other bloke in it. And as far as the orderlies are concerned, let's not ask them to go without any of their Red Cross tucker; just get them to scrounge those spuds and anything else they can from the kitchen.'

Just at that moment the door of our room crashed open and Johnny Rawson came breezing in.

'Johnny …' I said, just as he tripped over a loose board and measured his length on the floor. We helped him up, and as he dusted himself off he was swearing like a trooper.

'Hang on Johnny,' I said, trying again. 'I want to ask your opinion on a little idea we're …'

'Stick it up your jumper for a sec, Champy!' he said. 'I've got some great news for you. Someone must have been telling the bloody Poms about our Anzac Day, because Micky Burn has just been asking me about it. I was telling him what we do back home when I had this fair dinkum brilliant idea of getting a bit of tucker together on the day, and then having a gigantic bloody piss-up for all comers and …'

'We're getting it all organised now, Johnny,' interrupted Rex. Rawson stopped in midstream and looked at Baxter. 'Well that was bloody quick, mate!' he said, astounded. 'I've only just left Micky.'

Mark chimed in. 'Great minds think alike, Johnny,' he said, tapping the side of his head with his finger.

'Well I'll be stuffed!' Rawson responded, and the three of us left him standing there in all his confusion, wondering about the powers of telepathy.

And so the plans were laid. The meeting took place in Mac's room, and the other Australians agreed that it was a great idea. The orderlies were thrilled at being made a part of it when I told them.

Not being officers, and having been consigned to Colditz simply as working orderlies, they sometimes felt out of it in such an elite escaping society. A little snobbery did go on, particularly amongst the Brits, and so they were more than happy to be included in anything worthwhile. Sapper Lionel Archer from West Australia worked in the camp kitchen, and he assured me it would be no problem to 'liberate' a few potatoes from the German storeroom. In this way, the Germans would unknowingly contribute to the dinner. Bush Parker readily agreed to provide the grog.

In mid-April printed invitations were formally delivered to the officers on the guest list. Head of the list was our SBO, Lieutenant-Colonel 'Willie' Tod, who would represent Scotland; Colonel 'Tubby' Broomhall would represent England, and South African-born Jim 'Old Horse' Rogers would represent that country. Other guests were Flight Lieutenant Peter van Rood (Holland); Captain Charles Upham, VC and bar (New Zealand); Lieutenant Paddy Martin (Ireland); 'Checko' Chalupka (Czechoslovakia); and so on it went.

The replies came in, and everyone accepted. Ralph Holroyd printed out some menu cards, and Bruce MacAskie painted flags on the covers in watercolour. We were granted the use of a fairly large unoccupied room in the Saalhaus wing, and on the morning of 25 April festooned it with makeshift blue streamers and three paper flags: the Union Jack and the flags of Australia and New Zealand. The trestle tables were covered with white paper for tablecloths, and copies of the menu placed at each seat.

After decorating the room we adjourned to the courtyard for a friendly Australia vs England cricket match. The skies were overcast and threatened rain, but we made a start, with referees Lieutenants Barton and Burdeyron officiating. By the time the game was over (and sad to say won by the English team) it was a very wet wicket indeed, for as we pulled up the 'stumps' it began to rain and hail like mad. By late afternoon, however, the storm had passed and we looked forward to our dinner that night.

Two of the fellows in our mess, Douggie Moir and Micky Farr, donned black ties and coats borrowed from the camp theatre and acted as ushers and waiters. At 8.15 that night, dressed in the best uniform we could muster, we were all seated. Rex, acting as Duty Officer, proposed the Royal Toast, and everyone agreed that the booze from Bush was just right.

Our waiters served the soup (Consommé de Volaille). It was a bit thin, but the Oxo cubes gave it a satisfactory flavour. Then came the cold buffet; thin slices of Spam with some carrot cubes and a few peas, but loads of puréed potatoes courtesy of Archer's kitchen. Then followed Gateau aux Pruneaux.

When the coffee was served and the King had been toasted, Malcolm McColm rose somewhat nervously to his feet to propose the toast to the Anzacs. He shuffled the notes he had been compiling from library books the past few days, and then spoke.

'Gentlemen,' he began. 'Twenty-nine years ago today, in 1915, Australian and New Zealand forces landed just before dawn on the desolate beaches of Gallipoli, in Western Turkey. In the face of fierce opposition from the well-entrenched Turkish garrison they established a beachhead at the foot of the forbidding cliffs. Despite strong support from the British Navy, with a continuous bombardment of the Turkish positions, the casualties were considerable. At the end of that day, 16 000 men had been put ashore, and 2000 of them had been killed. Thousands more were wounded.' He coughed, and turned to the second page.

'When the peninsula was finally evacuated on 19 December, after some eight months of dogged, and at times fierce fighting, over 9000 Australian and New Zealand soldiers had lost their lives. The evacuation was finally ordered when Lord Kitchener declared that he could no longer spare any men to provide reinforcements. It had been a futile and fruitless campaign, but the Australians and

New Zealanders had won their spurs, so to speak. A new national image had emerged, albeit at a terrible cost.

'And so the Australian and New Zealand Army Corps, or Anzacs as they had become known, went on to fight in France and Palestine, until the end of the Great War. By Armistice Day in November 1918, the Australian army had suffered 215 585 casualties from a total enlistment of 331 781. Of these, 61 862 had paid the supreme sacrifice.

'Every year on this date in Australia, Anzac Day is commemorated throughout the country. There is a march through the streets of all cities and towns, followed by a service. It is a closed, solemn day when we remember those men who gave their lives for King and Country.' He put down his papers.

'It is because of this tradition that when Hitler declared war on England, our Mother Country, we could not turn our own cheeks even from the other side of the world. Our fathers fought for freedom and we, in turn, are taking up the cudgel once again.

'So today is Anzac Day, and before I propose the toast to the Anzacs I would ask you all to rise, and observe with me a two-minute silence.'

We all stood and bowed our heads, and offered silent salutation to the men of Gallipoli and other campaigns, including those who had fought and died alongside us.

'Thank you gentlemen. I now give you the toast: the Anzacs.'

After this, Lieutenant-Colonel Broomhall proposed another toast to the Allies, and then we got down to a little drinking and lots of talking. When the grog had finally expired the guests began drifting out. It had been a very remarkable and memorable observance of Anzac Day in what was unquestionably a most unusual place.

* * *

On 28 March I was on the tail end of a small drama concerning an abortive escape attempt, and the exposure of two of our camp 'ghosts'.

I was sitting on the edge of my bunk, idly flipping through a copy of *My Love Must Wait* – the excellent story of Matthew Flinders, which I had borrowed from our camp library – when all at once a squad of goons burst in.

'Herr Lieutenant Champ?' asked the leader. Rather startled, I replied that I was, and was instantly taken downstairs and marched to an area near the Saalhaus. Eggers, now the camp Security Officer, was there together with a closely guarded prisoner. I recognised him as Dennis Bartlett, who had won a Military Cross while serving with the Royal Tank Regiment, before being bagged in Greece. He was in on the Eichstätt escape, and was part of the Escape Committee at Colditz. I wondered what the hell was going on, and how it concerned me. Hauptmann Eggers looked up, and came over to me.

'What is your name, please?' he asked in English.

'My name is Champ, Lieutenant Champ,' I replied quite innocently.

Bartlett groaned. 'Bloody hell, Jack, didn't someone tell you?'

I sensed somehow I had given the wrong answer to Eggers's question, but what was the right answer? I had absolutely no idea.

The story had begun several hours before in the wee small hours, when Bush Parker and Mike Harvey had made a bold escape bid and been caught. They had cut the bars of a window in the third storey of the Saalhaus near the German quarters and climbed down a rope in the twenty seconds during which the sentry was out of sight around the corner.

The escape had been carefully choreographed after months of patiently watching and timing the movements of the three guards who patrolled the immediate area. Their objective was a small slatted door in the causeway between the Saalhaus and the high outer wall. It bore a sign *Luftschutzraum* (air raid shelter). Lengthy observation of the locked door, although restricted by a limited view, indicated that more people seemed to enter the room than leave it; the logical assumption being that there was another exit, possibly to the outside of the camp walls.

On reaching the cobbled causeway, Bush scampered away from the dangling rope into the shadows of the doorway and tried out some keys he had manufactured for the job. Mike Harvey followed him, but some movement – either by Mike or the rope being withdrawn – was noticed by a sentry, who fired a shot into the air and ran to press an alarm bell. In those few precious seconds Bush had opened the door to the shelter and both he and Mike slipped in. He then slid his hand through the slats in the door, turned the key and removed it. The door was now firmly locked. They ran down some stone steps into a cellar, but their search for another exit was fruitless. Outside, the Germans were raising a grand hue and cry, running in every direction, and two of them even stopped to rattle the door, although they did not bother going into the shelter.

The whole scheme was a disappointing failure, and with nowhere to go the would-be escapers finally gave themselves up to the searchers.

The German security staff were now in for a big headache, as Mike Harvey was one of the long-serving castle 'ghosts'. Together with Jack Best he had been registered as having successfully escaped from Colditz nearly a year before. The balloon was about to go up as Eggers asked these newest escapers for their names. Parker gave his, and Eggers confirmed the identification, but then Harvey gave the name Dennis Bartlett, which had been arranged earlier in the event of his recapture. It may have succeeded except that Eggers smelled a rat. He sent Parker to a small temporary cell in the courtyard, and asked that Bartlett's papers be brought to him. When he checked the official photograph against the face in front of him, his suspicions were confirmed. He handed the identity card to his riot squad and ordered them to bring the man whose photograph it bore. After a good search they located Bartlett and took him to Eggers. Then Hauptmann asked Bartlett to identify himself, and realising what had happened he gave the name of an officer he somewhat resembled: me.

The trouble was that I had not been privy to this deception, and as a result I was sent straight back to my quarters after giving Eggers my name. Bartlett was now correctly identified, and to the great satisfaction of Eggers a full identity card check revealed the mystery escaper to be none other than the long-absent Mike Harvey.

Eventually Eggers realised that if one 'ghost' had turned up, then the other missing prisoner, Jack Best, might also be at hand. Indeed he was, and after a thorough identity card check he too was revealed, although he in turn pretended to be Bob Barnes. The grand deception was at an end, and our two 'ghosts' were given a stiff sentence in the cells.

In the interim, Bush was in his courtyard cell, still with much of his escape paraphernalia. Before the inevitable search he cut a hole in the cell's wire grille and passed his cut-down naval greatcoat, maps and money to a fellow conspirator waiting outside. When the Germans noticed the damage to the cell they added another fourteen days to Bush's sentence.

* * *

On 16 June the Germans caught three kriegies in the main sewer under the outer courtyard, chipping away at a stone obstruction. Dominic Bruce, Bos'n Chrisp and Dick Lorraine were ordered out through a manhole that the guards opened, and the three were put in the cells.

The entrance to the sewer pipe was from a tunnel the Poles had dug in one of their rooms before they were shifted from Colditz, and it was hurriedly decided to block up the sewer access shaft before the Germans found it. Rex Baxter, Alan Cocksedge and Bob Barnes were given the job, but to their dismay fell into the arms of some Germans waiting in the sewer pipe who had already discovered the shaft. The three of them were promptly marched off to the cells.

It was a cardinal rule in POW camps that whenever you saw a queue forming you attached yourself to the end. You never knew what might be up front and generally it was nothing, but it could end up being food, cigarettes, lead pencils or anything. It happened that one day in the summer of 1944 I entered the recreation room on the top floor to see a queue of about fifteen men lined up behind an officer, near a window that overlooked the countryside to the south-west.

'What's going on?' I asked the chap in front of me.

'Don't know,' he replied. 'Have to wait and see.'

Half an hour later I was two from the front, and there to my amazement I saw an officer looking intently through what was obviously a telescope. A tall lieutenant I knew in passing was coordinating things, and soon it was my turn.

'You get five minutes,' the Lieutenant said. 'At the moment we're on to two nurses from the local hospital who are sunbathing in a small clearing about half a mile away. Not much to look at, but it's interesting to think we can see them quite clearly when they think they're completely hidden!'

The telescope was constructed of strong cardboard tubing, and was about four feet long. At intervals in the tubing someone had placed disused spectacle lenses of varying strengths, arranged so that maximum distance magnification took place. It really was very clever.

Not knowing quite what I would see I took up position and peered into the telescope. To my complete astonishment two naked women came into view. They were stretched out on their stomachs, and certainly weren't great beauties, but nevertheless my mouth went quite dry at a sight I hadn't seen for many years. Just before my time was up one of them graciously got to her feet and towelled herself down, and then my five minutes had expired.

I'd seen enough anyway.

Other people built these telescopes, or 'lecherscopes' as they became known, and gradually a list of libidinous 'targets' was compiled, including the upstairs bedroom window of one lass who regularly entertained her soldier boyfriend, not realising that their antics were fuelling the lust of some very red-blooded males. After a while most of the men realised that such sights were not doing their hormones any good, and the 'lecherscopes' were eventually put to more practical uses, such as spying on German soldiers during their training (as opposed to carnal) manoeuvres.

As the war in Europe drew to a close we knew by the news from our secret radio that the Americans were within striking distance of Colditz. We were organised into a small battalion with company and platoon commanders, section leaders, a signal unit, intelligence officers and all other necessary ingredients. We were prepared to fight if need be, although of course we were unarmed.

The former 'lecherscopes' were now put to good use, with observation posts set up at various points on the top floors. When the Americans did attack the village of Colditz the following year our CO was able to get excellent reports of their progress.

By now we had a new Senior British Officer, Lieutenant-Colonel Tod of the Royal Scots Fusiliers, who had arrived from Oflag IXA/H, Spangenberg. 'Tubby' Broomhall handed over the reins after his five-month term as SBO, having earned the respect of not only the men he represented, but the Germans with whom he had continuously negotiated on our behalf.

'Willie' Tod, as he quickly became known, was with us for the rest of our stay in Colditz. His firmness, fairness and unending representations in order to maintain or improve our welfare made him a popular and well-respected leader.

Clive Dieppe was still suffering the consequences of his earlier escapes, and during his incarceration at Colditz was hospitalised twice with bad stomach trouble and recurring anaemia. He also received a series of Swiss-sent injections for second-degree frostbite in his toes. Through all this he applied himself to studying accountancy under the tutelage of Ralph Holroyd, and the two of them became firm friends.

At one time Clive received a clothes parcel from Australia, which included a brand-new slouch hat complete with puggaree and badge, but to his great indignation was told it could not be issued. Hauptmann Eggers was at the bottom of this, saying the slouch hat was too easily converted into a civilian hat. His argument was without any merit, as Lionel Archer and I both had slouch hats, and had retained them all through our months in Colditz. Dieppe went to see Colonel Tod, and he in turn did his best, but Eggers remained adamant.

Not long after, a Swiss Commission visited the castle to check continuing applications of the rules of the Geneva Convention. Among other matters of contention, Colonel Tod brought up the matter of the slouch hat and they readily agreed that as it was part of Dieppe's uniform it should be issued. Pressure was brought to bear on Eggers, and with undisguised reluctance he ordered the hat to be handed over to the Australian.

11

The Colditz Glider

On a number of occasions since the war people have asked me questions about the famous Colditz glider. Was it really built? How was it possible in a POW camp with such tight security and unknown to the Germans? Would it really have flown? And finally, where is it now?

I had the privilege of working on this masterpiece of ingenuity, inventiveness and careful planning. So the answer to the first question is yes – it did exist.

A good deal of confusion has arisen in recent years, mainly due to an American film company's rather preposterous movie, *The Escape of the Birdmen*, which seized upon the idea of the glider as the basis for a fictitious POW adventure. In this film, at a non-existent German castle called Bechstätt, an Office of Strategic Services officer organises the building of a secret glider in order to get himself and a nuclear physicist out of the 'impenetrable' castle. Had security at Colditz been as lax as at Bechstätt, there would have been no need for a glider – we could have all shinnied out of the drunken

Kommandant's unbarred window and walked the movie's ten miles to Switzerland! However, the glider in the movie flew, and over the years fact has unfortunately become intertwined with fiction, and many people are now convinced that such an escape actually took place.

Here, for the record, is my story of the real Colditz glider.

I sat perched on a rafter high up in a small room, right on the top floor under the gable roof of the attic in the north-east wing of Colditz Castle. Through a small opening between two of the roofing tiles my eyes were glued on a second-floor window on the opposite side of the courtyard. An officer was gazing out of the barred window and occasionally glancing down at a book he was pretending to read. On the windowsill was an empty green soft drink bottle. This told me that all was clear.

In the small room below me, five other officers were toiling industriously. Two of them were Lieutenants – Jack Best in the RAF, and Tony Rolt in the British Rifle Brigade – and they were going over a set of plans laid out on the floor. The other three were hard at work with needles and thread. They were sewing blue and white checked cotton bed sheets together. This material was to form the fabric for the glider we were building. It was slow and painstaking work.

Occasionally the German sentry patrolling the courtyard came into view. When I couldn't see him the stooge at the window could. I could also see the main gate into the camp, which he couldn't. If any Germans entered through that gate I would quietly say 'Yellow alert!' Once my colleague saw the Germans he would replace the green bottle with a round yellow tobacco tin as all work in the small room ceased.

The tobacco tin would stay in place until the Germans left the camp or their whereabouts were known and it was safe for the work to proceed. The green bottle would take the place of the tin, and I would give the all-clear message. More than an hour spent at this duty was hard on the eyes, so we would change over every hour.

One day I was busy helping with some sewing when Mark Howard, who was sitting at the small opening, called out 'Red alert!' This meant that some Germans had entered the wing of the castle where we were working. Soon we heard them tramping up the spiral stone staircase. They unlocked the door of the room below and we could hear them talking as they examined the area. Apparently satisfied, they left, and a minute later Mark gave us the all clear.

At 4.25pm Tony said, 'Okay chaps, pack it in.' He opened a small trapdoor in a corner of the room, dropped a rope ladder to the floor of the room below, and all but Tony climbed down. He then pulled the ladder up before lowering himself through the trapdoor until he was standing on Jack Best's shoulders. He then closed the trapdoor and sprinkled some dust from his pocket around the edges.

We formed up at the locked door and a few seconds later heard two light taps from the other side. Tony replied with three taps and the door swung open, revealing the grinning face of Bush Parker. Once we were through the door Bush locked it again and we followed him along a passage, down some stairs through two other doors, which Bush opened with his set of skeleton keys, and then we were back in our quarters. Twenty minutes later the siren sounded the five-minute warning for the five o'clock Appell. This was pretty much the routine every day, but up in the attic room we had just come from, something was very definitely taking shape.

It was now September 1944. Rex, Mark and I had been part of a team numbering something just over a dozen who had been helping Jack Best, Bill Goldfinch and Tony Rolt build their glider for the past two months. They were the experts, we were the workers.

The scheme had been conceived some eight months earlier when detailed plans were drawn up by the three men with help from experts in design and aerodynamics. It was planned to construct the smaller wooden parts, struts and so forth, in the security of their own room, and when the time came for the assembly of the glider, and the covering of the wings and fuselage, the operation would be moved to a place yet to be determined, The code name for the operation was 'Heavy Industry'.

There were four main living quarters in Colditz, and each could only be reached from the courtyard through a narrow doorway, from where one climbed a spiral staircase to the three floors used for living and recreation. Should a German enter the doorway the first British officer to see him would shout at the top of his voice, 'Goons up!' This cry would be echoed through the quarters so that within seconds everyone knew there were Germans about. This gave plenty of time for any nefarious activity to be halted, and escape gear and tools quickly concealed in well-prepared hide-outs. Should some special work be under way, such as listening to the six o'clock BBC evening news on our secret radio, then three stooges would be spaced out on the stairway. Everyone (and there were about 200 of us in Colditz at this time) was rostered for these duties. Thus Tony Rolt and Jack Best were able to work with reasonable security in the early stages.

We knew Tony Rolt from several previous escape attempts, so we were pleased when he asked the three of us to help him on what he said was a rather unique idea. He was a tall, good-looking fellow, and a keen motor racing driver. In post-war years he rose to prominence by winning the Le Mans Grand Prix, but that was a few years hence as he settled down to tell us what he had in mind.

'We're on a scheme to get out,' he said. 'Jack Best and I. It's very hush-hush but the time has come when we need a few more reliable bods. Mostly stooging to start with, but later things will change and it will be more interesting, I can assure you, and it's not a tunnel. No need to tell you any more at this stage, and in fact the less you know right now the better. Will you help?'

Almost a silly question; of course we would. We all liked Tony and anything was better than sitting around all day reading, playing endless games of cards or board games, and generally growing idle. And so, the following morning, I found myself stationed at a window in a room on the second floor pretending to read a book placed on the sill with a yellow tobacco tin, a red one, and an empty green soft drink bottle sitting on the table beside me. My instructions were simple: if the regular sentry was the only German in the courtyard I placed the bottle on the sill. If any other Germans came into the courtyard I replaced the bottle with the yellow tin, and if they entered the unoccupied north-east doorway I was to display the red tin. Ours not to reason why. At 11am Mark relieved me, and at 12.30pm operations shut down for the lunchtime Appell.

We continued with this task for nearly two weeks, averaging about a two-hour shift per day. Finally the day came when we were let into the secret. Tony told Rex and I to be in his room at 8.30am the next day, wearing gym shoes. The two of us were there right on schedule, and Bush Parker led us to a locked door on the third floor. We were through in seconds, then up some stairs, along a passage, through two more locked doors, and soon we were in a long, narrow empty room about 70 feet long. I realised we must be very near the top of the castle, above the unoccupied north-east wing.

Bush departed, and Tony led us to the far end of the room. When we reached the far wall Tony climbed onto Jack Best's shoulders, from where he could easily reach the ceiling. A gentle shove upwards, and like magic a small trapdoor opened upwards. Tony heaved himself through and a perfectly made rope ladder with wooden steps snaked down. One by one we went up, through the trapdoor into a small room about ten feet wide and twenty long. 'First stooge up!' said Tony. Douggie Moir climbed onto a cross beam and started peering through a gap in the tiled roof.

I looked around. In orderly chaos stood various components made of wood. There was no doubt about its purpose. 'My God,' I said to Rex. 'It's a bloody aeroplane!'

'Well, not exactly,' said Tony. 'It's actually going to be a glider, and all going well Jack and I will leave this dismal place in about five weeks' time, fly over the river and land on some open ground. We're estimating we'll make around 500 yards, which will do, but depending on weather conditions we may glide a little further. From then on we plan to travel south by train.'

I stood and gazed in wonder; the workmanship was perfect. The fuselage had already been assembled, as well as the single wing, which was still in two sections.

'But how on earth did you discover this ideal workshop?' asked Rex.

Tony smiled. 'The wall on the right is false. The other side of it is an exact replica of the one you see on your left. We made it to look the same so that when the Germans enter from the other end, having just come from the room below; they don't realise that the wall is false and that the room below us in now in effect ten feet longer. The distance deceives the eye. They seldom come up this far anyway, and to date it has worked perfectly.'

Completely ingenious, I thought. Simple, clever and effective.

Jack Best showed us the detailed plans together with a scale drawing of the finished article. They were perfect. He explained that the end wall was made of old bricks, and when the time came this wall would be bashed down and they would be out in the open. The wings would be clipped into place on either side of the fuselage and the whole affair mounted onto a special track fitted at the time over a roof peak immediately outside the hole. There was nothing beyond this steep roof but a 500-foot drop to the ground.

Launching presented something of a problem, but the current thinking was that a large number of rubber bladders from footballs and basketballs would be joined together, and this would be used to catapult the glider into the air. It might drop a little as it went beyond the roof line, but it was felt that control would be quickly achieved.

And so to work. It was sewing day, and we began working on the cover for one of the wings. The material we were cutting and sewing had been the blue and white check cotton sheets provided as paillasse covers by the Germans. Some weeks before volunteers had been sought to give up their sheets, and all we knew as we handed them over was that they were being used for an escape attempt, which was certainly reason enough. This material was now being used to cover the wings and fuselage of the glider.

The wing was constructed in conventional fashion with spreaders of varying lengths connecting to the outer section. We used large needles and strong thread, and we carefully pulled the cotton fabric into place as we slowly worked our way along the edge. Every hour the stooge looking through the tiles was relieved. By mid-morning it was difficult to see what had been achieved, but the ever-cheerful Tony was satisfied with the progress.

By the end of September the sewing had been completed, but there was still a lot of work to be done. Cotton by itself is rather flimsy, but after some experimentation the experts had come up with a novel way to stiffen or dope it. They used boiled, crushed millet, an inferior grain, but one which was in adequate supply. One such brew was tested on a stretched section of cotton in the workshop and it worked perfectly, the material setting stiff and firm. We were confident it would stand up to the stress of wind and possible rain. The full doping would not take place until a few days before the escape.

Next came the fitting of controls and once again the experts went to work. The glider had two cockpits and was designed to be flown by Jack Best from the front. Electric light wire purloined from around the camp was stripped of its outer coating and then threaded expertly through the various control points. Using my pre-war yachting experience I carried out all the wire splicing. Quite a lot of it was necessary, and as the wire had eight strands it was painstaking work. A handmade marlin spike fashioned from a piece of iron by that jack of all trades Bush Parker helped considerably. The glider was completed towards the end of October 1944. Douglas Bader paid a visit to the site and expressed his approval and complete confidence in the ability of our glider to function when put to the test. In fact it was sad that this beautiful craft had been built in the knowledge that it would only ever make one flight.

Meanwhile, events outside the castle were accelerating; the Allied landing in France had succeeded, Italy had capitulated, and Allied forces were advancing north towards Rome. Winter was setting in, and soon the first snowflakes began to drift down into the courtyard.

Although the Allies seemed to have bogged down a little in their advance, the nightly BBC news was very encouraging, and it was apparent that the end of the war in Europe was nigh.

All work on the glider ceased, as it was now finished apart from the doping process. Wisely, the decision was taken that it would not be prudent to attempt to fly it, not only because the weather was prohibitive, but we had learned of a strict German curfew outside the castle. Anyone caught outdoors after 6pm who did not have a satisfactory explanation would be shot. With the end of the war now imminent, it would be foolish to risk the lives of two men just to prove that the bird could fly. An organised liberation would soon see us released without risking further lives.

The secret workshop was sealed, and Colonel Tod finally declared that the glider would only be used as a last resort, and then only to save any lives in peril.

In fact the glider was never used, and never discovered by the Germans – apart from one guard who, for reasons known only to himself, decided against telling his superiors. He came instead to our senior officers and told them he knew of the glider in the secret workshop, but asked only for 500 Players cigarettes in exchange for his silence. By an incredible coincidence that same guard died of natural causes just a week later. Unless one of the last great Colditz secrets has never been revealed, there was absolutely no foul play in his rather timely demise, but it was with great relief that the Escape Committee heard about his passing.

Johnny Rawson always regarded himself as something of a loner in his escape attempts, and made four of them before being brought to Colditz. Although Bill Fowler had scarpered long before we got there, to Johnny falls the distinction of being the only Australian AIF officer to make his escape from Colditz Castle. He takes up the story.

> This chap Aitken [Captain A. H. Aitken, New Zealand Expeditionary Forces] came into Colditz as a dentist on 1 November 1943. I found out that he was going to Stammlager IVB, Mühlberg, which was on the Elbe in Saxony, and as this was an NCOs camp I felt there might be a good chance to escape from a working party – something like the Hohenfels affair. I saw Andy Aitken, and he agreed to allow me to impersonate him and go in his place. He knew that there would be two weeks in the bunker for him when they found out who he was, but he readily agreed to the change.
>
> I went to see the Escape Officer at that time, Tom Stallard, and explained my plan to him. Andy was leaving the camp in two days' time, on 25 November, so there was a degree of urgency in my request, and quite happily Stallard allowed me to proceed.
>
> Two days later, as scheduled, a single guard arrived from Mühlberg, and I was handed over and marched out of Colditz with very little trouble. When I got to Mühlberg I was very well received by the chaps there; a cosmopolitan bunch indeed, but some very fine Australian airmen were in their midst. I got to know a couple

of them, told them my true identity, and said that I wanted to get onto a work party and escape while outside the camp.

I was called before the Senior British Officer – a colonel I knew by reputation from Crete, and a chap I had absolutely no time for. There was no way I was going to tell him who I really was, and he asked me when I was going to hold my first surgery as a dentist. I quickly explained that I had arrived with absolutely no equipment, and it might be a while before I could start seeing any patients. To my chagrin he said that they had plenty of instruments for me, and that I should start as soon as possible. I hustled up the Aussie airmen and asked with some urgency when the next morning party would be, and said that if it got to the situation where I had to start extracting teeth, it would hurt them a lot.

A couple of days later the colonel cornered me, and said he had arranged for me to see some patients the next morning. I was in a real pickle, and the next day I looked into close on sixty mouths, saying that I would fix them up in order of dental priority. But somewhere the balloon went up, and one of them must have realised that I was not who I was making myself out to be. One of the airmen gave me a tip-off that the SBO was looking for me. I slipped out of the building and was hidden in the attic of a disused storehouse nearby. I was there for about 24 hours, but in the end decided to see this colonel and try to explain my actions. A mistake! He was far from amused, and accused me of impersonating protected personnel. I reminded him that it was every officer's duty to escape by whatever means necessary to the job, but he wouldn't have a bar of it. When he told me that he was going to turn me over to the Germans I rather blew my stack, saying that they had it pretty good in the camp, and had no comprehension of what it was really like to be a prisoner of war, which was quite true.

Anyway he did as he had threatened, and turned me over to the goons. Later, when I got back to England, I put in a report on his actions – I felt he should have been court-martialled for preventing me from carrying out my duty to escape. Nothing ever came of it, but I've never forgotten that colonel and what he did.

I was returned to Colditz, and apart from a scheme I evolved with David Walker, which entailed crossing a plank from one third-floor window to another, I was not really involved in any other escape bids myself.

Captain Aitken, meanwhile, was taken off parade at Colditz two days after assuming Rawson's identity. It cannot be determined whether the masquerade was first uncovered at Mühlberg or Colditz. But the time had come when Johnny Rawson had to answer for his sins. His escapes from Eichstätt and Hohenfels were excusable under the terms of military procedure, which state that it is a soldier's duty to try to escape enemy captivity, but breaking and entering during a blackout, and stealing bicycles belonging to German civilians, were considered crimes outside the allowable conduct for escapers. He was told to prepare himself for a court-martial in Leipzig's High Court.

Rawson, and many other inmates of Colditz, were fortunate enough to have a legal whiz in their midst – Lieutenant Alan 'Black' Campbell of the Royal Artillery, and a barrister in peace time. His shrewd mind and professional manner unquestionably saved many prisoners from being railroaded through the complex technicalities of the German legal system, and his resolution was steadfast.

Campbell readily agreed to accompany Rawson to Leipzig, and to represent him in court.

Rawson made himself as presentable as possible by borrowing a fine pair of shoes from Jack Millett, a cap from Laurie Pumphrey, and a shirt from Peter Greenwell. Thus attired, he and Campbell were put aboard a train with a watchful armed escort and given a seat next to a vigilant Feldwebel. Two armed guards were also positioned just outside the compartment in case there was any mischief.

Sitting opposite Rawson and Campbell were three elderly women, who peered anxiously at the prisoners and whispered amongst themselves. Eventually they could not contain their curiosity any longer, and one asked the Feldwebel about the two men.

'These men are British prisoners of war,' he bragged, enjoying his importance in the matter.

'And what is to happen to them?' asked another of the ladies.

The Feldwebel pointed at Rawson. 'This one gets the lot,' he said, rather ungraciously. He drew a gloved finger across his throat. 'Today he gets the lot!'

To Rawson's embarrassment the old lady burst into tears, and soon her two companions had joined in. The Feldwebel was stunned with surprise. Fortunately for all concerned the women got off at a stop soon after to do their shopping, but one lingered long enough to say that she would include Rawson in her prayers that night.

Once they were in court, things didn't seem to be going all that well for Rawson. There was a lot of finger-pointing and shouting, and even though he knew a little German, much of the heavy legal terminology was beyond his comprehension. Finally, 'Black' Campbell asked that a speech made in 1941 by Franz von Werra concerning an officer's duty to escape be submitted as a defence argument. Lieutenant von Werra was the only German to ever escape from Allied custody during the entire war, and the young airman (killed in a plane crash in November 1941) was a national hero in Germany. One of his most salient comments was now read out by Campbell, and Johnny's hopes rose as the court listened with increasing interest. The airman had said, 'It is the sworn duty of every officer to escape, regardless of means, other than committing actual physical damage.'

The court went into an uproar, but in his later summation the judge accepted the fact that Rawson's actions were in keeping with the code of escape as laid down by von Werra, and the case was dismissed. Johnny came back to us a very relieved fellow, grateful not only to 'Black' Campbell, but to the precedent set by an heroic enemy airman!

Escaping was by now quite a serious matter. It could be dangerous, as guards were under specific orders to shoot at escaping prisoners. A notice to this effect was posted in POW camps all over Germany following the cold-blooded murder of the fifty air force escapers from Stalag Luft III. Many of those in Colditz knew some of the officers shot in this tragic episode. Bush Parker had worked as part of Roger Bushell's 'X' organisation during his four-week stint in the Sagan camp, and was distraught at the news concerning many of his former friends. There's little doubt if Bush had stayed in Stalag Luft III he would have been one of the prime members of Bushell's escape team, with its obvious ramifications, and I think this also crossed his mind more than once.

Up to this time, the closest we had come to tragedy in Colditz was during a bold attempt by an officer Hauptmann Eggers later described as 'the greatest escaper of them all'. Mike Sinclair, a red-haired lieutenant in the Rifle Brigade, was known with open respect by the German guard company as the Red Fox. Mike was an incredibly persistent and determined escaper, and his passion to make it back to England was little short of an obsession.

In September 1943, during an impersonation scheme which came within an ace of succeeding, Mike was shot at point-blank range and badly wounded by a guard after he'd all but relieved the guard company with disguised British officers. Despite not having any medical attention for 35 minutes he managed to survive and eventually made a full recovery.

Undaunted by this setback, he later made another courageous escape over the west terrace in January 1944, but was unfortunately caught literally within sight of the Dutch border. It was a great tragedy that he did not make it on this attempt, as his next bid was a rash and suicidal scramble for freedom. This time, on his eighth escape attempt, the Red Fox's luck ran out.

It happened on 25 September 1944, while on a walk with a small group in the castle park. The others had no idea what he was contemplating, but then an ashen-faced Sinclair took his final, awesome gamble. The next few moments were graphically described by Security Officer Reinhold Eggers in his 1961 book, *Colditz: The German Story* (Robert Hale Publishers):

> Suddenly, without warning or any foreknowledge among those present, Lieutenant Sinclair broke away from a small group walking around inside the wire. He sprang across the tripwire and reached the main fence. Up over it he went, his thick gloves helping him to grip in spite of the barbed wire. Down he came on the other side.

> An NCO close by shouted to him to stop. His revolver misfired. Sinclair ran forward down the ravine to where 150 yards away the stream ran through a grid under the foot of the ten-foot park wall. He could not climb this wall. He could not get through the grid. What could he have hoped to do?
>
> Several sentries opened fire. Even then, the shot that killed Michael Sinclair was not aimed true. Fate seemed to hold just one more chance in store. But just as one year previously a bullet from three-foot range had glanced off Sinclair's ribs and out of his body, this time the bullet glanced off his elbow and inwards to his heart. He died instantaneously – 'Shot whilst escaping.'

The Red Fox was gone. Who knows what final desperation could have urged him into such an impossible act? Was it a moment of madness, or the action of a man for whom the thought of not escaping was unbearable? In recent years, Colditz researchers have argued that Sinclair did indeed have a plan, and was making his way towards the inlet that spanned the small stream, giving access to the outskirts of town. He realised that the guards would shoot at him, which is why he was zig-zagging as he ran to the wall, but gambled that the moments it took them to reload would give him a slim chance of making it through the inlet. Despite what Eggers wrote, it is believed Sinclair could have made it through the inlet grid. But this can only remain a cause for conjecture, as Mike Sinclair did not confide his final, desperate escape plans to anyone.

Two days later he was buried with full honours in the town's military cemetery. Padre Heard officiated and ten prisoners from Mike's old regiment, as well as Colonel Tod, were present.

Willie Tod addressed us on parade a few days later, reminding us that the war would soon be over, and any further escape attempts were not only futile, but dangerous in the extreme. Escaping would not be forbidden, but such attempts would be deemed ill-advised. The Wehrmacht no longer considered us as officers duty-bound to escape; Hitler had personally directed that recaptured POWs were to be shot.

As the notice posted in all camps stated, escaping could no longer be considered a sport.

Picture a rather glum day on 7 December 1944. Lieutenant John Hyde-Thompson, a pleasant young fellow from the Durham Light Infantry was enveloped in misery. Things were just getting him down, and the thought of languishing in Colditz for several more months – as it now seemed – filled him with despair. He badly needed some sort of lift, a morale boost, and as he wandered into the room where Johnny Rawson and George Bolding were sorting out a parcel from Rawson's folks back in Australia he sighed deeply, little realising that providence had brought him here at this exact moment, and his gloom was just about to vaporise. He stopped and idly watched as Rawson pulled out some paper-wrapped bundles, and then an incredulous look swept his face as he realised what the Australian was stacking into a careless pile was milk chocolate. And if there was one great weakness John Hyde-Thompson had in life, it was chocolate. He could never get hold of more than a morsel or two, and the thought of it pervaded many a dream.

'Good God!' he exclaimed breathlessly. Rawson looked up.

'Hello mate,' he said. 'Be with you in half a mo' – just want to get this stuff unpacked.'

The young lieutenant repeated himself. 'Good God.' He found it rather hard to talk. 'Just … just how much chocolate have you got there, Johnny?'

Rawson looked around nonchalantly. 'Oh, about twenty pounds of the stuff I suppose.' Incredibly, he didn't care too much for milk chocolate. 'George and I pool what we get together, and trade it for other essentials. We've got a lot more in some boxes under our bunks. Comes in very handy at times, as most blokes love the stuff!'

Hyde-Thompson couldn't believe his ears, but what Rawson had said was quite true. He and George received several personal parcels from Australia, which were limited in weight to ten pounds (six kilograms), and these generally contained some blocks of chocolate, which they bartered for other commodities.

Then Johnny looked up and saw the unconcealed longing in his fellow prisoner's eyes. It was more than a mere mortal could stand.

'Here John,' he said, thrusting out a whole block. 'Be my guest.'

'I say, Rawson, that's awfully decent of you,' stammered the overwhelmed recipient. 'But you must allow me to pay you for this.'

'Forget it,' Johnny responded. 'I use those bloody Lagermarks to light my fags, and we've got heaps of chocolate anyway.'

Hyde-Thompson was adamant. 'No, I insist. Fair's fair.' His mind went over his immediate possessions; not much there to interest anyone but himself. Then suddenly an inspiration hit him.

'I say, Rawson, what would you say to a perfectly good 1938 14-horsepower Renault coupe? Practically brand new.'

Johnny and George looked curiously at Hyde-Thompson, wondering if he had finally popped his cork.

'No, really – I'm quite genuine. It's at home of course, back in Oxfordshire. But I've got other cars there, and none of them much bloody good to me under present circumstances. Tell you what – the car for … five pounds of chocolate. Deal?'

Rawson, a slick entrepreneur himself, laughed at this rather innovative offer. He looked across at Bolding, who merely smiled and winked at him. 'Okay, you silly Pommy bastard,' he said at last, still highly amused. 'You're on. Here's your chocolate, and I'll have one of my chauffeurs pick up the car once we leave this bloody awful place.' He heaped some more bars in front of Hyde-Thompson, who gathered them up eagerly and headed off for his own bunk and some privacy.

'Thanks, Johnny,' he called out over his shoulder. 'And I mean what I say!' Rawson just shrugged and dismissed the whole incident as he continued to sort out his parcel. George Bolding still had a huge smile on his face, and occasionally shook his head in wonder. What some guys would do …

The next morning Hyde-Thompson swept in again, and planted a document in front of a surprised Rawson. 'Here we are, old boy,' he exclaimed. 'I've had "Black" Campbell draw up a contract of sale for the car. I've signed the contract, and he's notarised it. If you'll just care to sign it as well I'll get it back to him for safekeeping!'

Thus, an amazed Johnny Rawson became probably the only POW to ever purchase a car. Following our liberation he received an urgent summons from Hyde-Thompson's mother, requesting that he come to Redholme Manor before he went back to Australia. Johnny took George Bolding up with him, and found the large estate easily. A deep crater from a V-1 'buzz-bomb' was the only visible sign of the war in the area. Hyde-Thompson's mother explained that her son had gone grouse shooting in Scotland after his arrival home in order to be by himself for a while, but he had insisted that Rawson be contacted.

The Renault was up on blocks in the garage, along with several other vehicles. The tyres weren't the best, and the battery was flat, but apart from that it was in excellent condition.

Mrs Hyde-Thompson insisted that Johnny take the car for looking after her son, and two days later he managed to sell it in Eastbourne for 250 pounds. A very tidy profit indeed on a car bought for five pounds of chocolate in Germany.

12

Beginning of the End

Christmas Day of 1944 began as an uninvitingly frosty morning. The temperature was 12 degrees Fahrenheit – well below freezing point. We celebrated by digging into our meagre rations, and breakfasted on porridge, some powdered eggs, coffee and toast, and then attended Padre Platt's morning service.

Lunch, or rather dinner, was available from the kitchen. We had to wait our turn and then line up for the turnip soup and potatoes, and each received a good ration of this, but as usual it was lukewarm. We made our own supper of toast and marmalade, then enjoyed some lovely hot tinned Christmas pudding courtesy of the Red Cross. Finally we solemnly toasted what must surely be our last Christmas in captivity.

On Boxing Day Johnny Rawson organised a mammoth whist drive with some chocolate as first prize. It was a fine contest, finally won by Major Victor Campbell. At 5.30 that evening we attended the Christmas pantomime, *Hey Diddle Snow White*, which was specially written by Micky Riviere, adapted and produced by

Charlie Hopetoun. It was great fun, with a Wicked Duke, Good and Bad Fairies, Prince Charming, Gangster Bodyguards and Japanese Torturers. The music was written by the very likeable Jimmy Yule.

The year 1945 was ushered in on a cold note, and the mere fact that another year had begun weighed heavily upon us. As well, there was very little coal for heating, and the only salvation occurred on 3 January when we were issued three Red Cross parcels per five persons.

Three days later Doug Crawford heard the news he had been waiting for. He was to go to the repatriation centre at Heilag, Annaberg, and from there he would be shipped home to Australia. Doug was not very well, and suffered badly from his haemorrhoids.

At 8pm the next day Doug left Colditz, together with Major Miles Reid, Captain Victor Vercoe and Flight Lieutenant Dan Hallifax (who had been badly burned in his aircraft). All four were finally sent home, where they were able to receive specialist treatment for their disabilities.

Doug was sorely missed, as he had been a popular character in the camp. He had been involved at various times with the excellent camp library, had been a cook in the kitchen, and did a fine job as our Tobacco Officer. To pass some of his spare moments he studied to be a naval architect, and even designed a yacht with Ralph Holroyd's assistance for the *Yachting Monthly* (which, sadly, was never submitted for publication). Together with Bush Parker he had often figured in raids on the camp parcels office in order to liberate some rather dodgy parcels they were expecting from other prisoners' kinfolk in England. Much-needed contraband was thus diverted into the Escape Committee's hands before it was discovered by the Germans. Bush would pick the locks, and Doug then absconded with the appropriate parcels while the guard's attention was distracted, usually by a fight laid on for his benefit. Punches couldn't be pulled in these torrid diversions, and many a parcel was retrieved in exchange for a bloody nose or a black eye.

Having left Colditz behind them, the four being repatriated were sent to Stalag IVD for two nights, where they somehow arranged for a truck full of Red Cross parcels to be diverted to us as a parting gift. Then it was onto a train that went down through Switzerland, and then another took them to Marseilles. Here they were placed onto the SS *Letitia*, a Canadian hospital ship which docked at Liverpool on 20 January. After a few days in England Doug embarked on the *Empress of Scotland* and sailed to Australia via Panama. Once back in Queensland he was placed in a convalescent home, received further treatment, and was eventually released as fully fit. The first 'new guy' was home!

Another Australian officer joined us in Colditz on 13 January. Lieutenant Howard K. H. (Jack) Goodwin of the 2/7th Battalion had been sent under guard from Oflag IXA/Z at Rotenburg, and he joined the mess of Charlie Upham, the double Victoria Cross winner from New Zealand. I am afraid I don't recall meeting Jack, and he is only vaguely remembered by the others.

Howard Goodwin was born in Moonee Ponds, Victoria, in 1904, and when he enlisted was a publican in Woodbridge, south of Hobart, in Tasmania. He was battalion adjutant to the commanding officer of the 2/7th on Crete, Lieutenant-Colonel Theo Walker DSO, having been appointed to that position shortly before embarkation for Greece. Following the debacle on Greece the 2/7th were deployed to Crete. At the time Crete fell to overwhelming German forces, battalion headquarters were situated on the beach at Sfakiá. Walker and Goodwin had actually been on a landing craft which would take them out to one of two destroyers lying offshore, but when Walker learned he was on the last craft to be used in the evacuation it is said he yelled, 'My battalion is there on the beach!' and jumped off to rejoin his men. Goodwin followed his CO, and early on the morning of 1 June 1941 heard the bitter news that the Navy had gone and they were stranded on Crete. Soon after, orders came through for Walker to surrender his men, so he told them to destroy their weapons and equipment and escape if they could. In company with Goodwin, Walker then climbed to Komitadhes where they met an Austrian officer, to whom they formally surrendered the battalion. The Austrian was puzzled by their presence on Crete, and asked, 'What are you doing here, Australia?'

Walker responded, 'One might also ask what are you doing here, Austria?'

The man shrugged. 'We are all Germans,' he replied.

On 2 June, the day after their capture, Walker and Goodwin managed to escape, but were recaptured two days later. After a time in Salonika, Goodwin was sent to the POW camp at Lübeck, then on to Warburg, arriving two days before our arrival from Biberach. When we left Warburg for Eichstätt in early September 1942, 38-year-old Howard Goodwin was transferred to Oflag IXA/Z at Rotenburg, together with all the 'over 35' officers.

When we heard that Goodwin was in Colditz, Mark Howard went to say hello to his fellow officer from the 2/7th. To this day neither Mark nor I know why the man ended up in Colditz, as the camp at Rotenburg was still several weeks away from its eventual evacuation. But knowing the 'graduation' requirement for passage to Colditz, the Tasmanian had probably been up to no good – from a German point of view. It will be appreciated that the war was obviously drawing to a conclusion, and we were far more interested in the progress of the rapidly approaching American army than the arrival of another Australian in Colditz.

Howard Goodwin was not in touch with anyone from Colditz after the war, and the 2/7th Battalion newsletter reported his death in 1989. But for those who are interested in the numbers of Australian officers who 'graduated' to Colditz, his arrival made the number thirteen, including three RAF and ten AIF officers, as well as a medical officer and seven orderlies – a total of twenty-one.

On 3 February Rex Baxter departed from Colditz, and was destined never to return. In fact he disappeared for several weeks, and I only learned of his movements once I was back in Australia. Our eventual reunion in Victoria was a marvellous occasion, and the following account of his post-Colditz saga is presented in Rex's words.

> Looking back, there is one story about my time in Colditz which, in retrospect, is surely ridiculous, but it caused me to have some doubts about my future at the time it occurred. There was this cellar in the castle, on the left-hand side as you came in the main gate, and although it was getting pretty late in the war and most avenues of escape had been well sealed off, someone decided we should have a look to see if there was anything interesting there – maybe a tunnel or something. Food was pretty tight at that time,

and when we finally broke into the cellar the first thing we saw was all these potatoes!

Well, you have to get your priorities right, and we immediately suspended all other thoughts and began filching these potatoes, which we guessed were German stores – not for the POW population. We must have knocked off dozens of them, shooting them out in Red Cross boxes, before our luck ran out. We were busily engaged in packing some spuds when the chief ferret, named 'Auntie', happened to walk past the cellar window. His practice was to wander around the compound with eyes and ears alert when you least expected him (the most efficient method of all) and he must have heard us. Probably we were a little incautious, but to us those potatoes were like receiving Christmas parcels from America, and we had been flat out to get as many as we could before anyone came snooping about.

Anyway, the next thing of course the goons came crashing in, complete with rifles and dogs, yelling, screaming and threatening in their usual hysterical fashion. Peter Winton and I were marched unceremoniously down to the Kommandantur, where we were told that the most serious of charges would be laid against us. For stealing German potatoes we were to be court-marshalled, and when found guilty we would be shot! On return to our quarters we sought out that brilliant legal mind 'Black' Campbell, who agreed to represent us should it come to a court hearing.

At this stage I must go back a little further in time to an earlier camp I was in – Oflag VIB, Warburg. A very large red-headed Scot from the 51st Highland Division was teaching me how to box. I wouldn't keep my guard up and so collected a thunderous left jab on my nose – which broke. In due course it set itself comparatively well but with a restricted air passage which was inclined to make me snuffle noisily. Not long after the potato incident at Colditz, I exploited an opportunity to have my nose 're-bored' at Obermaasfeld, a hospital camp staffed primarily by British doctors, who appeared to handle any surgery required by captured American airmen – and any other prisoners. The operation was performed by an Australian doctor who, after finding out that my father had been an eye, nose and throat specialist in Collins Street for about twenty-three years, reluctantly told me that he was only a general practitioner! Anyway he operated, but really it only made my nose worse, and it's been worse ever since.

I was then transferred to Meiningen, an off-shoot convalescent camp to which patients were transferred to recover. It was a wooden hutted camp with minimum facilities – a hospital in name only – located between Fulda and Coburg. As far as I was concerned I was to proceed back to Colditz after my nose had been fixed. The incident of the cellar and the threat of the court-martial I had almost forgotten. One day the senior surgeon came up to me, and he looked troubled.

'Captain Baxter,' he said. 'I've got this communication here from the Oberkommando der Wehrmacht, and you are to go by train to Berlin for court-martial!'

'On what charge?' I protested. 'Trying to escape again?'

'Oh no,' he replied, 'much more serious than that; sabotaging the German war effort by stealing potatoes from the German army. You could end up being shot, you know!'

So, I thought as I lay in my bunk, the bloody war's all but over, and they want to shoot me for pinching a few lousy rotten spuds. Not the most heroic way to give one's all for King and Country!

Fortunately the senior surgeon was a good type, and he told me that he thought he could help. Dysentery was rife in the hospital, and by convincing the German doctor that I was a genuine dysentery case it might delay my departure enough that the imminent liberation would take place ere I was 'well enough' to go. And so the stage was set; a couple of buckets of genuine dysentery 'samples' were placed alongside my bunk – compliments of some genuine Yank patients – and the surgeon fed me some horrible potion. Goodness knows what it was, but it shot my temperature up to about 104 degrees. I felt ghastly – sweating and feverish, and sick with the smell of all the trappings of genuine dysentery cases around me. And when the doctor arrived I hoped I looked pathetic enough, for I was due to go to Berlin the following day. The doctor examined me, and samples of my adopted diarrhoea were sent to be tested. I could sense that he was a bit puzzled, and not entirely convinced, but on collating all the conclusive results he reluctantly reported that 'Captain Baxter, due to very bad dysentery, is unable to proceed to Berlin at this time.' I did a mental cartwheel.

Once he had gone I relaxed – we had done it, and straight away I stopped taking that foul potion, bringing my raging temperature down to normal, and my groaning guts reverted to their normal function. But the old German doctor was perhaps not as dumb as I had thought; two days later he appeared unexpectedly at my bunkside.

'I've decided to examine you again, Captain Baxter!' And without warning he thrust his thermometer into my mouth. 'Ach so, 98.4. That is very good, very normal, And your dysentery, there is no sign of this. You have obviously made a remarkable recovery, and can now travel to Berlin!' Just like that …

However, time and the advancing fortunes of war were to save me. The hospital was situated maybe 190 miles from Berlin, and even as I was being prepared for my train trip, the Yanks – bless 'em – began shooting up the train line in their Thunderbolts. The din was awful, and as we were only 130 yards from the station, I began to have these visions of being shot up by our own Allies on a trip I would much rather have done without. Some of the more haphazard cannon shells actually sprayed the hospital. I remember one missing us by only five yards, blowing out the corner of the room. But with all the confusion, two trains exploding, and the tracks and sidings scattered all over the place, the Germans who were to escort me to Berlin decided the trip was not a good idea at all, and took off. And so this very relieved officer was left at the hospital, from which I was soon liberated by the Americans.

Thus was I saved from being probably the only POW ever shot for sabotaging the German war effort – by pinching spuds!

There were 300 American airmen in the hospital at Meiningen, all waiting to be liberated. Rex Baxter had befriended a tubby little Scotsman named Bob Laurie. As they were virtually the only two who were ambulatory they spent much of their time reassuring the Yanks and spreading the latest news. Finally, they heard the sounds of battle in the village below them, and after a very short time the skirmish died down to some sporadic gunfire. Knowing that Patton's Third Army was at hand the German guards at the hospital made a hurried exit. Baxter, Laurie and the senior surgeon organised a few of the less badly wounded airmen to take up guard duties within the hospital to warn of any hostile actions from overzealous German citizens or soldiers.

A few hours passed, and then a rather large and agitated German officer was seen marching into the grounds, accompanied by six guards. Baxter's heart sank – surely their newly realised freedom was not going to be taken away from them now. A small deputation met the elderly officer at the door. The German stopped, clicked his heels and saluted – military style.

'Gentlemen,' he wheezed. 'I find myself in an awkward situation. The hospital is, of course, to be surrendered to the American forces. However, I have been informed that our guards here have deserted, and you are left to your own devices. This is a dreadful situation; you cannot possibly be surrendered unless you have someone to surrender you! I have issued orders that the guards who were here are to be found and brought back.'

Baxter and Laurie looked at each other with astonishment. The Germans were proving sticklers for correct military procedure right to the end.

Several of their former guard company were then rounded up and brought back. They were made to surrender all their weapons, and while the officer and his two aides waited to surrender themselves and the hospital the remainder of their guard was placed under observation in the guardhouse. Rex Baxter decided to go down into the village to make sure the Americans were aware of their presence, and he slipped on his field tunic for identification. Making his way to the central square he observed several Sherman tanks barging up the narrow streets. Eventually he moved out into the square from between two buildings, and found himself staring down the barrels of two rifles. His hands shot up and he yelled out, 'Don't shoot! I'm an Australian officer, and don't point those bloody things at me!'

The two American corporals approached cautiously. 'Just who the hell are you?' one asked.

'I'm a captain in the Australian Imperial Forces!' Baxter replied.

'Did you say Austrian?' shouted the other corporal. 'Are you one of those bastards who have been sniping at us from the rooftops around here?'

'Hell no!' was Baxter's retort. 'I'm from Australia – Down Under – the land of the kangaroo! Just look at my uniform and you'll see – it's covered in rising sun buttons.'

Still not entirely convinced, the corporals stared at Baxter's buttons but they might have been lumps of coal for all it meant to them.

'Look here,' he said, 'can you take me to your divisional commander or whoever's in charge? There's a lot of your fly-boys in a hospital across that bridge, and I've got to get the news to him.'

The men shrugged and beckoned Baxter to go ahead of them. They were still not taking any chances. He was taken to the tank commander, who listened to Baxter's story and summed up the situation quickly. On hearing that there were 300 American flyers in the hospital he gave the appropriate orders and a detachment of men crossed the bridge and marched up to the hospital. This done, the commander accompanied Baxter to the building where General Wyman, the Divisional Commander of the 71st Infantry Division had set up his forward command post. Once again Rex explained who he was, where he had been, and about the Americans in the hospital. He was presented with a very welcome cup of coffee while the General issued instructions to his aides regarding the hospital and its inmates. He finally looked at Rex.

'You say you speak fluent German, Captain Baxter?'

'That's correct, General. It's come in pretty handy over the years. But may I ask what is going to happen now? Obviously I want to get out of here and go home as soon as I can.'

General Wyman tapped his pencil on the arm of his chair. 'Not possible at the moment,' he said firmly. 'What with the way things are now as far as transport and communications go, I'd say it would be close to six or eight weeks before you could leave here. We're on a rapid advance, as you will appreciate, and we couldn't possibly spare the means to get you back to your people for quite a while.'

Rex slumped back into his chair. *Six to eight weeks?*

The General continued. 'What I want you to consider is that you are in a very unique position under the circumstances. We desperately need a German speaker to interpret for us, and to lay down the ground rules to the village Bürgermeisters as we go through. Would you consider hitching up with us for a while? You'd sure be a big help.'

Rex thought about it. Getting back into an operational unit was something he'd wanted to do during his years as a prisoner of war, and now he was being offered the chance, albeit not as an operational soldier. The thought of two months inactivity was the clincher, and so Rex Baxter of the AIF became a captain in Patton's Third Army, sweeping rapidly south. He was assigned to the Military Government section of the division, under the command of Major John Hudson.

Rex became part of a small unit made up of two trucks and a jeep, which followed the tanks into villages in their path, and it was their job to advise the local Bürgermeisters through Rex that the infantry would shortly be moving into the area, and he should advise the local populace to surrender their arms and not offer any resistance. Any defiance would result in the offenders being shot.

The Germans had had enough, and the section encountered very few problems as they raced south through Germany. By now Rex was attired as an American captain, and the sight of the uniform was enough to subdue any stubborn Bürgermeisters.

The 71st Infantry passed through Velden, Sulzbach and Amberg, crossed the Regen River at Regenstauf, the Danube at Regensburg, the Isar at Landau, and the Inns on dams east of Branau (which were only secured following some vicious fighting and major labours of the engineers). They stopped only at their objective – the River Enns at Steyr – although some patrols thrust deeply into enemy territory at Waidhofen and Armstollen – the easternmost point reached by American ground forces of any US army in the European theatre. Once at Steyr several men, including Baxter, were asked to go down to release a small concentration camp at Kirchdorf near Sierning, about 19 miles from Steyr. Baxter writes:

> I stayed at Sierning for about a week while the Americans tried to clear the camp. The concentration camp was small by comparison with such infamous places as Auschwitz, but there were still three or four thousand people there. When we arrived at the camp there was a huge pile of bodies in the centre of the compound where the SS and Hitler Youth had done them over. We caught one kid of 17 who had personally despatched 150 people with his rifle butt – men, women and children, the adults weighing only four or five stone. The dead were everywhere, and in each long hut, which would normally take about 30 people, they had about a hundred stacked like sardines and lying about in several inches of excreta, urine and filth; some dead, some barely alive. The stench was indescribable.
>
> The American colonel in charge did what I thought was

> a splendid thing; he rounded up all his vehicles – about 40 altogether – and headed back into Steyr where he picked up nearly 200 German civilians, put them in the vehicles, and took them back to the concentration camp, both men and women. Once there, they were forced to walk right around the camp, past all the bodies and through the filth. He ran a shuttle service from the village until enough Germans had seen the horrors inflicted on innocent people by the monsters of Hitler's 'master race'.

Once back in Steyr, and with their objective now reached, Rex again requested permission to be allowed to return to England, and this time he was successful. Altogether he spent about eight weeks with the Yanks, and still recounts many stories, both amusing and horrifying, of his time as a Captain with the US Army.

Our living conditions in Colditz were to alter considerably at the end of February with the arrival of 1500 Frenchmen who were being evacuated from Oflag IVD, about 80 miles away. For a start we had to shift quarters to the first three floors of the Kellerhaus, with our orderlies taking the fourth floor, and then the Germans cut our rations by twelve percent. Because of the recent bombing not many Red Cross parcels were getting through, and we'd had to tighten our belts. Although we were crowded the French were worse off; the sanitary facilities and food and water supplies just could not cope with the massive influx.

We still had Appells, although these were now conducted in the corridors of the Kellerhaus wing. Rather pointless really, as it was impossible to count the French who milled around in the courtyard, making a proper tally impossible. We still received our morning ersatz coffee, and a soup and potato ration for lunch. The French began demanding that the British share their remaining stocks of Red Cross parcels, but this was vetoed.

It was now becoming almost impossible for us to maintain proper levels of hygiene. The French always seemed to be three deep behind the wash basins, while nearly all the toilets were blocked up and stank to high heaven. Civilian bread loaves were now being issued to us instead of the usual Wehrmacht variety. The same weight, but only half as sustaining.

The Germans were forced to remove the window bars from the first floor as a fire precaution, and placed buckets of water in the lavatories to aid flushing. Hot showers were now a thing of the past. Clive Dieppe had some of his food pinched, and he was absolutely livid.

On 21 March a relief consignment of food from the Danish Red Cross arrived, and despite some bitter argument it was determined that each man would get one pound of porridge oats, three ounces of bacon, and a tin of condensed milk. The rest of the food went to the French, who tore into it with gusto.

On Friday the 13th, despite the Kommandant's assurances to the visiting Foreign Office representative, orders were given for the 'Prominente' (Romilly, Alexander, Haig, Lascelles, Hopetoun, de Hamel and Elphinstone) and the Polish General Bor-Komorowski and his staff to be removed from the castle. Colonel Tod was in a particularly hostile mood and argued heatedly with Prawitt, who said he was acting under Himmler's direct orders, and he dare not disobey. He finally agreed to send some of his own guard company along, who would report the group's safe arrival at their unknown destination. It was the best compromise Tod could organise.

The 'Prominente', as Padre Platt records, 'had an adventurous and nerve-racking time. Romilly escaped, and several others tried to. They were eventually taken to Austria and handed over to the Swiss on 25 April.'

The day after the group's departure, Willie Tod had a two-hour interview with Prawitt, and came back to announce, amid loud cheering, that we were definitely staying put until liberated.

As March gave way to April we knew that our days in Colditz were drawing to an end. The Americans were rapidly approaching on one front, and the Russians on the other. Air raid sirens blared on and off throughout the days. Feelings were running high – not only because of liberation being so close at hand, but also the fear of an inadvertent air attack. We realised that as prisoners of war we were potential hostages, so we clung tenaciously to the belief that the Americans would reach us before we were evacuated away from the area.

Surprisingly, on 6 April, Clive Dieppe was taken into Leipzig for a medical examination – a rather late exercise by the Germans, considering the rapid encroachment of the war. He was escorted to a Catholic hospital in that town by a rather nervous-looking Feldwebel, for their visit coincided with an American air raid on the rail marshalling yards by 660 Flying Fortress bombers. Clive and his guard found their way into an air raid shelter. Padre Platt later recorded the ensuing events in his diary when they returned from Leipzig.

> The man in charge of the shelter had a map showing the sectors into which the town had been divided, and a radio told of the progress of the raid: 'Enemy planes are passing out of Sector P into Sector K,'

followed by a snatch of music, and then, 'Enemy planes are passing out of Sector K into Sector L.' Then the radio stopped, the lights were dimmed, and the thud and tremor of distant bombs became the shrill swish and whistle and horrible shattering of heavy bombs dropping nearby. The man in charge showed them on the map how the bombing tactics operated. The bombers first passed over the sector in which the target lay, and then turned to release their load. There was a time-lag of about three minutes between each wave attacking the target. He was explaining all this while the raid was at its height. Some of the women in the shelter heaved a sigh during the three minutes' relief, but none fainted or screamed.

The sector was all-cleared and the lights restored, and the radio told which of the other sectors were under bombardment. The planes were not out of hearing before the radio issued orders to fire-fighters and medical personnel, and the prisoners who were engaged in clearing the debris. When Clive (and his guard) emerged from the shelter the air was thick and acrid. Fires were raging, and in several places horses' entrails, feet, heads and legs were splashed about.

No one treated him unkindly, or spoke disparagingly of Britain, America or anyone. They had to walk several kilometres down what had been the railway track from what had been the largest station in Europe before they reached the point from where a train could travel.

As we had observed the severity of the raid from the comparative safety of our castle, I can tell you we were mighty pleased to see old Clive walk through the gate about six o'clock. He was immediately surrounded by a large group of kriegies eagerly asking him how it had been. Clive, stunned and angered by what he had seen in

Leipzig, was in no mood for conversation. He uttered a few choice words about 'bloody f…ng indesf…criminate bombing!' and strode off to be by himself for a while.

On 8 April, to our further amazement, and with the arrival of Patton's Third Army imminent, the Germans rounded up Clive Dieppe, Teddy Barton and an orderly and took them to a hospital camp at Hohenstein-Ernstabl in lower Saxony for the purpose of seeking their repatriation from the Mixed Medical Commission. They were still there when the Americans swept into the area and liberated the hospital. Thus Clive Dieppe was not in Colditz at the time of our own liberation just a week later.

On 10 April the possessions taken from us when we were made prisoners (with the exception of civilian clothing, compasses and money) were returned to us, and the following day Willie Tod spoke with Kommandant Prawitt, asking his intentions, as Colditz was fast becoming involved as a battle zone. Prawitt replied that he was expecting orders soon from Himmler, and Colonel Tod would be informed at that time.

Always a meticulous person, Ralph Holroyd recorded his personal observations on the liberation of Colditz Castle in superbly graphic terms in his war diaries. Here is that story, with explanatory interjections by Jack Millett, who had a bird's-eye view of the battle raging below.

> Though not listed in any official war history, the Battle for Colditz on 15 April had no little significance in the lives of some 350 British and Allied officers who had migrated to Oflag IVC. Naturally speculation

as to when and how liberation might ultimately take place was ever rife. The old cry 'Home for Christmas' had worn a bit thin over the years, yet about Easter 1945 there was good reason for conducting a sweep as to the actual date the gates would finally open. Leipzig and the synthetic oil plants in our immediate vicinity were the subject of terrific air raids. The camp's position on the pinnacle of a rugged hill overlooking the countryside gave us a grandstand view. Nor were these constant air raids unsupported. Bulletins from an illicit radio that had survived every effort of the Wehrmacht and Gestapo to discover it were now issued six times daily and gave news of the approach of General Patton's Third Army and the rapid fall of towns in their path. Then the more ominous news of the evacuation of other POW camps in the vicinity leaked through.

Finally the dreaded moment came, and it looked as though it would be our turn. The Kommandant had received orders for the immediate evacuation of all British prisoners at Oflag IVC and these orders were conveyed to the Senior British Officer. Colonel Tod refused to budge and the Kommandant phoned the General at Dresden. The conversation went something like this:

'The British refuse to move.'

'They must!'

'I can't move them without shooting. Will you take the responsibility?'

'No!'

'Neither will I,' said the Kommandant, and banged down the receiver.

We did not move! Nor was this the only outcome, for a division of elite SS troops had already moved in to defend Colditz and could be seen erecting tank blocks, putting up wire defences and preparing rifle pits. The air force's objective now moved on to the local station and marshalling yards. We had every reason to believe that General Patton's forces would be here in less than 48 hours, for our receiving set kept us posted as to American troop movements. By the same means we heard that the Americans had crossed the river ten miles downstream and in addition to their frontal artillery attack were making a flanking movement headed by Sherman tanks.

Artillery fire was now trained on to the town and on to a battery behind Colditz Castle. In an effort to effect recognition from the air, a huge home-made Union Jack was spread out in the courtyard and an immense POW spelled out with sheets. Then the Union Jack was hoisted to the head of the Kellerhaus and the French flag in front of the Saalhaus. All windows of the castle, with their perfect view of the battle, were packed with cheering kriegies.

The American artillery, whose policy during their rapid advance had been to stop at nothing, finally ranged on to the castle itself in the firm belief that it housed the remainder of the German garrison. They moved up in front of Colditz on the range due west about 700 yards away and started zeroing in on the castle. Came the order: Battery, one round, fire!

(J. M.: Technically we weren't fired on – we were ranged on. Before the Yanks saw our flags they let go a few rounds; they were ranging on us, and this means estimating the range and firing off a small round. The sights are then adjusted, another round fired off, and any further corrections made before the actual order to fire the artillery is given. For our own safety we were told to go down into the cellars, but I stayed at an upstairs window; I certainly didn't want to miss all the fun, and I saw all that went on. I've read where Douglas Bader was knocked off his tin legs by an airburst, but this is not so – he wasn't

> in his room at all. He was down in the courtyard gleefully calling, 'Where is the Luftwaffe? Where is the Luftwaffe?' to the cowering guards. But there was certainly some hot metal flying around, and I've still got a piece of shrapnel that came flying in through the window.)
>
> At this moment Driver MacAusland (US Army) saw the French flag through the window of the Saalhaus and yelled: 'Hey, Lieutenant, hold it! They've just stuck some flags out!' The lieutenant called down the phone 'Better reduce the place.'
>
> 'No, Lieutenant, don't do it. I'm sure some of our boys are in there.'
>
> The lieutenant took his advice, grabbed a couple of prisoners and demanded: 'What is that building over there?'
>
> He was told that it was a POW camp. Lieutenant Kenny Dobson, the genial but efficient American artillery officer, later confessed to us that they had planned to blast the castle with high explosive and then fill it up with phosphorus. Ten seconds … and this story would not have been written.

The following morning the Americans crossed the river in strength. One German was seen sauntering across the bridge, and was ordered to halt. He did not do so, and was immediately shot dead. The American soldier who shot him later told us that the German was just unlucky, as the soldier had seen his platoon sergeant killed only a few minutes before. 'I just let him have it!' he said.

We were liberated at 0800 hours on the morning of 16 April. Jack Millett remembers the moment:

> I saw the first two Yanks come in the yard, and everyone was quite calm, cool and collected. But I do remember one of them offering

his Tommy gun to us, with the suggestion that we could get rid of any Germans we wanted to. Nobody took him up on it.

The tables had turned completely on our former captors, for they were now our prisoners. Kommandant Prawitt surrendered his 17 officers and 350 guards to Colonel Leo Shaughnessy of the liberating US Army. We rounded them up and began to prepare for our imminent departure from Colditz. This took many different avenues, and our primary objective was food. Fortunately the Americans had brought copious supplies with them, and we gorged ourselves silly on tinned peaches and cream, chicken, condensed milk and other luxuries. As a consequence, many brought the rich food straight back up.

Some of us broke into the Kommandantur and took a souvenir or two, including our camp photographs. Mark also seized a fistful of rice-paper maps that had been confiscated as contraband over the years, and he still has them to this day. The French were plundering and pilfering shamelessly.

Colonel Tod, following the formal surrender by Prawitt, wisely put it to us that we remain in the precincts of the castle until a proper evacuation could be organised. As well, there were still pockets of German resistance outside the walls, and it would be rather foolish to venture far and end up full of lead.

That same afternoon, in a joyous mood, the glider was brought from its hiding place and assembled in the large attic below the workshop. It was a beautiful thing, perfect in every detail, and we all had an opportunity to go up the spiral staircase for a good look at it. Later we took it apart and returned it to the workshop above.

In 1978 I arranged for a friend of mine, who had a visa to visit his parents in East Germany quite near to Colditz, to see what he could find out about the glider and its eventual fate. I gave him a detailed plan of the castle. Helmut visited Colditz, managed to get into the castle, and took some excellent pictures, which are now in my possession. He learned the sad truth that the glider had been taken to the town museum where the Germans, not realising its historic value, eventually destroyed it.

These days a faithfully accurate half-scale model of the glider is on display at the Imperial War Museum. It was built from the original plans by Englishman Martin Francis, and on 1 November 1981 the model was successfully flown, hand-launched from the top of a ridge and facing into the prevailing wind. That first flight lasted about twenty minutes, and proved that our original Colditz glider would have flown.

The record of escapes from Colditz is a handsome one, and stands as its own tribute to the sheer audacity and clever planning of the inmates: 300 were caught in various escape attempts; 130 actually got clear of the castle, and 30 made successful 'home runs' – fourteen French, eight British, six Dutch, one Pole, and one Australian (although in official records Bill Fowler is listed as British).

On 19 April, just three days after our release, we were evacuated from Colditz. We were each allowed to take only one piece of baggage on the open trucks that would be our transport. I took a piano accordion and Mark carried our essential possessions, rolled up in a German blanket.

Departing Colditz about midday, we travelled about 100 miles back through the sparse lines of communications, with the sounds of battle rumbling ominously on both sides of the convoy.

Our American drivers sent the vehicles along at full pelt and we arrived at the captured Kolleda airfield late in the afternoon. The Americans provided us with an excellent hot meal and sleeping accommodation was quickly organised in the buildings around the field.

In the gathering dusk Mark and I strolled off around the airfield. Soon we saw a light in one of the buildings and picked up sounds of laughter coming from inside. Brashly we knocked on the door and entered the smoke-filled room. The dozen or so American NCOs in the mess greeted us with great cordiality and soon we were swigging down copious quantities of Coke, heavily laced with 'liberated' German schnapps. For the first time in four years we felt the warm glow of real alcohol seeping through our veins and it was two very contented officers who wandered back to their billet around midnight. We were soon fast asleep on beds of clean-smelling straw. We couldn't have been more content had we been bedded down in the Ritz. In fact I doubt we could have slept in a comfortable bed so soon. At 1.30 the following afternoon we watched as a flight of nine Dakota aircraft came in to land. Soon, after some top level negotiations, we were loaded on the aircraft in groups of 25 and were soon airborne, bound for England. It just seemed too much to assimilate. Less than five days earlier we had been locked up in Colditz Castle!

Our Dakota landed at Westcott aerodrome near Aylesbury, where we received a tumultuous welcome. As we stepped from the aircraft RAF ground personnel rushed up and grabbed our baggage, and then we were escorted to a huge hangar where an RAF band deafened us with some rousing welcome music as we made our way to seats around trestle tables groaning under plateloads of sandwiches, pies, cakes and large pots of steaming hot English tea. Our waitresses were wonderful ladies from a local volunteer organisation, and for the first time in over four years we listened, fascinated, to the sweet lilting sound of an English woman's voice.

The following day, after spending a comfortable night in the barracks of the nearby British army camp at Wotton Underground, we were given a brief medical examination and a ten pound advance on our pay. Mark phoned his mother in Sussex; he had not seen his parents for over seven years. She found it difficult to believe that it was really him. Meanwhile Johnny Rawson and George Bolding took off to collect Hyde-Thompson's 'chocolate' car. Enquiries revealed that we Australians were to proceed to Eastbourne on the south coast, where a reception centre for POWs had been established. Just 36 hours after we arrived in Eastbourne we went on leave. Mark went home and I went to London to buy a new uniform and other knick-knacks.

There is one highly amusing story with which to complete the story of our return to civilisation. Back in Eastbourne a few days later, I was approached by an officer who informed me that I was to attend an audience with Princess Mary, the Princess Royal (and sister of the King). He explained that she was anxious to talk to some of the Australian officers from Colditz, as we had known her son there.

Apparently the Viscount Lascelles (known as George Lascelles to us) had not returned to England as yet, but had spoken very highly of his Aussie mates. The Princess Royal was keen to hear of his activities and treatment in Colditz.

I caught the train back up to London, hailed a cab, and made my way to the Dorchester Hotel, where I was to be presented. As

I walked in I spotted Johnny Rawson and George Bolding. Judging from Rawson's rather boisterous mood and Bolding's careful speech, I gathered that they had not spent the afternoon in a cinema.

I felt somewhat nervous as we waited by the dais to be presented, but not so my two companions. Rawson simply exuded confidence, while Bolding appeared solemnly determined not to put his foot in it. Soon it was our turn, and we were ushered onto the dais and presented to the Princess. What a wonderful person she was. While she must have been concerned, not knowing where her son was or what had happened to him, there was no visible indication of her concern.

Princess Mary asked us many questions about life in Colditz – living conditions, food, accommodation, and how we filled in our time. Most of the answers to her questions were supplied by Rawson, with a few by me as we began to feel more relaxed in her presence. Bolding managed a stoic but attentive silence. The Princess cocked an eyebrow when Johnny inadvertently disclosed that while in Colditz we had run a poker school on a credit system, gentlemen's agreement, with payment after the war.

'You mean to say George played poker for money?' she said, in a disbelieving tone.

It was all too much for George Bolding, and now for the first time he entered the conversation. Nodding his head vigorously he drawled, 'I'll say he did! 'smatter of fact, he still owes me twenty quid!'

One of the aides, who had been hovering in the background, moved in quietly. 'Thank you gentlemen,' he said. 'We have some other guests waiting to be presented.'

The Princess graciously extended her gloved hand, and in turn we each grasped it gently and bowed. As Bolding leaned towards her she gave an almost imperceptible wink. 'Thank you,' she confided. 'I'll see that you get your money!'

I was in England for VE Day, and it was a colossal celebration. On 18 May I sailed for Australia on the *Dominion Monarch*. The ship was under British naval command and carried some 1500 Australian POWs as well as other personnel. On 15 June 1945, just as dawn was breaking, hundreds of excited Aussies lined the rails of the ship, straining to catch a first glimpse of the New South Wales coastline.

All of a sudden there it was. Firstly a dim haze on the horizon, but gradually forming into trees, cliffs and buildings.

'That's Sydney, mate,' said a soldier by my side. 'And isn't it bloody beautiful?'

And bloody beautiful it was. It had been just over five years since most of us had departed these shores. Five long years, and four of them behind barbed wire.

The following day we entrained for Melbourne. I met my parents, my sister and my fiancée at Albert Park and returned to Geelong by car.

A week later I was married. After all, five and a half years *is* a long engagement!

Epilogue

INEVITABLY, FATHER TIME catches up with us all. When this book was first published back in 1985, the majority of Australian officers once held in Colditz were still very much alive. It was a young author's pleasure to be in their company, eagerly listening to and recording their wartime memories.

From the first contact I had with Jack Champ, as recounted in this book's introduction, he and his wife, Pat, supported my plans to put this book together and we quickly became close friends. I would often visit them at their home outside of Geelong, Victoria, bearing a bunch of flowers for Pat and clutching a bottle of the finest scotch whisky for Jack. Even after our book had been published we would still spend many pleasant hours in his lounge room discussing the indomitable personalities who once inhabited Colditz Castle. I can still recall Jack's unbridled joy when our newly published book was listed in the *Geelong Advertiser* as the No. 1 bestselling book at the local, historic Griffiths bookstore – no doubt aided by Jack calling on everyone he knew in Geelong to make their way to the store and purchase at least one copy.

Jack could best (and easily) be described as a true inspiration in my own life. The more I found out about his wartime experiences, not only in battle but his evasions and escapades, the more my admiration for his bravery and sheer audacity grew and his recollections of these events continued to astound me. Every hour spent in discussion with him was an hour spent in fascination. The Warburg Wire Job, the tunnel escape from Eichstätt – these were two of the greatest mass POW escapes of the European war and Jack was fully involved in both. Even in Colditz, as the war drew ineluctably to an end, Jack was still assisting in such incredible escape schemes as the renowned Colditz glider.

To continue his story post-war, Jack Wilton Knox Champ returned to Australia aboard the *Dominion Monarch*, arriving home on 16 June 1945. One week later he married his fiancée of five years, D'Arcy Shoebridge, and the year after, their son John was born. D'Arcy died in 1954 after a long illness, and Jack married Patricia Brisbane twelve months later. They had a son, Peter, born in October 1958. Meanwhile Jack had returned to the Ford Motor Company three months after his return, first in the accounting department (where his studies in Colditz proved invaluable), and then a year later transferred to their marketing section. At the time of his retirement he was Ford's Market Representation Manager for Australia. The author of several published short stories, Jack wrote and organised publication of *The Wind is Free* in 1989, a 285-page history of the Royal Geelong Yacht Club. From 1951, he was an active member of Legacy in Geelong and Melbourne, serving as President of Geelong Legacy in 1983–84 while living a quiet life in the Geelong suburb of Highton. Although it had once played a major part in his life, Jack Champ never returned to Colditz.

A worried Pat Champ let me know when Jack entered Geelong hospital in the latter part of 1998 for a major operation to repair a twisted bowel. Tragically, the onset of Alzheimer's Disease had robbed him in his last few months of the ability to focus on writing letters – a passion throughout his life. Despite being hospitalised, Jack still managed to maintain that wonderfully stoic sense of humour he had displayed all his life Sadly he slipped into a coma and died peacefully on 13 August. Just a week earlier his hospital bed had been surrounded by his loving family in order to celebrate his 85th birthday. I was truly devastated when I was told he had lost his final battle that year. He and I had shared so many experiences in putting this book together, and afterwards, and I will always be grateful that our lives came together when they did and we remained great friends for more than 17 years. That was an aspect I always admired in Jack Champ – a man who remained fiercely loyal to the friends he had made throughout his life, but especially during the four difficult and demanding years he spent as a reluctant prisoner of war in Greece and Germany.

People always want to know what became of the subjects of books such as this, so in this revised edition I can tell in brief the post-war stories of the Australian officers with whom Jack Champ shared – and endured – his 663 days in Colditz.

Rex Ransley Baxter (1916–1991): Rex returned to Australia in August 1945 and a joyful reunion with his wife, Kathleen. Later he joined the staff of the Vacuum Oil Company and was employed in their publicity office. He remained with them until his retirement in 1989. Rex devoted a lot of his energy in his later life to his children and grandchildren.

George Bolding (1911–1955): George came back to Australia and was formally discharged from the army in Victoria on 27 July 1945. On his return to Morwell he had received a tumultuous welcome from his family and friends. He and his wife, Jean, then lived in peaceful seclusion at 'The Grange', his boyhood home in North Hazelwood. In October 1955, George died when his car smashed into a tree outside of Morwell. It is believed he had suffered a stroke behind the wheel.

Alexander Douglas (Doug) Crawford (1914–1999): Following his repatriation from Germany, Doug Crawford arrived in Australia in April 1945, where he was greeted by his wife and four-year-old daughter, whom he was meeting for the first time. He elected to stay in the army and rose through the ranks until his transfer to the retired list with the rank of Lieutenant-Colonel in 1983. For a time he operated as a professional fisherman until becoming a wine consultant, first with the Wine Information Bureau and then as an independent. A member of Brisbane Legacy since 1977, he always remained active in that organisation.

Clive Ivor Charles Dieppe (1911–1999): On his return to Australia, Clive bought and ran an orchard for a short period, then returned to the cinema business in which he had been a contract officer pre-war. He subsequently joined the public service and in 1973 published a book of World War One front line photos titled *As It Was*. One of his great passions in his later years was building intricate models of famous sailing ships, including a magnificent replica of Captain Cook's *Endeavour*.

Hedley Nevile (Bill) Fowler (1916–1944): As related in this book, Bill Fowler successfully escaped from Colditz Castle and made a 'home run' back to England. A year to the day after he'd called his father to say he was safe, Bill was killed during an RAF dive-bombing exercise in Dorset on 26 March 1944, aged just 27. He received a Military Cross for his escape, and is buried in Durrington cemetery, Wiltshire.

Howard Kingsley Hill (Jack) Goodwin (1904–1989): Jack was held in Colditz for just 12 weeks before the castle was liberated. On 6 December 1946, following his return to Australia, he was made a temporary captain on the army's Permanent Supernumerary List and settled in Mt Colah, New South Wales, with his wife, Dawn (the former Dorothea Power). They later moved north to Chevron Island on the Nerang River, Surfers Paradise, Queensland.

Ralph Holroyd (1913–1990): Ralph joined the Kodak Company after the war then, after a succession of jobs, he was offered a position with a tobacco and coffee importing and distributing company. A tireless worker for Legacy, he suffered a debilitating and memory-sapping stroke as the result of an aneurism in 1982, only a week after being interviewed for this book. He never recovered, although his fighting spirit kept him alive until he passed away peacefully on 11 December 1990.

Mark Alfred Howard (1918–1999): After spending time with his family in England, Mark returned to Australia in August 1945. A medical examination prior to his discharge revealed he had tuberculosis, and he spent a year in hospital at Bonegilla. Discharged from hospital and the army, he spent 12 months at an agricultural college before successfully applying for a Soldiers' Settlement block near Dunkeld in Western Victoria. He married, and successfully operated the property with his wife, Judy, until ill health forced him to retire and settle in Peterborough on the west coast.

Malcolm Llewellyn McColm (1914–1966): Malcolm stayed on with the Royal Air Force for a time, before returning to Brisbane in 1947. He became an outspoken Liberal Party member for Bowman in 1949, a seat he held with dignity until 1961. He then championed the cause of the Royal Flying Doctor Service and the Queensland Cancer Fund. Sadly, he died of a cerebral haemorrhage in 1966, two weeks after marrying his second wife, Nell.

John Robert (Jack) Millett (1912–1999): Jack returned to Perth after the war, and went into the panel-beating business for private firms and later for the government. Quitting this, he worked for a company that supplied steel furniture, and then for another steel and wood furniture company, where he stayed for 21 years until his retirement. Divorced from his first wife, Jack never remarried, and always maintained a deep interest in the study of military history and strategies until his death.

Vincent 'Bush' Parker (1918–1946): Like Malcolm McColm, Vincent decided to stay on in the RAF before returning to Australia, and flew with No. 56 OTU (Operational Training Unit) in Milfield, Northumberland. On 29 January 1946, he was flying north from his base in a Tempest aircraft when for some unexplained reason it crashed into a field, and one of the most popular young men in

Colditz was killed at the age of 27. It is believed he was engaged to be married at the time. According to his sister Mona, a gypsy once told Vincent that, like his mother, he would not live to be 30.

Dr Roger Andre Playoust (1900–1962): After his three-month stint in Colditz, 'Doc' Playoust was sent to other camps at Warburg and Rotenberg. Treating thousands of ill and diseased men, together with a poor and inadequate diet and a lack of proper medicines, he fell victim to the insidious actinomycosis – an infectious bacterial disease. Eventually he was deemed eligible for repatriation exchange and sent to Stalag IID at Stargard to await his return home, which occurred early in 1945. Once back in Sydney and reunited with his wife, Olga, and two sons, he resumed his general practice, but never regained full strength. He would eventually succumb to his illness at just 62 years of age.

John Gerald Rawson (1917–1990): Johnny Rawson came home in June 1945 where he was greeted by his wife, Kit. For a short while he remained in the army and was promoted to captain. He then went dairy farming and grazing in the Kyneton district. Returning to Melbourne, he became involved in a series of enterprises, which included running a service station and gold mining in Gippsland. In 1989, he was diagnosed with cancer and, typically, fought the disease for many months. At one stage he had to have the lower part of one leg amputated, but he battled on until he finally succumbed to the disease on 25 August 1990. In recognition of his initiative, resourcefulness and bravery as a prisoner of war, he was Mentioned in Despatches.

Australia Will Be There

How the Hell was I to know,
That THIS is where he meant –
When Menzies said, in '39,
To some top-hatted Pommie gent –
'Australia will be there!'

'Australia will be there,' he said,
'Australia will be there!
'We'll send you ships, we'll send you guns,
'And what is more – we'll send our sons!
'The Diggers will be there!'

My Dad was there, a long time back,
Four bleedin' years he spent,
Marching, fighting, eating tack,
And came back home without a cent!
I tell you mate – he did HIS whack!

I've done mine too, I reckon mate,
I've done my bloody whack!
From Alamein – to Tripoli,
From Crete to bleedin' Germany.
From prison camp to prison cell –
From turnip soup to kartoffeln,
From ersatz marge to hedgerow tea –
And endless dreams of liberty.
This year? Next year? Who can say?
I tell you mate – I've earned my pay!

'Australia will be there!' he said –
I lent a willing ear,
But how was I to bloody know
That what he meant was HERE!

Lieutenant Commander J. M. ('Mugsie') Moran, R.N., formerly of Oflag IVC, Colditz. Based on words scratched on a prison cell wall, circa 1942.

Index

Aitken, Capt. A. H. 257–259
Alexander, Lt. Michael 282
Allan, Lt. Anthony 'Peter' 162–164, 166
Archer, Sapper Lionel 230, 237, 239, 247
Arkwright, Major Albert 82–83, 95
Ashton, Lt. Bill 99–102
Atkinson, Dennis 32
Augustus the Strong 142
Ayers, Sir Henry 200

Bader, W/Cdr. Douglas 197–198, 231, 255, 287–288
Barnes, Lt. Bob 243–244
Barr, Lt. Bobby 34–37, 75, 89–90
Barter, Ronnie 31
Bartlett, Lt. Dennis 243, 243
Barton, Lt. Teddy 238, 285
Baxter, Sgt. Bill 218–219
Baxter, Capt. Rex 12, 23, 42–49, 54–55, 60, 62, 69–70, 72, 75–76, 78–79, 81–89, 107–114, 126–135, 157, 212, 235–239, 244, 251–253, 272–281
Beaumont, Lt. John 9–13, 129
Benns, Lt. Andy 56–65, 213
Best, F/Lt. Jack 242–243, 249–255
Blair, Lt. Chandos 29
Bolding, Lt. George 67–69, 137, 264–266, 292–294, 298
Bor-Komorowski, Gen. 282
Borwick, Michael 79–80
Boulay, Lt. 158
Boyce, Lt. 97
Broomhall, L/Col. 'Tubby' 143, 238, 240, 246
Brown, Arthur 215
Bruce, F/O Dominic 4, 164–166
Brush, Major Peter 31, 74
Buckley, L/Cdr. James 190
Burdeyron, Lt. Noel 238
Burn, Capt. Micky 237
Bushell, S/Ldr. Roger 190, 261
Butterworth, Lt. Peter 190

Campbell, Lt. Alan 'Black' 259–261, 266, 273
Campbell, Major Victor 268
Campbell-Preston, Capt. Pat 90
Casey, F/Lt. Mike 193
Chalupka, F/Lt. Cenek 'Checko' 238
Champ, Finlay 31
Chrisp, Bos'n Jack 154, 244
Christie, Capt. Hector 29, 116, 128
Clisby, F/O Leslie 201

Cocksedge, Lt. Alan 244
Codner, Lt. Michael 122
Coombe-Tennant, Capt. Henry 95
Courage, Col. 17
Crawford, Capt. Alexander (Doug) 73–75, 89–95, 137, 230, 269–270, 298
Crawford, Mimi 168
Cruickshank Lt. J. 79–80

Dakeyne, F/Lt. 191
Davis, Capt. Dick 110
de Hamel, Lt. Max 282
Dickinson, F/Lt. J. 'Bag' 193–194
Dieppe, Lt. Clive 96–105, 137, 246–247, 282–285, 298
Dobson, Lt. Kenny 288
Donaldson, F/O Don 'Weasel' 4, 195
Donkers, Lt. H. G. 205–206
Drew, Lt. George 113–114
Dulag Lufts
  Oberursel 170–171, 189–190, 202
Dulags
  183, Salonika 21–24
Duncan, Lt. Michael 32, 34, 36
Dupree, Lt. John 79–81

Eberhardt, Sonderführer 171
Eggers, Hauptmann Reinhold 12–13, 149–150, 232–233, 241–243, 246–247, 261–263
Elliott, Capt. Harry 154
Elphinstone, Capt. John 282
Evers, Capt. Brian 125, 128–129, 136

Fanshawe, L/Cdr. Peter 190
Farr, Lt. Micky 157, 238–239
Fergusson, Lt. Pat 113
Flinders, Matthew 241
Fortune, M/Gen. Victor 27, 35–36, 37
Fowler, F/Lt. Bill 167, 200–210, 257, 290, 299
Fowler, Florence 200, 210
Fowler, Maxwell 200, 210
Francis, Martin 290
Fuller, Capt. Robert 95

Gee, Dr Howard 154–155
George VI, King of England 210, 239
Gephard, Oberstabsfeldwebel 204–205
German, L/Col. Guy 143–144, 198,
Gestapo 137, 164, 182, 190, 207–208, 286
Gill, Lt. Derek 205
Gilliat, Capt. Martin 46, 90
Godfrey, L/Col. Arthur 14
Goldfinch, F/Lt. Bill 251
Gomel, Hauptmann 26, 36
Goodwin, Lt. Howard (Jack) 270–272
Gray, Capt. Ab 15, 20–21, 28, 60–61
Greenwell, Sir Peter 260
Griffiths, Capt. 190

Haig, Capt. Earl 282
Hallifax, F/Lt. Dan 269
Hamilton, Lt. Hamish 137–139
Hamilton-Baillie, Lt. Jock 4, 80–81, 111, 125
Hand, Jack 89, 90
Hann, Cecil 169
Hannay, Lt. Ed 153–154
Harrison, Lt. 'Rex' 194
Harvey, L/Cdr. Mike 144–145, 241–243
Heard, Padre Dick 232, 263
Himmler, Heinrich 282, 285
Hitler, Adolf 52, 123, 133, 185, 231–232, 240, 264
Holroyd, Charles 185, 231–232
Holroyd, Paula 185, 231–233
Holroyd, Lt. Ralph 145–147, 167, 175–186, 212, 230–234, 238, 246, 269, 285–288, 299
Hooper, Jessie 187
Hooper, Major 97
Hopetoun, Capt. Charles 135, 144, 269, 282
Howard, Charles 168
Howard, Henry 51
Howard, Lt. Mark 21, 23, 29, 50–52, 54–55, 60, 62, 69, 82, 88, 107–110, 111, 113, 126–135, 147–148, 157, 230, 235–237, 250–252, 271, 289–292, 299–300
Howe, Capt. Dick 9–10, 194
Hudson, Major John 279

Hurley, Frank 175
Hyde-Thompson, Lt. John 264–267, 292

Isherwood, Lt. Len 60

Jackson, Capt. 128
Johnstone, Capt. Johnny 78, 80, 83, 89
Joyce, William 185

Kelly, Ned 57–59, 67, 213
Kennedy, Col. G. W. 40, 77, 79, 81
Kirkwood, Alan 89–90
Kitchener, Lord 239
Klau, Hauptmann 217–218

Lascelles, Lt. Viscount George 282, 292–293
Laurie, Bob 276–277
Lawton, Capt. Bill 'Lulu' 194, 204
LeRay, Lt. Alain 157–158
Levante, The Great 188
Lewis, W/Off. 213–218
Littledale, Major Ron 175, 209
Lockett, S/Ldr. Charlie 171–172, 174
Lorraine, Major Dick 244

MacAusland, Driver 288
MacAskie, Lt. Bruce 157, 238
MacKenzie, Lt. Colin 135
Macky, Col. Neil Lloyd 176
Mairesse-Lebrun, Pierre 158–159
Marchand, Lt. Roger 136
Martin, Lt. S. 'Paddy' 238
Mary, The Princess Royal 292–294
Max and Moritz, dummies 160
McCall, Lt. Alan 157
McColm, Adelaide 167
McColm, Alberta 169
McColm, Don 168, 169
McColm, S/Ldr. Malcolm 167–174, 236, 300
McColm, Capt. William 167–168, 169
McCulloch, Capt. Jock 213–216, 218–223
McLaren, Lt. Pat 137
McNab, Michael 32
Millar, Lt. Bill 134
Millett, Lt. Jack 9–10, 116–123, 137–139, 231, 260, 285, 287, 288–289, 300
Moir, Lt. Douggie 134, 157, 238–239, 253
Molloy, Simon 32
Moran, L/Cdr. Mike 'Mugsie' 3, 234, 303

Neave, Lt. Airey 162, 202
Newman, F/Lt. Tim 170–171

Odry, Lt. Pierre 159
Oflags
  IVC, Colditz 7–13, 118, 135, 139, 141–167, 174–175, 186, 194–212, 230–293
  VB, Biberach 24–38, 73–75, 116, 271
  VIB, Warburg 37–95, 97–98, 106–107, 111, 114, 122, 271, 273, 296
  VIIB, Eichstätt 9, 90, 94, 96–140, 142–144, 150–152, 156, 212–218, 241, 259, 271, 296
  IXA/H, Spangenburg 246
  IXA/Z, Rotenburg 213, 270–272
  XC, Lübeck 40, 56, 74, 97, 121–122, 171–174, 271
O'Hara, Lt. W. 'Scarlet' 194
Onions, Peter 32
O'Sullivan, Barry 36
Owens, W/Off. 213–215

Page, Dick 81, 83, 90
Panton, F/Lt. Alastair 193
Pardoe, Lt. Phil 90, 152
Parker, Edith 187
Parker, Jack 187
Parker, F/Lt. Vincent 'Bush' 149–150, 167, 186–199, 236, 238–239, 241–243, 250, 253, 255, 261, 269, 300–301
Paterson, Lt. Jack 20, 60, 62, 71
Patton's Third Army 276, 279, 285–289
Penman, Lt. John 128–129
Perodeau, Lt. André 161
Perrin, Lt. Andre 174
Perry, S/Major 136
Peters, Major 122
Philpot, F/Lt. Oliver 122
Piltz, 'Charlie' 192–193

Plant, S/Ldr. 'Pappy' 190
Platt, Padre Ellison 268, 283–284
Playoust, Capt. Roger 'Doc' 234, 301
Pöhnert, Willi 160–161
Prawitt, Oberstleutnant 146, 282–283, 285, 289
Prittie, Terrence 31
Prominente 141, 233, 282–283
See also Alexander, Lt. Michael; de Hamel, Lt. Max; Elphinstone, Capt. John; Haig, Capt. Earl; Hopetoun, Capt. Charles; Lascelles, Lt. Viscount George; Romilly, Giles
Pumphrey, Lt. Laurie 145, 260

Rademacher, Hauptmann Friedrich 49–52, 87–89
Rawlings, Bill 89–90
Rawson, Lt. Johnny 56–67, 212–229, 236–237, 257–261, 264–267, 268, 292–293, 301
Reid, Major Miles 269
Reid, Major Pat 1–2, 162–163, 174–175, 195, 199, 205
Riviere, Lt. Micky 268
Roberts, Fred 121
Rogers, Capt. Jim 203, 238
Rolfe, Major Gordon 134
Rolt, Lt. Tony 12, 31, 249, 251–255
Romilly, Giles 282–283
Rowan-Hamilton, Major Angus 36

Sandbach, Lt. C. 'Sandy' 138
Savige, Sir Stanley 15
Schmitt, Kommandant 159
Sgouros, Dr George 181–183
Sgouros, Lysandre 182
Shaughnessy, Col. Leo 289
Shepherd, David 169
Sinclair, Lt. Mike 262–263
Slater, Major Alfred 184
Stalags
IVB, Mühlberg 257–259
XIIIB/344, Lamsdorf 183
XIIIC, Hammelburg 234
383, Hohenfels 218–223
Stalag Lufts:
I, Barth 170–171, 174, 190, 202
III, Sagan 122, 140, 190, 193–194, 261
Stallard, Major Tom 42–49, 53, 72, 75, 77–78, 81, 84, 90, 257
Stephens, L/Cdr. Billie 174–175
Stephenson, S/Ldr. Geoffrey 174
Stirling, Sgt. Jim 219, 222

Tito, Marshall 227
Tod, L/Col. Willie 13, 238, 246–247, 256, 263–264, 282–283, 285–286, 289
Tunstall, F/Lt. Peter 149

Upham, Capt. Charles 238, 270

van Doorninck, Lt. Damiaen 204–209
van Rood, F/Lt. Peter 145, 194, 238
Vercoe, Capt. Victor 269
von Werra, Lt. Franz 260–261

Walker, Lt. Archie 16–18
Walker, Capt. David 3, 9–12, 46, 48, 53, 72–73, 77–78, 90, 95, 112–113, 116, 259
Walker, L/Col. Theo 270–271
Wardle, F/Lt. Hank 174–175
Watson, George 4, 188
Wavell, Sir Archibald 117
Weldon, Capt. Frank 80, 110–114, 125–126, 128, 156
Westley, Capt. Tom 31–32
Williams, F/Lt. Eric 122
Winton, Lt. Peter 273
Wittet, Lt. Mike 157, 198–199
Woollatt, Capt. Hugh 36
Wood, Major A. 174
Wood, Lt. Jerry 186
Wright, Capt. S 'Screwy' 136
Wyman, Gen. 278–279

Young, Lt. Jack 20
Yule, Capt. Jimmy 269

About the Authors

JACK CHAMP was born in Geelong, Australia, in 1913. He fought as part of the 2/6th Infantry Battalion in Greece in 1941, where he was captured by German forces following the Battle of Crete. After escaping from each of the POW camps he was assigned to, he was sent to Oflag IVC, Colditz Castle, where he would see out the remainder of the war.

After the war, Champ published many short stories, as well as *The Wind is Free*, a history of the Royal Geelong Yacht Club. He was an active member of Legacy until his death in 1998 at the age of 85.

COLIN BURGESS was born in suburban Sydney, Australia, in 1947. In 2002, after 32 years' service with Qantas Airways in a variety of roles, Colin took an early retirement in order to concentrate on his writing career.

His first published book was *The Diggers of Colditz* in 1985, co-authored with Colditz veteran Jack Champ. This was followed by *Destination: Buchenwald*, the harrowing story of 168 Australian and Allied airmen illegally held in Buchenwald concentration camp. Since then, he has had numerous non-fiction books published on a wide variety of subjects. In recent years he has not only turned his attention to writing books on the history of human space exploration, but was appointed series editor for the Outward Odyssey series of books on that subject, published by the University of Nebraska Press in the United States.

His most recent completed undertaking was a set of six books relating the stories of each of the six manned Mercury flights in the early 1960s. To date, he has written or co-authored nearly 40 books.